Twayne's United States Authors Series

EDITOR OF THIS VOLUME

Mason I. Lowance, Jr.

University of Massachusetts, Amherst

American Political Writers: 1588–1800

TUSAS 343

AMERICAN POLITICAL WRITERS: 1588–1800

By RICHARD E. AMACHER

Auburn University

TWAYNE PUBLISHERS

A DIVISION OF G. K. HALL & CO., BOSTON

Copyright © 1979 by G. K. Hall & Co.

Published in 1979 by Twayne Publishers,
A Division of G. K. Hall & Co.
All Rights Reserved

Printed on permanent/durable acid-free paper and bound
in the United States of America

First Printing

Frontispiece of *The Declaration of Independence* by John Trumbull
reproduced with the permission of © Yale University Art Gallery

Library of Congress Cataloging in Publication Data

Amacher, Richard E.
American political writers, 1588–1800.

(Twayne's United States authors series; TUSAS 343)
Bibliography: p. 235–238
Includes index.
1. United States—Politics and government—Colonial
period, ca. 1600–1775. 2. United States—Politics and
government—Revolution, 1775–1783. 3. United States—
Politics and government—1783–1809. 4. Authors,
American—Political and social views. I. Title.
E188.A49   320.9′73   79–12158
ISBN 0-8057-7237-5

Contents

About the Author

Richard E. Amacher is Hargis Professor of American Literature at Auburn University, Auburn, Alabama, where he teaches graduate seminars in early American literature and literary criticism. He received his Ph.D. from the University of Pittsburgh in 1947. He also studied with Professors Clarence Faust and Walter Blair at the University of Chicago. He has taught at Yale, Rutgers, Henderson State (Arkadelphia, Arkansas), and at Auburn. He twice served as Fulbright lecturer in Germany—at the University of Würzburg (1961–62) and at the University of Konstanz (1969–70) in departments headed by Professor Wolfgang Iser. From 1977 to 1979 he was president of the Southeastern American Studies Association.

Dr. Amacher has published books on Benjamin Franklin, Edward Albee, and Joseph Glover Baldwin as well as short articles and reviews on a wide range of subjects in American literature. Currently he is editing with Professor Victor Lange a collection of essays entitled *New Perspectives in German Literary Criticism* (scheduled for publication in 1979 by the Princeton University Press).

Preface

Much early American literature is political. In the last quarter of the eighteenth century, for example, writers like Philip Freneau, Hugh Henry Brackenridge, John Trumbull, Francis Hopkinson, the Connecticut Wits, Jeremy Belknap, and others frequently expressed their political ideas in the form of satirical verse or fiction. A good deal of this material has already been closely studied and analyzed by literary scholars. But less attention has been paid to the *nonfiction political writings* of such seventeenth- and eighteenth-century authors as Roger Williams, John Winthrop, John Cotton, the Mathers, Samuel Sewall, John Wise, John Woolman, Anthony Benezet, Jonathan Mayhew, James Otis, the Adamses, Franklin, Paine, Jefferson, Freneau, Hamilton, and Joel Barlow—all of whom made important contributions, in one way or another, to the American political tradition.

There is a genuine need, therefore, for a study of the principal ideas and themes found in the printed political documents of these two centuries and for the study of techniques of rhetoric (persuasion) used to present them in nonfictional writing. An investigation of this kind presupposes an interest in the history of ideas, techniques of argument, and order of presentation in writing. It embraces two regular disciplines—analysis of ideas and rhetorical analysis.

This book aims at presenting a survey not only of the above-named authors but also of a number of less well known writers who helped shape public opinion on important political events and issues. When Dr. Sylvia E. Bowman suggested this book as a possible volume for the Twayne USAS, I had no idea of the difficult task awaiting me. My friend and esteemed colleague in the Auburn University History Department, Dr. Joseph Harrison, who had worked on the Jefferson papers, speedily informed me that there were at least 200 names that he considered "absolutely indispensable" for my bibliography. How to organize in a small volume these "names," many of whom had written not merely one but several works, then became my waking nightmare.

Needless to say, such a problem was unsolvable. My makeshift solution finally consisted in attempting in each chapter to organize the major figures and some significant though less well known writers around the theme of a period in early American political history. These chapters forthwith became the seven chapters of the present volume. I have tried to follow a roughly chronological arrangement of topics for these chapters.

The first chapter treats the growth of the Christian commonwealth in seventeenth-century New England, including the battle for freedom of religion and the separation of church and state. The second follows logically with the decline of the theocracy, principally seen in the career and writings of Increase Mather. Since Cotton Mather was an early writer on slavery in this country, and since some of the early Quaker writers on this subject worked in the 1730s, it seemed right to present next the discussions on slavery, even though some of these ran up to and beyond the Revolutionary War. Chapter four deals with resistance to the Stamp Act and other taxes. Here again I encountered some recalcitrance from my subject matter, since writers like Mayhew had already begun to preach resistance to such tyranny on general principles in the 1750s. For similar reasons it was necessary in chapter five to begin discussion of the Revolution in 1769 instead of 1776. Chapters six and seven posed no special difficulty, at least with the problem of chronology. But the plethora of writers on the adoption of the Constitution, most of whom wrote or published in 1787–1788, made necessary the omission of many names which I should have included if more space had been allowed. By the same token, in my final chapter, discussing the last decade of the eighteenth century, I was forced, in some cases, merely to list titles of works, because of the great complexity of events connected with the French Revolution and the conflict of parties in America at this time. Whole books have been written on this decade alone.

I would therefore gently urge the reader to view this book as a seven-chambered picture gallery in which some portraits are full-sized and others are, more by necessity than my own choice, slightly reduced. The catalogue of my little exhibit numbers approximately seventy writers.

I should add that I have proceeded on the assumption that a "political writer"—at least for the purposes of this book—is one who has written in an *ad hoc* manner about a specific event or situation. This excuse is the only one I can offer for excluding the numerous histories of the period, many of which contain, here and there, material relevant to this book. A guide to the events to which the writings in this work relate may be found in the Chronology section.

Because of the strictly limited size of this text I have had to concentrate almost entirely on main ideas and chief arguments. But I have also tried, by using copious quotations, to give the reader some idea of each writer's individual style. Each writer, in this sense, speaks for himself.

In general, I have modernized spellings for the benefit of the reader, but in one or two cases, where the archaic spellings did not interfere with clarity and enhanced the effect, these were retained.

In my research I have mainly used primary sources, and I owe a debt of great gratitude to the librarians of the Harvard libraries, particularly to Caroline Jakeman of the Houghton Memorial Library, the librarians of the Library of Congress, and those of the Ralph Brown Draughon Memorial Library at Auburn University. I cannot too much acknowledge my debts in the use of secondary material to Bernard Bailyn, Kenneth Murdock, and the late Perry Miller. These have been specifically indicated in the text. Mason Lowance read the manuscript and offered numerous helpful criticisms and suggestions. Finally, I am once again grateful to the Auburn University Research Grant-in-Aid Program for financial assistance and to Mrs. Gaylon Ponder, who typed the manuscript.

RICHARD E. AMACHER

Auburn University

Chronology

1584– 1587	Expeditions to area of Roanoke Island.
1607	Founding of Jamestown.
1619	First Negro slaves arrive at Jamestown.
1620	Mayflower Compact and landing of the Pilgrims.
1630– 1642	The Great Migration.
1636	Roger Williams flees to Rhode Island.
1637– 1638	Antinomian Crisis (Anne Hutchinson banished from Massachusetts).
1642	Puritan Revolution in England.
1643	New England Confederation.
1649	Execution of Charles I.
1651	Navigation Act.
1660	Restoration of Charles II.
1662	Half-Way Covenant.
1684	Revocation of Massachusetts Charter.
1685– 1688	Reign of James II.
1686	Dominion of New England under Governor Andros.
1688– 1689	Glorious Revolution (James II deposed).
1689	English Bill of Rights.
1691	Massachusetts made a Royal Colony.
1692	Witchcraft in Salem, Massachusetts.
1701	Increase Mather resigns as president of Harvard.
1723	Death of Increase Mather.
1734– 1750	The Great Awakening.
1754	Albany Congress (Franklin plans union against French and Indians).
1754– 1763	French and Indian War (terminating in Treaty of Paris, 1763).

1764	Sugar Act and Currency Act.
1765	Stamp Act.
1766	Examination of Dr. Franklin and repeal of Stamp Act.
1766	Declaratory Act.
1767	Townshend Acts.
1770	Repeal of Townshend Acts (except for duty on tea).
1770	Boston Massacre.
1773	Hutchinson Affair (Governor Thomas Hutchinson tries to curb liberties in the Colonies).
1773	Boston Tea Party (following Tea Act).
1774	Intolerable Acts.
1774	First Continental Congress.
1775	Second Continental Congress.
1776	Declaration of Independence.
1778	Treaty with France.
1781	Articles of Confederation
1783	Treaty of Paris (England recognizes United States independence).
1786	Shays' Rebellion (Massachusetts farmers resist foreclosure of mortgages on their farms and imprisonment for debts due to high land taxes).
1787	Northwest Ordinance (excluding slavery).
1787	Constitutional Convention.
1787–1792	Rise of Federalist and Anti-Federalist (Jeffersonian-Republican) parties.
1788	Ratification of the Constitution.
1789	George Washington elected president.
1789–1795	French Revolution.
1792	Washington reelected president.
1793	Washington proclaims neutrality in war between France and Britain.
1794	Jay Treaty (fails to control British trade privileges in West; French join British in attacking American shipping).
1794	Whiskey Rebellion (Western Pennsylvanians oppose Hamilton's tax policies with force).
1796	John Adams elected president.
1797	XYZ Affair (French raids on American ships lead Adams

	to send three envoys to France; French demand of bribe as condition to negotiations angers Americans).
1798	Alien and Sedition Laws (Adams attempts to restrict Anti-Federalist sympathies for French and freedom of press to criticize president).
1798–	
1799	Kentucky and Virginia Resolutions (Jefferson and Madison invoke state rights doctrine against Alien and Sedition Laws).
1800	Thomas Jefferson elected president.

CHAPTER 1

Freedom of Religion and
the Christian Commonwealth

I The Foundation of the Theocracy

TWO of the chief political controversies during seventeenth-century American history concerned freedom of worship, according to the individual conscience, and the determination of the dividing line between the power of the church and that of the state in a Christian commonwealth. The purpose of the early New England settlers was to build a commonwealth where the laws of God were clearly exhibited in both church and state.[1] Eventually this creative purpose resulted in a kind of theocracy. Then, because of objections to this form of government, as we shall see, the problem of separation between the powers of church and state arose.

Curiously enough, one of the earliest works to allude to the possibility of theocracy in early America was a promotion tract written by an English mathematician, Thomas Harriot. Some thirty years before the first permanent English settlers arrived in New England, in *A Briefe and True Report of the New Found Land of Virginia* (London, 1588), Harriot's short "description of the nature and manners of the people of the countrey"[2] described the government of the native Indians in such a way as to stress the role of their pagan religion in maintaining "law and order" among them. According to Harriot—who was writing prior to the establishment of any permanent English settlement in America—the Indians' belief in an afterlife

worketh so much in manie of the common and simple sort of people that it maketh them have great respect to their Governours, and also great care what they do, to avoid torment after death, and enjoy blisse; althought [sic] notwithstanding there is punishment ordained for malefactours, as stealers, whoremoongers [sic] and other sortes of wicked doers; some punished with death, some with forfeitures, some with beating, according to the greatness of the factes.[3]

This passage, one of the earliest comments in English on a political subject in America, emphasizes religious sanctions which Harriot throught undergirded the political order of some North American native Indians.

With the Pilgrims and Puritans, who settled respectively in Plymouth and Massachusetts Bay, the religious framework for the political order was revealed in one, and only one, place—the Bible. The Bible was God's word, his one and only revelation. Practically every seventeenth-century New England writer who handled any subject even remotely "political" accepted this point as a basic truth. Consequently every theory of politics, every *statement* of it, had to be justified by scriptural quotation. To be sure, writers like William Bradford might refer to special providences,[4] but these were not considered *bona fide revelations*, in the strict sense of that word.

Perry Miller explained this distinction very well when he wrote, "He [God] converses with men only through His revealed word, the Bible. His will is to be studied in the operation of His providence as exhibited in the workings of the natural world, but He delivers no new commands or special revelations to the inward consciousness of men." [5]

More specifically, God's will as revealed through the Bible rested upon the idea of a covenant. According to Covenant theology, before the fall of Adam and Eve, man had been under a *covenant of works* in obedience to God. After the fall, God had drawn up a new contract, a *covenant of grace*, in which he had laid down conditions for man's salvation and had "pledged Himself to abide by them." Moreover, in the covenant of grace God "pledged Himself not to run athwart human conceptions of right and justice." [6] Man, on the other hand, after agreeing with God to be contractually bound by His law, had then naturally to "establish a government to see this law enforced." [7] Thus the new covenant provided a theological foundation for the legal system that developed in Massachusetts Bay.

The new covenant clarified the reasons and circumstances according to which only a very limited number of persons (the elect) were to be saved. Sidney E. Ahlstrom stresses the fact that the covenant was "irreducibly personal," at first to Abraham and his seed, but later to individuals in New England through the conversion experience required for church membership.[8] Since in the early days of Massachusetts Bay Colony only church members had the franchise, this Covenant or Federal theology (as it is sometimes called) was an important element in the politics and law that grew from it. Although Covenant theology was developed and expanded by a long line of theologians from Calvin to William Ames (1576–1633),[9] its first statement had, of course, been made by God himself in the Bible.

As one would expect, then, when a Puritan writer like John Cotton turned his attention to codifying the laws of Massachusetts Bay, he took great pains to indicate the scriptural sources that provided proof or precedent for these laws. Of the twenty-four crimes listed as deserving "capital punishment" in an anonymous work entitled *An Abstract[,] or the Lawes of New England, As they are now established* (London, 1641), nineteen carried the death penalty; five, banishment.[10] Each was supported by a marginal reference to the Old Testament that was very explicit about the exact form of punishment. The following excerpts from Chapter VII of this *Abstract* will give an idea of the style and the rationale of the argument:

Blasphemy.
Lev. 24. 11
to 16.

1 First, Blasphemy which is a cursing of God by Atheisme or the like, to be punished with death.

Idolatry.
Deu. 13. 10,
15, 16.

2 Idolatry to be punished with death.

Witchcraft.
Ex. 22. 18,
20, 27.

3 Witchcraft which is fellowship by covenant with a familiar Spirit to be punished with death. . . .

....

Sabbath.
Num. 15. 32.

11 Profaning of the Lords day, in a careless and scornefull neglect or contempt thereof to be punished with death. . . .

....

Rebellious *Children* Deu. 21. 18, 19, 20.	16 Rebellious children whether they continue in riot or drunkennesse after due correction from their parents, or whether they curse or smite their Parents, to be put to death. . . .

....

Sodomy, *Buggery,* *Pollution, etc.* Lev. 20. 18, 19.	20 Unnaturall filthinesse to be punished with death, whether Sodomy, which is carnall fellowship of man with man, or woman with woman. Or Buggery which is carnall fellow- ship of man or woman, with beasts or fowles.
	21 Pollution of a woman known to be in her flowers to be punished with death.
Whordome. Ex. 21. 16	22 Whordome of a maiden in her fathers house, kept secret till after her marriage with another, to be punished with death.
Man-stealing. Deu. 24.	23 Man-stealing to be punished with death.
False witnesse. [illegible]	24 False witnesse bearing to be punished with death.[11]

The building of a Christian commonwealth, then, had to be carried out, however severely, according to God's plan as revealed in the Bible.

But this did not mean that it was to be a *theocracy*, if by that term we mean government by the clergy. As Edmund Morgan makes clear, the founders of Massachusetts Bay colony—leaders like John Winthrop and John Cotton—had no intention of imitating or reviving what they considered the errors of the Roman Catholic Church, particularly the history of its political power in the pre-Reformation period. Although ministers like John Cotton and Roger Williams might be consulted by Winthrop, they themselves did not seek or hold office during Winthrop's time in Massachusetts

Bay colony.[12] And although at first only church members had the right to vote, their power over the person elected ceased the moment they had exercised it. From that moment on he was responsible only to God, not to the people. At least this is what Winthrop argued in his famous speech to the General Court of July 3, 1645. But even fifteen years earlier, in his sermon preached on the *Arbella* on his way to America in 1630, Winthrop had made use of a similarly undemocratic proposition as a starting point:

God Almightie in his most holy and wise providence hath soe disposed of the Condicion of mankinde, as in all times some must be rich[,] some poore, some highe and eminent in power and dignitie; others meane and in subjeccion.[13]

While such an assumption might be considered highly debatable, if not entirely wrong today, Winthrop had little difficulty in convincing his audience that such an inequitable distribution of wealth and power was not only quite proper but also smacked of the wisdom, justice, and mercy of the Creator!

The reasoning he used in defense of this position will bear looking into. First, he argued that as it was "the glory of princes to have many officers," or servants, so it was to God's glory to have "many Stewards," "counting himselfe more honoured in dispenceing his guifts to man by man, than if he did it by his owne immediate hand." (Although such an argument would be speedily rejected as feudalistic today, apparently his auditors accepted it as right and reasonable.) Second, he argued (in a circle) that such a system actually gave God a better chance to display "the work of his Spirit: first, upon the wicked in moderateing and restraineing them: soe that the riche and mighty should not eate upp the poore, nor the poore, and dispised rise upp against theire superiours, and shake off theire yoake." Also, he contended, such a system would enable both the "regei[erate" and the "poore and inferiour sorte" to exercise their better natures. In the "greate ones" (the so-called "regenerate") it would bring out the best in them—"love[,] mercy, gentlenes, temperance etc."—while in the "poore and inferiour" it would exercise their "faithe[,] patience, obedience etc." Lastly, he argued that such a system would bring about greater solidarity among rich and poor alike, insuring both the common good of all men as well as the glory of their Creator. (Winthrop himself was quite wealthy, an exception among Puritans. But, as Morgan shows, the remarkable thing was that while the charter of the Bay company gave him and others of its members absolute governmental power and while temperamentally they might have been inclined to exercise such power, they did not do so.)[14]

The structure of this sermon by Winthrop follows the typical pattern—*text*, and proof of text; *doctrines* (which were drawn from the text) and their proof (called *reasons*); and *uses* or applications to daily life.[15] In his development of the *doctrine* part of this sermon Winthrop explains that they are two in number—Justice and Mercy—and related to a generally accepted distinction between the so-called Law of Nature and the Law of Grace or the Gospel.[16] The "lawe of nature was given to man in the estate of innocency"—in the Garden of Eden. Having violated this "law," man encountered the wrath and justice of God and was expelled from the garden. But God in his mercy offered man a new covenant by sending his son, Christ, to earth and by His revelation in the Bible. Thus the Law of the Gospel (the Bible) resembled a binding legal contract by which man was to direct his entire life in order to make the best use of his second chance for salvation. In this sermon Winthrop uses the phrase "the practice of mercy" to indicate this kind of direction expected of the ordinary saint or church member. Specifically, it had to do with such matters as lending money and covering bad debts. Money might be lent according to the law of Justice, but for bad debts the law of Mercy or forgiveness had to be invoked. If it is asked how these superficial resemblances between law and theology are related to politics, Winthrop's answer is that love, the affection from which the "practice of mercy" arises, operates as a kind of binding element among the members of the church, like ligaments in the human body. Ultimately the source of this love is Christ; it is the love of Christ that holds the Church (his symbolical body) together. But it was also this same Christian love that was to hold together his fellow travelers aboard the *Arbella* in a "due form of Government both civill and ecclesiasticall" once they had arrived in the New World, as he clearly indicates in the *Uses* at the end of the sermon. Consequently this "Modell" of "Christian Charitie," as the sermon is called, presents Winthrop's first statement of his interesting fusion of theological and political ideas, a fusion that he later developed in his manuscript war with Henry Vane, in his account of the Antinomian controversy, and in his *Discourse on Arbitrary Government* and in his above-mentioned speech to the General Court.[17]

II *John Winthrop and the Antinomian Controversy*

The significance of the Antinomian controversy and the banishment of Anne Hutchinson was far greater than the number of writings which resulted from these events. This exile of Anne Hutchinson marked the beginning of the running skirmish for religious toleration and freedom from persecution waged by Roger Williams against John Cotton during the period 1636–1652, and it also served as a prelude for the first appearance of the Quakers as a force to be reckoned with in the future of American history. For what was it, after all, this Quaker doctrine of the "inner light," but a heretical challenge to the accepted Puritan conviction that the Bible was the *only* revelation of God? If God revealed himself directly to the consciences of Anne Hutchinson and her followers, as well as to the Quakers, the keystone of Puritan faith in the Bible as the one direct revelation would fall, and the whole arch of associated doctrines (civil and religious) would crash down with it. Hence this religious controversy signaled a real political crisis for Massachusetts.

Winthrop was governor during much of the Antinomian trouble and during most of the ensuing dispute between Williams and Cotton, and he sided with Cotton. John Cotton had been the teacher of Anne Hutchinson in Boston, England, and his migration to New England had been one of the main reasons for her exodus from her mother country. Ultimately, however, it was he and Winthrop who were responsible for her forced departure from the Bay colony.

All we know about Anne Hutchinson was written by contemporaries who were unfriendly to her and who were disposed to discredit her.[18] Winthrop, for example, wrote "A Defence of an Order of Court Made in the Year 1637," in which he attempted to rationalize not only her banishment and that of Roger Williams before her but also a recently passed court order which limited the stay of visitors to the colony to three weeks. He had managed to pass this order against his rival, Governor Henry Vane (a follower of Anne Hutchinson whom Winthrop had succeeded in unseating), for the express purpose of hindering the growing political power of the Antinomians because of immigration.[19] The argument is worth noting.

Winthrop begins with a question about the essential nature of a commonwealth. He answers this question by saying that it is the "*consent* of a certain companie of people," to live together under a form of government that will insure their "mutual safety and welfare" (my italics). The desire for such security causes people to subject themselves to "rulers and laws; for no man hath lawfull power over another, but by birth or *consent*, so likewise, by the law of proprietye [proprietorship], no man can have just interest in that which belongeth to another, without his *consent*" (my italics). From these initial premises he then concludes that commonwealths can be founded only "by free consent," that any claim of "privilege" in the government of the commonwealth must rest on "free consent," that persons thus incorporated into a commonwealth have responsibility for maintaining its welfare and "to keepe off whatsoever doth appeare to tend to theire damage," and that the good of the whole must be put before that of any private citizen. From these conclusions he reasons: that "no man hath right to come into us &c. without our consent," that "if no man hath right to our lands, our government priviledges, &c. but by our consent, then it is reason we should take notice of before we conferre any such upon them," and that "it is lawful to take knowledge of all men before we receive them" and to refuse them entrance into the commonwealth if their "dispositions suite not with ours" or if their society would be "hurtfull to us. . . ." Miller and Johnson point out that the Congregational churches at this time admitted only those who bore "visible marks of regeneration upon them." [20] And Winthrop urges that this precedent of the churches "to receive or reject at their discretion," as well as the similar practice in the governments of towns, should not be denied to the commonwealth—"why then should the common weal be denied the like liberty and the whole more restrained than any parte?"

He continues. Obviously everyone would admit that "Jesuits, &c." should not be admitted. (The "&c" would certainly include the Quakers.) Furthermore, "if any should be rejected that ought to be received," that would be the fault of those entrusted with execution of the law rather than the fault of the law itself.

This brought up the question of *intent*. "The intent of the law," writes Winthrop, "is to preserve the wellfare of the body; and for this ende to have none received into any fellowship with it who are likely to disturb the same, and this intent (I am sure) is lawful and good." He then offers a word of advice to those who had charge of executing this law, urging them to "follow theire owne judgments, rather than the judgments of others."

Two objections remained to be refuted. First, it had been

objected "that some prophane persons are received and others who are religious are rejected." By way of answer, Winthrop replied that no case of this kind had as yet occurred, but that if it did, it might be justified, for he considered that "younger persons (even prophane ones) may be of lesse danger to the common weale (and to the churches also) than some older persons, though professors of religion." Here he cited Christ's intimacy with publicans and his rejection of the Pharisees as the definitive word on this matter. Second, it was objected that by this law "good Christians and so consequently Christ himselfe" might be rejected. Again he answered that he knew of no such case's having as yet occurred. He added that it was possible to deny a true Christian entrance to the commonwealth without rejecting Christ. Here he offered a few examples—a person who believed in "community of goods," a person who believed that the magistrates (governors, deputy governors, and their assistants) should not punish the "first table" of the commandments,[21] a person who thought that church members should not be punished for criminal offenses, a person who believed himself not subject to any laws or magistrates to which he had not given "an explicite consent," etc. Such opinions, wrote Winthrop, might be "maintained in simple ignorance" by good Christians in "a state of grace." But it would be dangerous, even sinful, for members of the Christian commonwealth "to receive such among us, except it were for tryall of theire reformation." He denies that the law was aimed at Rev. John Wheelwright, Anne Hutchinson's brother-in-law who shared some of her opinions. But even if it were, "where is the evil of it?" he asks.

If we conceive and finde by sadd experience that his [Wheelwright's] opinions are such, as by his own profession cannot stand with externall peace, may we not provide for our peace, by keeping [out] of such as would strengthen him, and infect others with such dangerous tenets? and if we finde his opinions such as will cause divisions, and make people looke at their magistrates, ministers and brethren as enemies to Christ and Antichrists, &c. were it not sinne and unfaithfulness in us, to receive more of those opinions, which we allready finde the evill fruite of: Nay, why doe not those who now complayne joyne with us in keeping out of such, as well as formerly they did in expelling Mr. Williams for the like, though lesse dangerous?[22]

Wheelwright was "disfranchised and banished," according to Winthrop's *Journal*, in October of the same year (1637). He appealed to the King, but the appeal was overruled on a

technicality—that the Massachusetts Court "by the power of the
King's grant . . . had power to hear and determine without
reservation." [23] Anne Hutchinson was also banished at this same
time, although sentence was not carried out against her, "because it
was winter," and she was pregnant. Winthrop says that she was
committed to a private house where only elders of the church and
friends were permitted to visit her (145). She did not leave the
colony until March 28 (151). According to Winthrop her "two
dangerous errors" were: "1. That the Holy Ghost dwells in a
justified person. 2. That no sanctification can help to evidence to us
our justification" (111). At a conference of Massachusetts ministers
held in Boston regarding this latter point it was agreed that
"sanctification did help to evidence justification" (111). Anne
Hutchinson ran into trouble, too, for reproaching ministers (with
the exception of her teacher John Cotton) that they did not "preach
a covenant of free grace" (145). Her view was that by maintaining
that sanctification was evidence of justification, they contradicted
the well-known doctrine that man was saved by God's grace rather
than by any good works that man himself might perform.

III *Winthrop's* Journal *and the Liberties of the People*

Winthrop's *Journal* also reveals interesting sidelights on the
Abstract. Evidence of John Cotton's part in the drawing up of this
Abstract is mentioned during the entries for the year 1636:

Mr. Cotton being requested by the general court with some other
ministers, to assist some of the magistrates in compiling a body of
fundamental laws, did, [during] this court, present a model of Moses his
judicials compiled in an exact method, which were taken into further
consideration till the next general court. (111)

By March 1638, the *Abstract* had not been sufficiently published to
send three adulterers to death. (They got off with whipping and
banishment—149). Winthrop mentions, however, the publication
(in 1641) of the *Body of Liberties* (Nathaniel Ward's new codifica-
tion, but partly a reworking of the *Abstract*). The careful process
whereby these were ultimately adopted as the law of the colony
shows regard for the democratic process:

This session continued three weeks, and established 100 laws, which were
called the *Body of Liberties*. They had been composed by Mr. Nathaniel

Ward (sometime pastor of Ipswich: he had been a minister in England, and formerly a student and practiser in the course of the common law) and had been revised and altered by the court, and sent forth into every town to be further considered of, and now again [during] this court, they were revised, amended and presented, and so established for three years, by that experience to have them fully amended and established to be perpetual. (237)

A brief chronological survey of Winthrop's *Journal* during the 1640s will acquaint us with a few other occurrences that had taken place in the colony. For example, in 1641 the colony had rejected Lord Say and Seal's proposal for an hereditary nobility. During this same year, too, a very exceptional event had taken place: Israel Stoughton's maid had been baptized and accepted into church membership. A few years later, in 1644, it was proposed as a general principle that citizenship be extended to nonchurch members; previously, only church members held citizenship. Also in 1644, the General Court had been divided into two houses, magistrates and deputies (representatives of the various towns [328]). Finally, in 1645, had come the famous impeachment trial—generally acknowledged the first in American government.

The background of this trial is complicated, but basically it concerned a disputed election of an artillery officer in the town of Hingham. According to Winthrop's journal, one Lt. Emes had held the office of chief commander for seven or eight years and had been recently reelected. But before his confirmation by the Governor's Council (magistrates), "the greater part of the town took some light occasion of offence against him, and chose one Allen to be their captain," and presented him for approval. The magistrates, however, favored the incumbent Emes and told the two parties of disputants, into which the military company had split, to go home to await further orders. Resenting this treatment, the artillery company then complicated matters by holding an election of their own, which Allen won by a two-thirds vote.

The fact that Allen was supported by the deputies and Emes by the magistrates resulted in a power struggle between the two houses—a power struggle that appears to have reflected some popular disaffection with the magistrates' degree of control over the people. Mr. Hubbert, a minister of Hingham, having three brothers who sided with the Allen faction, attempted to *excommunicate* Emes. He did not succeed. In consequent legal action Winthrop, who sided with Emes, had three of the Hubberts and others of the

Allen faction bound over to appear at the next meeting of the Court of Assistants. When some of them refused, he had them "committed" (jailed). The Hubberts then presented a petition (signed by about ninety persons in Hingham) concerning the violation of their liberties, the liberties of the church, etc., by the magistrates. Upon further inquiry Winthrop was singled out as defendant and underwent trial.

After acquittal at this trial, Winthrop made his well-known speech on liberty, arguing:

The great questions that have troubled the country, are about the authority of the magistrates and the liberty of the people. It is yourselves [he tells his audience] who have called us to this office, and being called by you, we have our authority from God, in way of an ordinance, such as hath the image of God eminently stamped upon it, the contempt and violation whereof hath been vindicated with examples of divine vengeance.[24]

Although he acknowledged that a magistrate was bound by his oath to the people, he nevertheless took the position that, once elected by the people, in every other way except in the obligation of the oath, he was responsible only to God. In this same speech Winthrop also took occasion to correct a misapprehension about *liberty*. Liberty, as he saw it, was of two kinds—natural and civil.

The first is common to man with beasts and other creatures. By this, man . . . hath liberty to do what he lists; it is liberty to evil as well as to good. This liberty is incompatible and inconsistent with authority, and cannot endure the least restraint of the most just authority. The exercise and maintaining of this liberty makes men grow more evil, and in time to be worse than brute beasts: *omnes sumus licentia deteriores* [we are all the worse for freedom]. This is that great enemy of truth and peace, that wild beast, which all the ordnances of God are bent against, to restrain and subdue it. The other kind of liberty I call civil or federal, it may also be termed moral, in reference to the covenant between God and man, in the moral law, and the politic covenants and constitutions, amongst men themselves. This is the proper end and object of authority, and cannot subsist without it; and it is a liberty to that only which is good, just, and honest. This liberty you are to stand for, with the hazard (not only of your goods, but) of your lives, if need be.[25]

He contends that this latter kind of liberty is akin to the subjection a woman, having freely made choice of a husband, must feel to the authority of her husband, which is "in a way of liberty, not of bondage." It is, moreover, the kind of liberty the church has "under the authority of Christ, her king and husband." And he closes his argument by urging the people to abandon their "natural corrupt liberties" and enjoy only "civil and lawful liberties, such as Christ allows. . . ." [26] Thus he would preserve the liberties of the people!

There can be no doubt concerning Winthrop's sincerity. But Charles I had to be beheaded and James II removed from the English throne before this "divine right" theory was thoroughly discredited.

IV   *The Question of Religious Liberty and the Powers of Church and State: Roger Williams and John Cotton*

Closely related to Winthrop's writings and to the Antinomian controversy, the long debate between John Cotton and Roger Williams had important political repercussions, since it also involved freedom of worship according to the individual conscience as well as the determination of the proper limits of the powers of church and state. This debate began in 1636 and lasted until Cotton's death in 1652. John Cotton, Jr., continued it after his father's death, for as late as March 25, 1671, there is a letter of Williams answering certain charges related to this long and complex altercation. [27]

This controversy has been treated in different and more detailed ways by other writers. [28] Here there is space only for a few main arguments and for touching on a few high points of political significance in the controversy.

Cotton and Williams differed on *separation*; Williams insisted that the Puritans should withdraw altogether from the Anglican church. Beyond that Williams grew unpopular with church leaders at Salem for three "heresies" bearing on the authority of conscience or church versus state. First, Williams denied the validity of King James's charter, claiming that the land had been illegally seized from the Indians. It followed logically from this fact, he argued, that Massachusetts Bay had no valid legal power to prohibit churches from separating. He therefore urged separation. Second, he denied that a magistrate could administer an oath of civil obedience to an "unregenerate" person, one who had not received *grace*, a non-church member. (After all, could one trust the oath of such a person?) Third, he also denied that magistrates had power to adjudicate violation of the first four commandments, those dealing with God and man. [29]

At the same time Williams was escaping to Rhode Island in 1636,

as a result of his banishment for holding these "heresies," Cotton
was busy writing. Two of Cotton's letters of this year illustrate his
powerful invocation of a religious principle as a basis for deciding on
issues of governmental structure. The first, "Certain Proposals
made by Lord Say, Lord Brooke, and other Persons of quality, with
the answers thereto," advised Lord Say that a hereditary aristocracy
such as the nobleman and his friends would have liked to set up in
Massachusetts was out of the question. Authority and power of a few
during one generation, Cotton admitted, the Bible did not
necessarily rule out of the commonwealth. But that such power
should be transmitted to the posterity of these few if the posterity
were not similarly qualified for posts of power and authority, he
opposed. Rather, he argued that ". . . if God should not delight to
furnish some of their posterity with gifts fit for magistracy, we
should expose them rather to reproach and prejudice, and the
commonwealth with them, than exalt them to honor, if we should
call them forth [i.e., elect them], when God hath not, to public
authority." [30] In the second letter (addressed to Lord Say alone)
Cotton made clear yet another principle of the Massachusetts
"theocracy," viz., that it was "better that the commonwealth be
fashioned to the setting forth of Gods house, which is his church;
than to accommodate the church frame to the civill state." [31] It had
apparently worried this same noble lord that only church members
had the right to vote, a principle of operation which Cotton also
politely but firmly defended on the authority of the Bible.[32]

Cotton was probably also busy at about this same time writing a
letter to John Davenport—A Discourse about Civil Government in
a new Plantation Whose Design is Religion.[33] This letter was not
published until 1663.[34] In it Cotton defends the limitation of the
vote to church members. He also clarifies the limits of the church
and state as "parallel institutions . . . with separate purposes."
"Man . . . may be the subject of civil power and state, but man by
grace called out of the world to fellowship with Jesus Christ and His
people is the only subject of church power." [35]

In the years 1644–52 Cotton and Williams fired a series of
pamphlets and letters back and forth at each other on the questions
of church government, religious persecution, and toleration.

It is impossible to unravel this series of pamphlets in the
Cotton-Williams controversy without considering some important
historical events of the previous year, 1643, in England. One of
these was Parliament's convening of the Westminster Assembly in

July. At this assembly five friends of Cotton had drawn up a work called the *Apologetical Narration*, which had argued for Congregational rather than Presbyterian church government, according to the *Model of Church and Civil Power*. The *Model* stated the nonseparatist position of the associated ministers of Massachusetts, and Williams thought Cotton had written it. Actually, according to the *Solemn League and Covenant* passed by Parliament on September 25, 1643, the Westminster Assembly was committed to maintaining the Presbyterian form of church government *by force* if necessary in both England and Scotland.

Williams's *Queries of Highest Consideration* (February 9, 1644) addressed these five friends of Cotton with an argument for religious toleration—of Catholics, among others! Approximately a month later, on March 14, 1644, he succeeded in obtaining a charter for Rhode Island (the main reason, ostensibly, for his visit to London). On July 15, 1644, just before he embarked for America he released anonymously *The Bloudy Tenent of Persecution, for cause of Conscience, discussed, in a Conference betweene Truth and Peace*. This work is in two parts. In the first, Williams attacked Cotton's defense of persecution; in the second, the nonseparatist ideas of the Massachusetts Bay ministers association.[36]

Cotton's response was delayed until 1647, but he then exploded with a double-barreled retort: *A Reply to Mr. Williams his Examination*, which defends his part in the banishment of both Williams and Anne Hutchinson, and *The Bloudy Tenent, Washed And made white in the Bloud of the Lambe: Being Discussed and Discharged of Bloud-guiltinesse by just Defence*, which argued a distinction between just and unjust persecution, defending the former. Both of these tracts were bound together.

Williams's reply was also delayed. Miller thinks that Williams probably wrote *The Bloudy Tenent Yet More Bloody: by Mr. Cotton's endevour to wash it white in the Blood of the Lambe* sometime in the later months of 1651, while still at Providence, before beginning his second trip to London (to protect his charter). At any rate, *The Bloudy Tenent Yet More Bloody* was not printed until May or June of 1652. Williams's timing was strategically perfect, for he had let his work be immediately preceded by that of his close friend John Clark, *Ill Newes from New-England: or a Narrative of New-England's Persecution* (May 13, 1652).

Ill Newes was a true report of an incident that had happened to Clark and Obadiah Holmes a few years previous when they had returned to Lynn, Massachusetts, to comfort a dying Anabaptist. Both had been shamefully treated—fined and whipped—by John Endecott, the new governor after Winthrop's death in 1649 and a bitter enemy of Williams from Salem days. *Ill Newes from New-England* shocked and aroused the London reading public. It focused the limelight on these two friends of Williams and, indeed, on his whole colony and its *raison d'être*. Although it covered essentially no new ground beyond Williams's previously stated position, it did add, as Miller says, *much rhetoric*.[37] Williams had also included in the edition of *The Bloody Tenent Yet More Bloody* the letter he had written to John Endecott, "his former friend and betrayer," objecting to the treatment of Clarke and Holmes.

Another related work that deserves mention is Williams's twenty-three-page pamphlet written in support of Major Butler, fellow advocate of religious toleration, *The Fourth Paper, Presented by Major Butler, To the Honourable Committee of Parliament* (March 30, 1652).[38]

Although John Cotton died in 1652, this was not the end of Williams's concern for or writings on religious toleration. In his already referred to letter of March 25, 1671, to John Cotton, Jr., a minister at Plymouth, Williams defends his career and convictions.[39] " 'Tis true," he writes, "my first book, *The Bloudy Tenent*, was burnt by the Presbyterian party (then prevailing) but this book whereof we now speak (being my reply to your father's answer) was received with applause and thanks by the army, by the Parliament, professing that, of necessity—yea, of Christian equity—there could be no reconciliation, pacification, or living together but by permitting of dissenting consciences to live amongst them. . . ."[40]

An unpleasant coda to this entire long controversy occurred in the year 1676 when Williams published in Boston his attack on the Quakers—*George Foxx Digg'd out of his Burrowes, Or an Offer of Disputation On fourteen Proposalls made this last Summer 1672 (so call'd) unto G. Fox then present on Rode-Island in New-England, by R. W.* Although the Quakers reminded him he was committing treason to his principles of toleration, Williams, orthodox Calvinist that he was, could not tolerate the heresy of accepting God's revelation anywhere other than the Bible. The Bible, at least for him, was still the law in 1676. Miller also defends Williams's opposition to the Quakers of the 1670s as being deserved because of their role as disturbers of the peace in Rhode Island.[41] Nevertheless, inconsistent as this last unfortunate act of his may seem, Williams remains a commanding force in the life and history of our nation. As Miller says, despite the paradox of Williams's views on the Quakers, "As a figure and a reputation he was always there to remind Americans that no other conclusion than absolute religious freedom was feasible in this society." [42]

Although Williams has often been criticized for poor literary quality and lack of clarity in his writing, he was certainly capable of good writing at times, too, as is evident in his letter to the town of Providence (*circa* January 1655).[43] This letter is a model of compactness, unity, and clarity. In it he corrects the mistaken idea of some of his fellow citizens that his argument for "liberty of conscience" might be construed as giving them the right not to obey the civil laws of Providence. By use of an effective analogy, he illuminates this distinction:

There goes many a ship to sea, with many hundred souls in one ship, whose weal and woe is common, and is a true picture of a commonwealth, or a human combination or society. It hath fallen out sometimes, that both papists and protestants, Jews and Turks, may be embarked in one ship, upon which supposal I affirm, that all the liberty of conscience, that ever I pleaded for, turns upon these two hinges—that none of the papists, protestants, Jew, or Turks, be forced to come to the ship's prayers or worship, nor compelled from their own particular prayers or worship, if they practice any. . . .

He adds that he

. . . never denied, that notwithstanding this liberty, the commander of this ship ought to command the ship's course, yea, and also command that justice, peace and sobriety, be kept and practiced, both among the seamen and all the passengers.[44]

And he goes on to detail the various obligations which citizens owed the commonwealth.

It is obvious, then, from this letter, as well as from his later attitude toward the Quakers, that for Williams "liberty of conscience" was a rather strictly limited and carefully qualified proposition. Miller calls attention to the fact that Williams's writing against the Quakers was probably the only one of his works that was enthusiastically received in Boston. The general climate there certainly was conservatively Calvinistic. Such people regarded "liberty of conscience" as dangerous.

V The Dangers of Religious Liberty: Hooker, Johnson, Ward, and Cotton

Two other writers who thought religious toleration a generally dangerous proposition were Thomas Hooker and Edward Johnson. Although he was an originator of Congregationalist polity (see his *Survey of the Summe of Church Discipline*, 1648), Hooker also sided against Anne Hutchinson and Roger Williams and was often of the same mind as Winthrop and Cotton in repudiating religious toleration.[45] In Connecticut, where he led his congregation after seceding from Massachusetts Bay, the franchise was not restricted to church members, but otherwise theory and practice were quite similar to government in Massachusetts.[46]

Hooker did differ from Winthrop, however, in placing less stress on the principle that "the wise, the able, and the good [in short, leaders like Winthrop himself] knew the purposes of the covenant better than most of those who entered it and should be allowed freedom to interpret it at their discretion." [47] (Hooker's idea of civil government was that it should follow the analogy of the church covenant.) He therefore tended to put more stress than Winthrop on the idea that "they who appoint officers have also the power to set bounds and limitations to them." In a letter to Winthrop, dated 1638, and reproduced by Miller, Hooker makes reference to Winthrop's having raised the question about the discretionary power of the judges to fix sentences. To this proposal of arbitrary power for the judges, Hooker strongly objects, saying, "I am afraid it is a course which wants both safety and warrant. I must confess, I ever looked at it as a way which leads directly to tyranny, and so to confusion, and must plainly profess, if it was in my liberty, I should choose neither to live nor leave my posterity under such a government." [48]

Edward Johnson, like other orthodox leaders, attacked "Familists, Seekers, Antinomians and Anabaptists," saying that there was no room in Christ's army "for toleratorists." Miller informs us that this statement was made at a time when Cromwell's Puritan army, because of difficulties in winning recruits, had had to enforce a policy of toleration. But whatever Cromwell might do, Johnson espoused a more rigid doctrine of church "purity." [49] Johnson was one of the founders of Woburn, near Boston, and supposedly he wrote his famous history of New England (from the year 1628) there. This work, entitled *Wonder-Working Providence of Sion's Savior*, appeared anonymously in London in 1654.

At nearby Ipswich, too, Nathaniel Ward, author of *The Simple Cobbler of Aggawam* (1647), had viewed religious "liberty" in this same light. Parrington describes this book as "bitter with the intolerance of toleration." In style Ward was "a belated Euphuist," a contemporary of Ben Jonson and much influenced by the satiric flare for word play and wit of Elizabethan culture. While he wrote like an Elizabethan, he nevertheless thought like an Anglican— Parrington says he knew and loved King Charles.[50] At the same time, he had been trained not only as a minister but also as a London lawyer and was deeply aware of the problem of defining the limits of political power between contending parties. It was his draft of laws in 1639, after Cotton's *Abstract or The Lawes of New-England* had failed to win adoption by the General Court, which ultimately became known as the Massachusetts *Body of Liberties* (enacted into law in 1641). Morgan calls this document a "bill of rights," which it certainly was.[51] At the same time he observes that Ward "had no more love for popular government than John Cotton, but like Cotton he believed that governments must be limited, and he thought the best form of limitation was a public statement of the rights of subjects." [52]

John Cotton was actually one of the earliest American writers to insist on limitation of the powers of the magistrates. In *An Exposition upon the Thirteenth Chapter of Revelation* (London, 1655) Cotton argues from the doctrine of the total depravity of mankind that "mortal men" should be given "no greater power than" the givers of such power "are content they shall use, for use it they will." He illustrates his thesis by citing the historical abuse of temporal power in the papacy. And, he concludes, "It is therefore most wholsome for Magistrates and Officers in Church and Common-wealth, never to affect more liberty and authority than will do them good, and the People good; for what ever transcendant power is given, will certainly over-run those that give it, and those that receive it. . . . It is necessary therefore, that all power that is on earth be limited, Church-power or other." [53]

Everett H. Emerson calls Cotton "the most representative and probably the most popular writer of his generation." [54] Cotton's ability to write with clarity, force, and intelligence was certainly a factor in his popularity. As a writer, he may have lacked warmth and enthusiasm, as Emerson points out; but, considering Cotton's basic religious zeal, perhaps this coolness was only one of his interesting complexities.

VI *Recapitulation*

In general, we have tried to show how different writers during the period *circa* 1588–1660 gave expression to a variety of opinions on the two chief controversies of the time—the struggle for religious freedom and the separation of the powers of church and state—in the Christian commonwealth. Since these two controversies developed concomitantly and often overlapped, they had to be considered together.

More specifically, we have seen how writers like John Cotton and Nathaniel Ward attempted to set up new bodies of law in Massachusetts Bay, thus showing the hand of the clergy in framing civil law. By way of clarifying the fundamental ideas of civil rulers like Winthrop on theocratic government, we have examined his sermon preached on board the *Arbella*, noting at the same time that in the Massachusetts Bay theocracy the clergy did not actually hold civil office—an important point in the separation of powers of church and state. Then, to show the development of religious toleration, we have taken up the Antinomian controversy and the long controversy between Roger Williams and John Cotton concerning persecution for cause of conscience. We have stressed the great difficulties attending this growth of religious freedom (especially for Quakers and other non-Calvinists) by presenting ideas hostile to religious liberty held by such leaders and writers as Thomas Hooker, Edward Johnson, Nathaniel Ward, and (in the case of the Quakers) even Roger Williams himself. Finally, we have hinted at limitation of the power of the magistrates—a concept that began to emerge in the work of writers like Hooker, Ward, and Cotton, all of whom opposed the general idea of religious liberty.

In the next chapter we shall trace the subsequent course of the struggle for power between church and state and the decline of the theocracy as it was exemplified in the careers of Increase and Cotton Mather during the period 1660 to 1728.

CHAPTER 2

The Decline of the Theocracy

I The Half-Way Covenant

ONE of the earliest indications that the New England way of Puritan life and congregational polity was experiencing a challenge may be seen in Thomas Lechford's *Plain Dealing: or, Newes from New-England* (London, 1642).[1] Lechford, who has been called Boston's first lawyer, was also probably America's first social critic. His preface mentions that he had been imprisoned earlier in England for nonconformity in religion. Arriving in Boston in 1638, he speedily became disillusioned with congregationalism in New England and returned to old England and the Anglican way. *Plain Dealing* may be viewed as his apology for his brief defection from the Church of England. But it is also an excellent source book, for Lechford reports critically and with valuable specific detail on some matters that plagued the civil and ecclesiastical government of Massachusetts Bay. The following statement by Lechford on the important matter of baptism might be hailed as a kind of prelude to the Half-Way Covenant of 1662: ". . . their children for the most part remain unbaptized: and so have little more priviledge than Heathens, unless the discipline be amended and moderated."[2]

It will be remembered that one could become a church member only by public profession of faith and examination by church elders. The single exception to this rule was that baptized children of church members could be considered as probationary members. This meant that they had all the rights of ordinary church membership except admission to the communion service. The idea, of course, was that as they advanced in their apprenticeship, or testing period, they would become converted and make public profession of faith, thus becoming full-fledged church members. But there were problems. Many of these apprentice members never experienced conversion. Then, too, the Cambridge Platform of

1648 [3] made the point, however lightly, that only children of church members were entitled to baptism. Thus an increasingly large number of persons were being excluded from church membership, which looked as if it were becoming an almost hereditary privilege. [4] Since one had to be a member of a church in order to vote, the whole matter smacked of political exclusiveness. Consequently one of Lechford's criticisms is directed at the fact "that the civil government is not so equally administered." [5] To illustrate:

Now most of the persons at *New-England* are not admitted to their Church, and therefore are not *Freemen* [i.e., citizens], and when they come to be tryed there, be it for life or limb, name or estate, or whatsoever, they must bee tryed and judged too by those of the Church, who are in a sort their adversaries: How equal that hath been, or may be, some by experience doe know, others may judge.

(p. 23)

The consequence was that increasingly the failure to extend baptism and church membership tended to divide the total population (in this case of Massachusetts Bay) into three groups: 1. a minority of church members; 2. a majority of non-church members who yet approved of the status quo; 3. a group, "consisting at first chiefly of servants and apprentices, but later recruited by newcomers and even the sons and grandsons of ardent Puritans, [who] were hostile to the 'theocracy.' " [6] This third group threatened the power of the clergy and challenged the civil government.

As early as 1662, one solution to this vexatious problem had been proposed—the Half-Way Covenant. Many of the early "probationary" members who had been baptized had *not* been converted; nor had they professed faith publicly. The question then was: should the children of these already "probationary" members also be admitted as provisional members without right of admission to the communion? Richard Mather argued affirmatively, and from this time onward the church was gradually forced into relaxing its originally strict standards for membership. This issue was also to be fought out orally later in the long duel between the conservative poet-preacher Edward Taylor and the liberal Solomon Stoddard, grandfather of Jonathan Edwards. [7]

To better understand the political significance of the period preceding this controversy between Taylor and Stoddard (and between Increase and Cotton Mather and Stoddard, for they, too, thought liberalization of standards for church membership a great danger to their ecclesiastical and political power), we must momentarily backtrack to a more detailed discussion of the Half-Way Covenant. The Half-Way Covenant was very important politically and related, as well, to the Covenant theology discussed in chapter one.

During the period 1646–62 children of full communing church members were regarded as "heirs to the covenant." But what if these children grew up and did not experience the saving grace of *conversion*? Were they still members? Or was the covenant relation broken? And what of the children of these unconverted or noncommuning "heirs of the covenant"? Could these latter children be baptized and similarly regarded as "heirs to the covenant"? Did the covenant last only three generations? Or did it extend to a *thousand* generations, as Peter Bulkeley and George Phillips, thought? [8] These and similar questions became matter for increasingly warm debate among the clergy during the decade before 1662.

In 1662 the Massachusetts General Court called a synod to solve this problem. The synod recommended that these third-generation noncommunicant children be baptized and considered "heirs." This recommendation (or Half-Way Covenant), [9] fathered by Richard Mather, John Eliot, Jonathan Mitchell, *et al.*, enlarged baptism and consequently church membership, despite the fact that not all churches immediately adopted the recommendation. (In fact, many of them opposed it; and frequently the congregation, or laity, opposed their own minister who, like Richard Mather of Dorchester, attempted to put it into practice.) [10]

According to Robert G. Pope, the ministers during this period (1648–62) were disturbed not so much by the backsliding of their members as by the growing members of the "unbaptized," by the "increasing chasm between church and community." [11] Pope also asserts that "nowhere in the debate over the Half-Way Covenant was the franchise mentioned." For as late as 1660 the Massachusetts General Court was still interpreting the church membership requirement for freemanship (citizenship) *strictly*—that is, the member had to be *"in full Communion."* [12] In 1664, however, the court did modify qualifications for such citizenship—in order "to mollify the King's Commissioners"—and only then "could anyone other than communicants acquire political rights." [13]

The opponents of the Half-Way Covenant often included certain ministers—such as John Davenport of New Haven and other so-called "Strict Congregationalists." Charles Chauncy, the president of Harvard, belonged to this latter group, as did Richard Mather's two sons, Increase and Eleazer. The New England Baptists also opposed this idea and its practice; in their view "children had no place in the covenant," for no one could tell if a child "had grace." [14]

In Connecticut the debate over the Half-Way Covenant flared into a new problem concerning church authority—both *within* the churches and *among* the churches. It appeared that the old Congregational polity (the autonomy of the individual church) was being challenged by a new party in this colony, one which advocated Presbyterian rule (government by the presbyters of groups of churches attempting to exercise control over an individual church). Eventually the Congregationalists began accepting the Half-Way Covenant—not because they approved of it, but because they regarded it as the lesser evil. By accepting it, they were able (to some extent) to keep their Presbyterian opponents at bay. Another important cause for their acceptance, of course, was the fact that in Connecticut both civil and church authorities had begun to question the old policy that kept "so many decent Christians" outside the churches. [15]

When John Davenport accepted a call to New England's "most prestigious" First Church in Boston in 1667, his opposition to the innovative Half-Way Covenant grew even stronger. Pope points out that Davenport's removal from New Haven to Boston coincided with the absorption of New Haven (as a colony) by Connecticut. One political effect of this merger was that (from Davenport's view) the "broad franchise" of Connecticut now "threatened New Haven." [16] Within two years of his arrival in Boston, Davenport had "disrupted Massachusetts politics, alienated the clergy, and split First Church." [17] Here the details grow complicated. Suffice it to say that the group that now split from First Church and set itself up as Third Church (against the advice of Governor Bellingham and five magistrates) ultimately succeeded in bringing the Half-Way Covenant issue into a battle between the two ruling houses (magistrates and deputies). After Davenport's death in 1670 his supporters in the House of Deputies drew up a report blaming the clergy for the woefully disturbed situation. The clergy struck back by campaigning for deputies supporting their view and succeeded in electing them. [18] This victory of the clergy over the House of Deputies (June 4, 1671) assumed an even larger dimension when the House of Deputies recanted and retracted its charges against the Third Church ministers, absolving them of any guilt.[19] The political significance of this episode lay in the fact that it helped define the limits of power between state and church. Increase Mather, the early opponent of the Half-Way Covenant, now, following the death-bed wish of his father in 1670, also recanted and in his *First Principles* (1671) listed evidence supporting the idea that "the founding generation had favored the principle of extended baptism." [20] Although some resistance to the Half-Way Covenant remained after 1671, in Massachusetts, this resistance was sporadic and localized. For practical purposes the battle was over. Mather's recantation marked the end of an era.

The years following 1675 saw greater implementation of the Half-Way Covenant, mainly as a response to a series of disastrous events—King Philip's War, two great fires in Boston, an epidemic of smallpox, and other threats to Puritan political control—all of which were interpreted as signs of God's wrath against his chosen people for neglecting the baptism of children in the church.[21] Thus the practice of "mass covenant renewals," as they were called, which were begun by James Fitch of Norwich, Connecticut, became increasingly popular. The sudden death of King Philip during the Indian war made them think this practice effective. (In renewing the covenant, or "owning" it, the second and later generation of "heirs of the covenant" had to answer certain questions publicly in church, affirming their acceptance of their obligations to God and man and their intent to meet these obligations "as far as it was humanly possible *unaided by grace.*") [22]

In sum, the political significance of the Half-Way Covenant was that it showed that although in Massachusetts (and elsewhere) church and state were separated, as Pope puts it, the two were nevertheless also "intimately related, and anything that affected religion ultimately had political ramifications. Religion and politics were too deeply interwoven at the center of men's lives to remain distinct." [23] Other points of significance were these: "Individual congregations and ministers applied it [the Half-Way Covenant] to fit their own theology and locale," with a resultant *individualism in local church government* in both Connecticut and Massachusetts.[24] There was also greater toleration of diversity within established churches, despite the fact that uniformity was considered desirable. Too, a critical attitude toward persons or groups holding political power began to emerge, as we have seen above in the quarrel of the deputies with the ministers, and along with it a principle of rectifying mistakes made by legislative bodies. If, as Pope says, the "half-way covenant occupies a central place in the transformation of New England" from an isolated "sectarian community" during Winthrop's day to a more prosperous " 'secular' society" during Cotton Mather's later years, the reason is that the churches in the later years of the seventeenth century had to reach out into the community for new members and to change their attitude toward the "unchurched." The old " 'tribalism' no longer sufficed; the churches became *evangelical*" (my italics). The "purity" of the old church thus became sacrificed to the idea of "community." [25] Half a century later, as we shall see, something similar to the Half-Way Covenant controversy arose again during the Great Awakening. In the heat of that great revival "many, if not most, of the new members joined the churches as half-way members. . . ." [26]

Since Jonathan Mitchell (1624–1668) has been labeled "the real leader of the movement for the Half-Way Covenant," [27] it might be helpful to look at an election sermon he delivered in 1667 in Cambridge as an illustration of one rather important political view that arose during the period of the controversy. Mitchell was the tutor and mentor of Increase Mather. He succeeded the well-known Thomas Shepard, even to marrying Shepard's widow.

In his sermon *Nehemiah on the Wall in Troublesome Times* he argued the old Roman maxim that the welfare of the people should be the supreme law. This was of course a far cry from Winthrop's assertion that a magistrate, once elected, was responsible only to God. Mitchell developed his principle logically, basing it solidly on "Reason and Equity" as well as on Scripture, contending that

. . . the Law of God enjoyns, that in Humane Civil Affairs, things be managed according to right Reason and Equity; and that Rulers, as they are for the people, so they are to make it their main business, and the scope of all their Actions, Laws and Motions, to seek the welfare of the people.[28]

Mitchell thought that "all other laws should be limited" by this principle. He writes, "This is the *Compass* that Rulers are to steer by, and the *Touch-stone* of Right and Wrong in all their Motions, *viz.* What is for or against the Publick good, and the welfare of the people." [29] He adds, "It is impossible that any thing should be truly right, that is destructive to the common good. . . ." And in his application of this doctrine (see *use* II) he impressed on his audience the idea that neither "hard times" nor "difficulties and troubles" should excuse or *"discourage* Rulers from doing the work of their Places which God calls them unto, or from seeking the welfare of the people." [30] Nehemiah had repaired the wall of Jerusalem during such "hard times," explained Mitchell, and he would have his congregation and their civil officers take this brave leader as their model.

II   *Increase Mather and the Andros Affair*

A second major factor in the decline of the theocracy centered around the Governor Andros affair, in which Increase Mather acted a major part. This Mather has been described as "the foremost divine of New England, its most prolific and widely read man of letters, and for many years a power in affairs of state." [31] The years of Increase Mather's presidency at Harvard (1685–1701) marked the high point of his career, but even after his withdrawal from this office until his death in 1723 he was a power to be reckoned with.

The background of the Andros affair dates from October 23, 1684, when the old Massachusetts charter which Winthrop had carried across the Atlantic was revoked by Charles II.[32] While the king's attempt to incorporate all the colonies under a Dominion of New England, headed by the cruel Governor Andros, failed, so did Increase Mather's lobbying for the return of the old charter, and Massachusetts became a royal colony in 1691. One important reform effected by the ensuing colonial reorganization was the disallowance of discrimination against religious minorities.[33] This reform curtailed the power of the Puritan theocracy which Mather represented.[34]

Mather's objections to the revocation of the old charter, which in practice had given the Massachusetts theocracy a great deal of power and independence, took the form of a trip to London in order to appeal to the king for a new charter. Many of his writings are related to this venture. Significant and paradoxical in Increase Mather's writings on this subject is the emphasis on explicitly *economic and political* concerns rather than on specifically *religious* matters. On the one hand, the fact that a clergyman of Mather's standing (President of Harvard and minister in Second Church in Boston) was chosen to represent colonial grievances at this time shows that the clergy still possessed great political-economic influence. But on the other hand the kinds and number of *secular* economic arguments and illustrations advanced by Mather show perhaps a decline in the relative role of religious and theological argument in political writing by New Englanders.

One of the earliest and most important of Mather's writings in connection with the Andros affair is an eight-page pamphlet printed in 1689 and entitled *A Narrative of the Miseries of New-England, By Reason of an Arbitrary Government Erected there.*[35] It begins by noting that it is against the national interest "that a Collony so considerable as *New-England*, should be discouraged," especially since the people there "are generally Sober, Industrious, well-Disciplin'd, and apt for Martial Affairs" (1).

The pamphlet presents in detail the reactions of the various colonies on discovering their charters withdrawn. A detailed list of grievances against the new administration under Andros follows in the next section (pp. 3–5), one of the chief of these grievances being that the colonists were being taxed without their own consent. Also listed is Andros's failure to print and publicize the laws and his having restricted the town meetings (which formerly had taken place sometimes as often as once a week—in order to act on cases of charity) to once a year. In addition, Andros had jailed some of the colonists arbitrarily—John Wise, among others—when they threatened to petition the king, and had refused those jailed the right of habeas corpus. Mather writes:

And yet these things (tho bad enough) are but a very small part of the misery which that poor People have been groaning under, since they have been governed by a Despotick and Absolute Power. For, their new Magistrates [Andros *et al.*] tell them, that their *Charter* being gone, their title to their Lands and Estates is gone therewith, and that All is the kings; and that they represent the King. (4)

It was this confiscation of their own private property that hurt most.

Mather's negotiations with James II ended with the dethronement of the latter and the ascent of William III to the throne in the Glorious Revolution of 1688.[36] Thus, whatever concessions Mather had managed to win from James II now had to be reexamined and granted anew by the new king, William III.

In an attempt at winning a new charter for Massachusetts from William III, Increase Mather wrote other works that were intended for the London reading public. Like his first pamphlet, these political writings of Mather aimed to persuade his readers that the mother country was *not* aiding the colonies but was instead exploiting it economically and politically. He tried, further, to show that the colonies were not trying to take advantage of the mother country.

According to his own statement before the Governor of Massachusetts in 1693, he wrote three different vindications of New England in a paper war with his opponents.[37] The first of these, entitled *New-England Vindicated*, has been described as "an answer to a pamphlet probably presented to Parliament in 1689, during the discussion of the Corporation Bill." [38] The pamphlet (written by persons Mather calls "Considerators") had charged that 300 ships had been employed to export from New England tobacco, sugar, wool, etc., for manufacture in France and Holland (the enemies of England) and also to import from these countries linen and woolen "and all other Manufactures" (112). Referring to this pamphlet as a "*Scandalous Libel*," Mather argues that New England could neither use nor sell so great a quantity of goods. Furthermore, New England had been subjected to a law prohibiting the export of wool, since it was extremely scarce. (At this time the principal exports were lumber, horses, and provisions for Jamaica and the West Indies. New England also built ships for old England.) The Navigation Act of 1663 constituted an additional complaint of the colonists, since by its terms officers appointed to take charge of vessels trading in New England were compelled to see that annual financial returns were sent to the governor and then forwarded by him to London.

Mather also attacks his opponents, the "Considerators," for blaming Massachusetts for the loss of its charter. Actually, the charter had been lost, he says, because it had been impossible for the colonists to appear in London at their own expense within the limited time allowed them by the *quo warranto* order and the accompanying royal declaration that challenged their old independent charter.

One of the charges brought against the colonists was that they had set up their own coinage—the famous pinetree shillings—and should be punished for debasing the coin of the realm. Mather first defended the New England coinage with respect to the excellence of the alloy. He then argued that the mint had been set up in 1652 (when Cromwell and the Puritans had been in power in England), but said that when Charles II had been restored to the throne in 1660, the colonists had complied with the king's rules for coining.

Maryland, Pennsylvania, and the East India Company had also altered the coinage, he points out. "Why then should *New-England* be esteemed more criminal than other Plantations? " (116).

To the accusation by the "Considerators" that New England had put a tax on imports from the mother country, he answered, "There hath been *none* imposed on Shipping but *Powder-Money*, and not half so much as is done in the other Plantations" (116). (*Powder-money* was tax money for the purchase of gunpowder.)

Other charges he refuted or attempted to refute were these: 1. that they had mistreated the captains of the king's ships for desiring permission to recruit victuals; 2. that they had entertained pirates; 3. that the New Englanders were free from taxes and contributed nothing to the crown; 4. that the settlers from other colonies did not want their charters restored to them, because it would expose them to French attack and make them independent of the English crown; 5. that the government of New England was "arbitrary" and was drawing wealthy investors away from England to settle there (this he answers with a show of loyalty but nonetheless scornfully—"As if People could live more easie under an unlimited and Arbitrary Power elsewhere, than under the regular Government of England" [120]); 6. that huge amounts of money had been invested in New England mines; 7. that if the charter were restored, the king would have no immunities to grant in New England (here he argued that the failure to settle the charter business was holding up the entrepreneurs who wanted to invest in the new world); 8. that Massachusetts had imposed upon their people an oath to their own commonwealth instead of to the king; 9. that Massachusetts had "*Encroached upon their Neighboring Colonies* in a hostile manner" (117); 10. that they had "affronted" the King's commissioners; 11. that they had made laws "*against all Opinions in Religion excepting those of the Congregational churches, and more especially against the Church of England*" (118); 12. that if the original charters were restored, many families who had recently cleared land (which had originally belonged to the older settlers) would be ruined. To this last charge Mather retorted that "the *Arbitrary Government*, which these men so much admire, hath not been there three years, and no Tracts of Land have been cleared since that Time" (121).[39] He admits that some people (under Andros's new rule) "have been enriched by invading other Men's estates" and that such people would quite rightly "be impoverished by the true Proprietors enjoying their own again" if the charters were restored.

Mather's first *Vindication* provoked an anonymous answer which repeated the original charges—*viz.*, that the colonists were bent on destroying the manufacture and navigation of the mother country. Mather then answered this latter work with his second "vindication," entitled *A Further Vindication of New-England, From False Suggestions in a late Scandalous Pamphlet, pretending to shew, The Inconvenience of Joyning the Plantation-Charters with those of ENGLAND.*[40] His third "vindication" might be the "Letter to a Person of Quality" entitled *A Brief Relation of the State of New England* (July 30, 1689),[41] in which he argues for the restoration of the Massachusetts charter, for the mercantile utility of New England in terms of its exports, and for its necessity as a military defense post against the French.

Thus far we have considered some, but not all, of the works Increase Mather intended for his London reading public. Just as he was about to embark for America, extracts from two of his letters back home along "with a paragraph from an English journal were printed as a broadside in Boston."[42] The title of the broadside was *The Present State of New-English Affairs* (1689), and its purpose, according to Murdock, was to prevent false reports.[43] The broadside assured the citizens of Boston that the new king approved of their rebellion against Andros; in fact, the last paragraph reported that "the king had commanded the return of Andros, Randolph, and the other captives of the Boston revolution, to answer the charges against them in England."[44]

When these culprits arrived in England, Mather was still there, having been delayed by his son's having contracted smallpox. Further complications took the form of a decline in the power of the Whigs (from whom he had most to gain) and in the increase of the number of agents now representing New England. When, on the advice of Sir John Somers, the colonists' chief legal advisor, the agents refused to sign the accusations against Andros, Randolph, and their henchmen, Mather's position became awkward indeed. Although he favored signing, he did not sign. The consequence was that Governor Andros got off very lightly; indeed, one year later, he was appointed Governor of Virginia. As Murdock says, "Mather inevitably lost ground" as a result of this episode.[45] He and the agents appealed to the king; but the king was busy with other matters. Randolph and other friends of Andros in England rallied to his defense. Under Randolph's auspices there appeared a pamphlet entitled *New England's Faction Discovered* and assailing "the colonial cause in general and Mather in particular." [46] Phipps's defeat at Quebec further weakened Mather's already tottering position. To make matters worse, King William left England for Holland early in 1691.

Nevertheless, Mather had not given up the fight during this period. He published *Reasons for the Confirmation of the Charters of the Corporations in New England* (1690). [47] This seven-page pamphlet listed eight reasons in as many paragraphs. Short as it is, it is a clever piece of rhetoric. It touched on the mood of the people in Massachusetts:

Some that know the Temper of that People, do confidently affirm, That there is not one in an hundred amongst the Inhabitants of that Territory, which does not desire that their Government by Charter might be continued by them: If the King shall please to gratifie them therein, They will cheerfully Expose themselves and all that is dear to Them in this World, to serve his Majesty. But if their former Rights and Privileges be with-held from Them, it will cause an universal dissatisfaction and discouragement amongst them. Nor can any thing be thought of, that will more Endanger their being ruin'd by the *French*, than the taking from Them their Charter Liberties: As is manifest in that, when They enjoyed their Charters, they easily subdued their Enemies, but since that it has been otherwise. (226)

The king was thus presented with a choice of alternatives, only one of which would be of mutual benefit to himself and the colonists. In a footnote it was explained that the colonists were asking only to "depend on the Crown" as did the corporations in England, that they had recently won a victory over the French, and that their capture of all of Canada would materially benefit "the *English* Crown and Nation"—by reason of the Beaver trade, the fisheries, and the "profitable and very considerable Addition" "to our King's Dominions" (229n). Thus Mather dangled the bait under the king's nose, at the same time stressing the dependence of the colonies on the crown and their attempt to revise or repeal such laws as might be "repugnant" to the crown (since by their original charter they were "bound" to make only such laws as he might not find offensive). He also stressed the fact that the colonists were bound to the king by an oath of allegiance, that they obeyed "all Acts of Parliament which concern[ed] the Regulating of Trade," and that all "Warrants" were issued in the "Kings Name." As if this were not enough to mollify his majesty, an additional material bait was mentioned—the fact that a fifth of mineral ores belonged by right to the crown.

It is hard to believe that Mather did not intend that some of the arguments in this tract should be drawn to the attention of the king himself. Murdock states that Mather put a copy of this work "into the hands of each member of the Privy Council." [48] Conscientious propagandist that he was, he not only wrote copy but also personally distributed it, in order to make sure it would reach the right people—i.e., those who might be most effective in advancing his cause.

Mather neither minced nor wasted words in his highly persuasive pamphlet. He pursued a somewhat different method, however, in a longer document, *A Brief Account Concerning Several of the Agents of New-England, Their Negotiation at the Court of England With Some Remarks on the New Charter Granted to the Colony of Massachusetts. Shewing That all things duely Considered, Greater Priviledges than what are therein contained, could not at this Time rationally be expected by the People there.* This pamphlet has Mather's name printed at its conclusion on p. 22, along with the place and date—"London, Novemb[er] 16, 1691." In the main this work is a pure *report* on the new charter and the long and complicated details of the three-year negotiation (1688–91) for it (see pp. 4–16). But Mather also had a job of persuasion to do here, too. He had to bring his readers (the Massachusetts colonists this time) around to willing acceptance of this new charter. The task was not easy, for he faced opposition from both the liberal and the conservative wings back home in Boston. The liberals wanted to elect their own governor rather than to accept one appointed by the king, even if he were (as in Phipps's case) a friend of Mather's. The conservatives did not want to relinquish church membership as a prerequisite for the franchise. To disarm those who still thought there should be some ecclesiastical test for the right to vote, he included at the end of this pamphlet a testimonial, signed by thirteen of his English friends, *An Extract of a Letter (Written by some of the most Eminent Nonconformist Divines in London,) Concerning the New Charter Granted to the Colony of Massachusetts in New-England.* The title page indicated that the letter was addressed "To the much Honoured *General Court* Assembled at *Boston,* in *New-England,*" where, writes Murdock, it was read. [49] The letter referred to Mather as "*our much Esteemed and Beloved Brother,*" cataloguing all his virtues.

Before passing on to the serious crisis that threatened Increase Mather soon after May 14, 1692, the day he arrived home from England, we should glance at one other writing, which has sometimes been attributed to him. This is *The Revolution in New-England Justified*, title abbreviated (Boston, 1691). The foreward "To the Reader" is signed E. R. and S. S. (6) and the work is thought to be by Edward Rawson, although others may have contributed to it, since the title page says that it was "Published by the Inhabitants of BOSTON" on the occasion of the overthrow of Andros.[50] The tract is a lengthy answer to Mr. John Palmer, one of Andros's defenders. Bound with it is a second pamphlet, entitled "A Narrative of the Proceedings of Sir Edmund Andros and his Accomplices . . . By several Gentlemen who were of his Council." [51]

The Revolution Justified was later reprinted by Isaiah Thomas (Boston, 1773) as a reminder of British tyranny.

III *Cotton Mather and Witchcraft*

When Increase Mather landed in Boston after his long sojourn abroad, he had no idea of what awaited him. Although he had written *An Essay for the Recording of Illustrious Providences* (1684), which dealt with, among other matters, some problems in witchcraft, his interest in the subject had been almost entirely that of a detached observer, and his point of view on such phenomena had been that of a "natural philosopher" or scientist.[52] He could have had little notion of the hysteria that was to occur during the Salem witchcraft trials, which began less than a month after his homecoming, or of other events during the forthcoming decade that, even more importantly than the witchcraft crisis, were to mark his decline from preeminence as a spiritual and political leader in Massachusetts. The year 1692 was to be the turning point in his life.

Until 1692 the story of Increase Mather's life is that of a constant development in leadership. In that year he was of unique rank in the colony. He had printed more books than any other writer in New England. He was the close friend and spiritual advisor of the governor. He was the sponsor of the new charter. Phipps and Stoughton owed their offices to him, and, until 1693, the Council members held their places because he had seen fit to choose them. He was in fact, if not in name, the leader of the local Congregational Church, and he was President of Harvard College.[53]

At this time (May 14, 1692) nearly 100 persons accused of witchcraft were in jail awaiting trial. As one writer described the situation, "The jails were crowded, the Salem court clerk had recorded hundreds of pages of frightening testimony, and the friends of both accused and afflicted were clamoring for trials." [54] Governor Phipps (a military man by the terms of the new charter) was preoccupied with the danger of an Indian attack. Accordingly, he appointed the deputy governor, William Stoughton, to act as chief justice at the trial that began on June 2. The eight associate judges included Samuel Sewall, John Hathorne, and other eminent citizens, some of whom were followers of the Mathers.

The Mathers, both Increase and his son Cotton, are often accused of having played an important part in these trials, which lasted until October 12. On that date, "a week after Increase Mather [had] read the ministers an essay demonstrating the unreliability of spectral evidence," [55] Phipps terminated the court. Contrary to popular belief, the Mathers probably did more to oppose the horror of this grave injustice than to promote it. Murdock states the facts. We know, he says,

that after the first execution [of Bridget Bishop], he [Increase Mather] publicly urged caution in the use of spectral evidence; that he did not attend the trials; that he cautioned a parishioner against spreading the excitement; that he made plain to Brattle his discontent with what was done; that he was chosen to write a full statement of the ministers' position; that the book which resulted was the first detailed argument against the procedure of the trials; and that after it was printed, no witch was executed in Massachusetts. [56]

The book here referred to was *Cases of Conscience Concerning Evil Spirits, Persecuting Men* (1693), which apparently also represented the Cambridge association of ministers' views, specifically their feeling that "spectral evidence" was not a valid proof for conviction of witchcraft. Increase Mather's position on this matter differed slightly from that of the ministerial association. He argued that "the Scriptures, the writings of scholars, and the observations of New Englanders, all prove that the Devil *can* disguise his agents in the shapes of the *innocent*" [57] (my italics).

Turning now to Cotton Mather and his writings in connection with witchcraft, we recollect that he had been concerned with this subject previous to its outbreak in Salem. This concern had taken the form of a book entitled *Memorable Providences, Relating to Witchcrafts and Possessions, etc.* (Boston, 1689). Unlike his father's work, Cotton Mather's *Memorable Providences* represented a more average or othodox Puritan view of witchcraft. But it, too, partook of the kind of scientific interest shown by the elder Mather. Part of this book, at least, was provoked by the hanging of one Goodwife Glover during the winter of 1688–89 for supposedly having bewitched some of the children of John Goodwin.[58] (Although there had been many previous outbreaks of witchcraft in the American colonies, probably the main reason that the colonists became so highly excited over this issue was their terrible fear of moral contamination or eternal damnation.)[59] *Memorable Providences* has been classified as "in part history, in part science, and in part . . . admonition and edification."[60]

The Wonders of the Invisible World. Observations As well Historical as Theological, upon the Nature, The Number, and the Operations of the Devils, etc. (Boston and London, 1693), was a similar kind of work. Briefly described, it consisted of a sermon on witchcraft and a record of five trials, including one of a clergyman, George Burroughs, who was convicted and executed. "Glad should I have been," writes Mather, "if I had never known the Name of this man."[61] And well he might say so, for if ever an event signaled the waning power of the theocracy, it was this one.

The Wonders of the Invisible World is a widely anthologized work. It is also the single work most people ordinarily associate with the name of Cotton Mather. It is a vivid account which Mather turned out in September and October of 1692, immediately following the summer outbreak and trials. Mather's intense interest in his subject communicates itself to the reader, and his feeling for baroque style (the very opposite of his father's plain and direct approach) is highly appropriate to the matter dealt with. It is well written, a classic in its own right.

Two of Cotton Mather's letters of the same period indicate that he was not at all as "benighted and superstitious" in his views on witchcraft as many later generations have thought him.[62] In his signed letter to John Richards, dated May 31, 1692, he writes, "I must humbly beg you that in the Management of the affair [the witch trial] . . . you do not lay more stress upon pure Specter testimony than it will bear." At the same time he thought the threat very real, for he says, "I begin to fear that the Devils do more easily proselyte poor mortals into witchcraft, than is commonly conceived." [63] Richards was a judge who had written to Mather, asking advice on the proper procedure for conducting the trial. In the second letter, dated Boston, June 15, 1692, and unsigned, Mather apparently voiced the consensus of several ministers who had been consulted by Governor Phipps and the council:

· We judge that in the prosecution of these, and all such Witchcrafts, there is need of a very critical and exquisite Caution, lest by too much Credulity for things received only upon the Devil's Authority, there be a Door opened for a long Train of miserable Consequences, and Satan get an advantage over us, for we should not be ignorant of his Devices. . . . 'Tis necessary that all proceedings thereabout be managed with an exceeding tenderness towards those that may be complained of ; especially if they have been Persons formerly of unblemished Reputation . . . and that there may nothing be used as a Test, for the Trial of the suspected, the Lawfulness whereof may be doubted among the People of God. . . . Nevertheless, We cannot but humbly recommend unto the Government, the speedy and vigorous prosecution of such as have rendered themselves obnoxious, according to the Direction given in the Laws of God, and the wholesome Statutes of the *English* Nation, for the Detection of Witchcrafts. [64]

In *More Wonders of the Invisible World* (London, 1700) Robert Calef, a Boston merchant, attacked the clergy, especially Cotton Mather, for aiding and abetting the witchcraft frenzy. Whereupon Mather, with *Some Few Remarks upon a Scandalous Book, against the Government and Ministry of New-England* (Boston, 1701), delivered a slashing attack upon Calef. [65] It is worth noting, too, that as early as 1692 Thomas Brattle had challenged the judges of witchcraft in *A Full and Candid Account of the Delusion Called Witchcraft*. Space does not permit presenting the detail of the argument of these works, but the significance of Calef 's attack for our purpose is that it shows a mounting tide of opposition to the Mathers. Brattle, on the other hand, was a close friend of Increase Mather, and his general view of witchcraft (i.e., in believing in it but urging "moderation and justice, not fanatical zeal" in trying accused persons) was probably very similar to the elder Mather's. [66]

But, everything considered, it was not witchcraft alone which brought about the decline of the Mather theocracy in the 1690s. When Increase Mather returned in 1692 he was vulnerable to attack by opponents of the new charter—largely centered in the person of

Elisha Cooke and his followers, who mainly objected to the institution of a royally appointed governor. In the election of 1693 the issue, as Murdock says, was the "old charter versus the new." [67] Witchcraft had very little to do with the results of this election. In the main it was a test of confidence for Phipps and the other officers whom Increase Mather had chosen for the colony. Mather himself preached a sermon on the day of the election, May 31, 1693. According to the new charter the new governor was to have a veto power over those elected. In short, he could refuse to accept any person elected by the people if, in the words of Mather's sermon, that person was "Disaffected to the best and highest Interest, or, to the Government of Their Majesties in *England*, or . . . an Enemy to the Government here. . . ." [68] Although he had fought fiercely against this very proposition in England, Mather now found himself obliged to defend, for political reasons, what he formerly had hated. Thus, in effect, he played straight into the hands of his enemies. And although but a few of these were elected on that particular day, Elisha Cooke, the arch-opponent of Mather and Phipps, was among those few. Phipps promptly vetoed the election of Cooke. The people forthwith blamed Mather more than Phipps for this act, possibly, as Murdock points out, because of what Mather had said in his sermon. At any rate, Samuel Sewall wrote in his diary for June 8, 1693, that there was "great wrath about Mr. Cook's being refused, and 'tis supposed Mr. Mather is the cause." [69] From this time until 1701, when his enemies succeeded in forcing his resignation as president of Harvard, the power of Increase Mather waned.

Cotton Mather has so often been identified with the witchcraft trials (see above) that his writings in defense of his father's work on the charter have often been overlooked. Murdock tells us that the younger Mather "played a leading part" in the rebellion against Andros and that it probably was he who wrote "the official declaration justifying it." [70] More importantly, he circulated in manuscript (*circa* 1692) certain *Political Fables*, four short animal allegories, to defend his father's acceptance of the charter against New Englanders who believed he had sacrificed their rights. The first of these, "The New Settlement of the Birds in New England," argues for the adoption of the charter, explaining its new provisions:

Jupiter . . . [King William] offered that the birds might be everlastingly confirmed in their titles to their nests and fields. He offered that not so much as a twig should be plucked from any tree the birds would roost upon, without their own consent. He offered that the birds might constantly make their own laws, and annually choose their own rulers. He offered that all strange birds [noncitizens, according to Murdock] might be made uncapable of a seat in their council. He offered that it should be made impossible to[o] for any to disturb the birds in singing their songs to the praise of their Maker, for which they had sought liberty in the wilderness. Finally, he offered that the king's-fisher [Phipps] should have his commission to be their governour until they had settled what good orders among them they pleased; and that he should be more concerned than ever now to defend them from the French kites that were abroad. The king's-fisher indeed was to have his negative upon the birds, but the birds were to have a negative too upon the king's-fisher; and this was a privilege beyond what was enjoyed by the birds in any of the plantations, or even in Ireland itself.[71]

The last paragraph of this fable tells of the birds' referring their problem to "reasonable creatures" for advice. The "reasonable creatures" all agreed that there could be no reason to question the new charter. Obviously the "reasonable creatures" were those of Mather's readers who might be inclined to agree with his position.

The second fable, "The Elephant's Case a Little Stated," is an argument in behalf of Sir William Phipps's policies. The elephant (Phipps) is presented as the defender of the other animals. Certain of the beasts, however, quarrel with him. "They had nothing to say against the elephant; he was as good as he was great; he loved his king and country better than himself, and was as universally beloved." The elephant then makes a speech, assuring the other animals that far from his being "the shoeing-horn" they had accused him of being, he really had kept off the shoe of a tyrannical governor that they were so much afraid of. He closes his speech thus:

And if, after all I have done for you, not only employing of my purse, but also venturing my life to serve you, you have no better name for me than a shoeing-horn, yet I have at least obtained this for you, that you have time to shape your foot, so as, whatever shoe comes, it shall sit easy upon you.

Mather then concludes, "Upon this the whole forest, with grateful and cheerful hearts, gave thanks unto the elephant; and they aspired to such an exercise of reason, in this as well as in other cases, that they might not be condemned to graze under Nebuchadnezer's [*sic*] belly."[72]

The third fable, the longest, is entitled "Mercury's Negotiation." Mercury, the messenger god, is obviously Increase Mather in his diplomatic function as go-between. In this fable Cotton Mather introduces the character of Orpheus, whose harp supposedly had on former occasions "reduced the beasts unto a temper little short of reason." Orpheus makes a long, impassioned defense of Mercury, who had acted as a kind shepherd to the sheep (supporters of Increase Mather), whom the foxes and other beasts of prey were now attacking. Mather's technique is the rather common one of a long string of rhetorical questions with a mounting feeling of indignation, but it is nonetheless effective:

Are you angry because he evidently ventured the ruin of his person and family by the circumstances of his first appearance in Saturn's palace for you? Are you angry because, for divers years .together, he did, with an industry indefatigable to a prodigy, solicit for the restoration of your old folds; but with a vexation like that of Sysiphus, who was to roll a great stone up an high hill, from whence he was greatly kicked down, so that the labour was all to begin again? Are you angry because he has employed all the interest which God has wonderfully given him with persons of the greatest quality, to increase the number of your powerful friends: addressing the king and queen, the nobility, the convention and the parliaments, until the resettling of your old folds was most favorably voted for you? Is your anger because the signal hand of heaven overruled all these endeavours? Or is your displeasure that he hath cost you a little money to support his negotiations? I am to tell you, that he spent two hundred pounds of his own personal estate in your service—never like to be repaid. He made over all his own American estate, that he might borrow more to serve you. At length he has obtained in boon for your college, and in the bounty, which he lately begged of the royal Juno, (a bounty worth more than fourteen or sixteen hundred pounds sterling,) got more for you than he has yet expended for your agency. . . . Are you troubled because your liberties, whether as Christians or as Englishmen, are fully secured? Are you troubled because you have privileges above any part of the English nation whatsoever, either abroad or at home? Are you troubled that your officers are to be forever your own[?] . . . So sang Orpheus. . . .[73]

The fourth and last fable, "An Additional STORY OF THE DOGS AND WOLVES, the Substance of which was used an hundred and fifty Years ago, by Melancthon, to unite the Protestants," shows the wolves (the French) and the dogs (the New Englanders) drawn up for battle. The dogs are quarreling among themselves. A wolf, sent out to scout them, discovers this situation and returns with this report: ". . . There was little among them but snapping and snarling at one another; And therefore, said he, monsieurs, let's have at them: we shall easily play the wolf upon them that have played the dog upon one another." The fable then concludes with this sentence: "This is a story so old, that, as the good man said, I hope it is not true." [74]

Murdock reminds us that Cotton Mather was a contemporary of Swift and Addison and that in these fables he appears less pedantic than in his usual writings. I do not recall any writer living in America before this time who had made use of the genre of the animal allegory for political purposes. But Mather was less original in this respect than one might think, for such fables were common enough in English literature, witness Dryden's "The Hind and the Panther," the contemporary popularity of Aesop's *Fables* and tales of Reynard the fox, etc., so that, as Murdock says, in England, at least, "there was nothing novel in pointing a political moral or telling a tale of current events through the medium of the fable." [75] In this context Murdock calls Mather "the kinsman of the eighteenth century essayist." [76]

We shall encounter Cotton Mather again in our chapter on antislavery. Any discussion of Cotton Mather's writings has, of course, to take into account his major work, *Magnalia Christi Americana* (1702)—that gigantic, epic-like source book (largely) of church history, although it also includes many other political and historical matters, such as the history of Harvard University, the biographies of the early ministers and governors, and memorable providences. One of the most interesting of the numerous "lives" in this noble monument is, as one might expect, that of Sir William Phipps, which apparently came out in 1697, five years before the *Magnalia* was published in London. [77] This is an eminently readable biography. "The whole story is well told, concisely and with an eye to dramatic effect." Mather does, however, gloss over Phipps's faults, leading Murdock to comment that

Phip[p]s was, in reality, no paragon. He was hot-tempered, injudicious, without usual statesmanship, and however pious in his relation to the Second Church of the Mathers, by no means free from the vices of a badly educated, adventure-loving sea-dog. . . . There is an interesting problem—and an insoluble one—in deciding how far Mather's book was written to exalt himself and his father and to defend their political tenets, and how far it was designed as a tribute to Sir William Phip[p]s. [78]

Cotton Mather sometimes wrote from a variety of motives. His mind turned as easily to politics as to pedantry and didacticism, and this predilection for instruction probably quite often affected his purpose in writings. As a writer he considered his chief aim to be instruction.[79] A voluminous author, he often covered a wide variety of subjects, in many different forms—history, biography, essays, sermons, fables, etc.[80] As already intimated, his style differed markedly from his father's, but it is usually clear, informative, interesting, and studded with allusions from his wide reading.

IV *The Paper War between Increase Mather and Solomon Stoddard and The Great Awakening*

The first decade of the eighteenth century marked a decided lessening in the ecclesiastical and political power of Increase and Cotton Mather. This decline took the form of a violent paper war between Solomon Stoddard and Increase Mather, although Cotton Mather, the poet Edward Taylor, and several other leading ministers of the time were also involved in it.

As early as 1677 Stoddard had announced to his congregation in Northampton, Massachusetts, that he planned to baptize everybody (adult or child) who accepted the creed, *and* to admit all "godly persons" to communion "without relation of a saving experience." [81] There was nothing new with respect to baptism in this announcement, but the admission to communion of "godly persons" who had not experienced conversion did indicate a radical departure from the older Half-Way Covenant. In an election-day sermon (May 23, 1677) Increase Mather attacked this "new liberalism," referring to it as a dangerous apostasy.[82] At the Reforming Synod in 1679 both Stoddard and Increase Mather debated "open communion," as the new policy was called. After 1679, according to James P. Walsh, Increase and Cotton Mather continued to make indirect attacks on "Stoddardism," although Walsh cites no specific writings.[83] In fact, until recently nobody had found a copy of any written work published before 1687. But a recent and important discovery by Mason I. Lowance and Everett H. Emerson of a manuscript (a fair copy, apparently intended for printing) in Cotton Mather's hand of a work by his father proves concretely that the Stoddard-Mather controversy—hitherto studied mostly from printed works and manuscripts of the period 1699 to 1709—had become a matter of serious and concentrated debate as early as 1680.[84]

Who was this man Solomon Stoddard who had so excited the ire of Increase Mather? Like Mather he was a Harvard graduate. (The date of his graduation, 1662, corresponds with that of the Half-Way Covenant.) Following graduation, he had served as college librarian at Harvard. From 1667 to 1669 he was a chaplain in Barbados. Three years later he became pastor at Northampton, a post which he held until his death in 1729. In 1670 he had married the widow of Eleazer Mather, the brother of Increase.[85]

It would have been bad enough, from Increase Mather's viewpoint, if Stoddard had limited his new liberal policy of "open communion" to his own church. But Stoddard had gone so far as to organize the Hampshire Association—a group of churches that followed the same practice. To make matters worse, several other churches in the Connecticut River Valley were also beginning to follow this "dangerous apostasy," as Mather termed it. According to Schafer, however, "Boston and the East did not . . . and when in 1700 Stoddard finally broached the subject in print, he became involved in a ten-year controversy with Increase Mather."[86] Actually, as Lowance and Emerson point out, Stoddard's first appearance in print on this issue was of even earlier date. In 1687 in *The Safety of Appearing at the Day of Judgment*, published in Boston, he had defended his standards of "free admission" and reminded his readers that he had discussed the matter at the Synod of 1679.[87] One of Stoddard's arguments in this work was that the sacrament of communion might be of help in bringing about conversion; ergo, half-way or any other members should not be kept from it—rather, they should be encouraged to attend it. This view was called a "converting ordinance," and Cotton Mather attacked it in *A Companion for Communicants* (Boston, 1690).

Ten years later, when Stoddard launched his full-scale exposition of this issue, *The Doctrine of Instituted Churches*, he had to have this work published in London, because of the Mathers' control of printing in Boston.[88] In *The Doctrine of the Instituted Churches* (1700), as in the earlier *The Safety of Appearing*, Stoddard discussed the communion question. But in *The Doctrine* he also set forth a new view of church government—the Presbyterian view of a "national church" as against the old Congregationalism (each congregation had independent power). Here Stoddard argued that God had made his covenant *with the whole people, or nation*, rather than with each single congregation. He therefore advocated government "by synods of elders after the manner of Scotland."[89] Massachusetts refused to accept this plan, but Connecticut eventually did, in the Saybrook Platform of 1708. Stoddard's espousal of this new form of church government was important politically, because it signaled a broadening of possibilities—not only as to the number of the elect (those who might be saved) but also as to the geographical area of control, or power, the ministers might aspire to—the synod or even the entire nation instead of the congregation. In reality, both Mather and Stoddard aimed to strengthen ecclesiastical control in New England; but they differed in the means they thought necessary to achieve this end.[90]

Mather's *The Order of the Gospel* (Boston, 1700) appeared in the same year as Stoddard's *Doctrine*, but it was actually a reply to another work, *A Manifesto* (November 17, 1699). The *Manifesto* embodied in its sixteen articles the aims of a new Congregational church (the Fourth or Brattle Street church), headed by Benjamin Colman, a follower of Stoddardism. It was the essence of these sixteen articles which Mather attacked with his elaborate answers to seventeen questions in *The Order of the Gospel*.[91] But of necessity his attack struck at Stoddard as well as at Colman, particularly at the former's notion of "open communion." Defending what he called "the Good Old way of the [Congregational] Churches," he argues from the precedent of the Bohemian churches, which had excelled in their "great strictness as to Admissions to the Lords Supper." [92] "Christ has taught us that we must not give Holy things, Except to Holy Persons," he writes.[93]

If we Espouse such principles as these, Namely That Churches are not to Enquire into the Regenration of those whom they admit unto their Communion. That Admission to Sacraments is to be left wholly to the prudence and Conscience of the Minister. That Explicit Covenanting with God and with the Church is needless. That Persons not Qualified for Communion in special Ordinances shall Elect Pastors of Churches. That all Professed Christians have right to Baptism. That Brethren are to have no Voice in Ecclesiastical Councils. That the Essence of a Ministers call is not in the Election of the People, but in the Ceremony of Imposing hands. That Persons may be Established in the Pastoral Office without the Approbation of Neighbouring Churches or Elders; We then give away *the whole Congregational cause at once,* and a great part of the *Presbyterian Discipline also.* (8)*

The Brattle Street group—Colman, William Brattle, Pemberton, *et al.*—continued their challenge to Mather's power to control church and town. By way of returning his uncomplimentary attack, in *The Order of the Gospel*, they issued *The Gospel Order Revived*, supposedly published by William Bradford in New York (again because of the Mather monopoly on printing in Boston).[94] In point of time, however, *The Gospel Order Revived* by the Brattle Street Group may have been published, or readied for publication, *before* Increase Mather's *The Order of the Gospel*, because in the Postscript of *Revived* the following note appears: "It is strange that our Review should be assaulted before it can be Printed." The Postscript also refers to *A Soft Answer to the Doctrine of Instituted Churches*, an apparent Mather-side rebuttal of Stoddard's work by this title. The rebuttal must have been something more than soft, for the Postscript reads: "Let them call it *soft* who have lost their feeling! For tho' tis confessed there are no very hard Arguments, yet Jealousie, Censures, Contempts there are, which grate hard enough" (37).[95]

The writers of *Revived*—Increase Mather thought Benjamin Colman had written it, but others like Mather's old friend of witchcraft days, Thomas Brattle, may have been responsible for its printing—accused Mather of having "*craftily & unfairly worded*" the prefatory statement referring to their ideas, so that they were completely misrepresented (5). They argued:

. . . it appears very strange that those who fled from an Act of Uniformity [Mather's ancestors in England], should presently impose on themselves, or their Neighbours, and entail the Mischief on their Posterity.

Some indeed would make the design of our first Planters to consist in some little Rites, Modes or Circumstances of Church Discipline, and those such as the Word of God no where requires. (4)

Regarding public confession of conversion, they write:

The Author [Mather] relates another story . . . of one who through importunity was brought to make a relation, and made the Congregation weep, when he did it; but whether for joy or grief, we are left in the dark. (6)

As Murdock says, *The Gospel Order Revived* is well worth reading. "There is a humorous tone in many of its pages, a satirical spirit, and an occasional passage of lampooning wit, which makes it seem like a cool breeze in a desert of too arid Puritan theological writing."[96] As a political document, it brought before the public—certainly to the

Mathers' embarrassment—a very potent challenge to the power of the theocracy, one that shortly was to result in the forced abdication of Increase Mather from his throne as president of Harvard.

In the following year (1701) the Mathers replied with *A Collection of Some of the Many Offensive Matters Contained in . . . The Order of the Gospel Revived*. Increase Mather signed the preface of this work, but Murdock thinks that Cotton Mather wrote it, because of its "brief and acid comments," one of which compared their opponents' work to "a considerable Dunghill." [97]

The main body of arguments in this Stoddard-Mather battle, however, emerged in three works published in the years 1708–1709. The first of these was a sermon—*The Inexcusableness of Neglecting the Worship of God Under a Pretence of being in an Unconverted Condition*—preached by Stoddard on December 17, 1707, in connection with "the Sitting of the Inferiour Court." [98] In this sermon Stoddard argued from the Jewish custom of permitting circumcised male strangers to attend the Passover, adding that "from the beginning of the World to this day, Men were never forbidden any duty of Worship, for want of sanctifying Grace" (3). "Ungodly men," he went on, must attend church in order to be converted. Christ, John the Baptist, and the Apostles had preached to the ungodly as well as the godly. While the preachers themselves should be "godly men," yet it was "lawful for men in a natural [unconverted] condition to Preach the Word. Christ Jesus sent out *Judas* to Preach the Gospel . . ."(6). From all this, of course, it was but an easy step to the proposition that the sacraments—baptism and communion—might be administered by the unregenerate. Here again he cited the practice of John the Baptist and the Disciples (10–11). Nor did the ministers of the sacraments necessarily have to be only the converted—"The blessing of this Ordinance does not depend upon the Piety of him that doth administer it" (13). Stoddard's reasoning behind all these then radical propositions rested on the fact that there was no certain way of telling who had "Sanctifying Grace" (14). But he still insisted that the sacraments were useful to conversion. Thus in his section on "Uses" at the end of the sermon he urges: ". . . Be not afraid to attend the duties of Worship, because destitute of Sanctifying Grace" (18).

The political consequence of arguments such as these was bound to be a leveling between Sanctified and Unsanctified, those who had experienced conversion and those who had not, since both groups could be more than half-way members and partake of communion. The prospect of such leveling threatened a breakdown in the old theological discrimination between these two groups, a discrimination that had permitted the Mathers and their cohorts to assert their power inside the church and outside it in the church-influenced community. Is it any wonder, then, that the Mathers battled so fiercely the ideas of Stoddard and his followers and called them "bastards of the valley"? [99]

The second work, Increase Mather's *A Dissertation, wherein The Strange Doctrine. . . The Tendency of which, is, to Encourage Unsanctified Persons* (while such) *to Approach the Holy Table of the Lord, is Examined and Confuted,* [100] claimed that Stoddard's ideas were "contrary to many Scriptures in both Testaments" (1). Mather takes up in this dissertation Stoddard's charge that "no country does neglect this Ordinance [the Lord's Supper] as we in New-England do, that in our own Nation at home [England], so in Scotland, Holland," etc., "they do generally Celebrate the memor[i]al of Christ's Death." Sarcastically he asks, "Would he [Stoddard] bring the Churches in *New-England* back to the Imperfect Reformation in other Lands, and so deprive us of our Glory for ever?" (85). (Here he alludes to the seventeenth-century theory of Winthrop, Edward Johnson, *et al.* that the Reformation had been incomplete, or "imperfect," in Europe, and was to reach its culmination in New England, as a kind of climax to all of world history. According to this theory, the Puritans were a hand-picked and specially covenanted group, commissioned by Christ himself—hence the "glory" of the task.) [101] In his conclusion Mather emphasizes the 1679 ruling of the General Synod that

Persons be not admitted unto Communion in the Lords Supper, without making a Personal and Publick Profession of their Faith & Repentance, either orally, or in some other way . . . to the just Satisfaction of the Church, & that therefore both Elders, & Churches, be duly Watchful, & Circumspect in this Matter. (89–90)

In the third work, *An Appeal to the Learned* (Boston, 1709), Stoddard refutes seven of Increase Mather's arguments in the first part (Bk. I) of this ninety-eight-page tract. In Bk. II (pp. 42–50) he attacks the arguments of Mr. Vines, Mr. Baxter, and Mr. Chadwick, whom Mather had cited as authorities. Bk. III is devoted to disproving Mather's "Exceptions" to Stoddard's idea that Sanctifying Grace was not necessary to lawful partaking of communion. Here is a sample of Stoddard's logic: he argues that if God commanded men to attend "Covenant duties," "then he don't forbid them; God does not require and prohibit the same thing, there is a consistency in God's commands" (83). God makes men promise to keep his covenant. "They cannot keep the Covenant if they don't come to the Lord's Supper, therefore it must be lawful for them to come" (83). Both Mather and Stoddard were skillful in logic and all three of these works make frequent references to logical terms such as fallacies, major and minor premises, consequents, etc.

Edward Taylor of Westfield, the poet-preacher and nearby colleague of Stoddard in Northampton, also played an important part in this long controversy. According to Grabo, he attacked Stoddardism as early as 1679 in *A Particular Church is God's House*. In 1694 he delivered a series of eight sermons directed at Stoddard's views on communion.[102] Until his death in 1729 he remained an adamant foe of Stoddard and a faithful disciple of Increase Mather.

Let us try to assess the political significance of this long and very complicated theological controversy. Mason Lowance defines the issue as a conflict between the idea of "a 'pure church' of visible saints" and "an impure congregation of political and ecclesiastical supporters."[103] "Increase and Cotton Mather," he writes, "were wise in the ways of church-state relations" and their "ultimate goal" was "to preserve the *idea* of a gathered church in the context of as much purity as . . . possible, while retaining their control over the community."[104] Like the Mathers, "Pope" Stoddard, as he was called, "not only ruled his congregation with a firm hand but engaged effectively in the civil affairs of town and province."[105] Lowance quotes Walsh to the effect that there was a contradiction in the kind of church established by the first-generation Puritans: they had tried to establish a "pure church by excluding the unregenerate from the Lord's Supper" and had assumed that this would be "a national church" and yet that "most of the community would be communicants."[106] Much of subsequent Puritan history was "the result of the inherent conflict between the desire to keep the church pure and the need to maintain the authority of the church over the entire community."[107] In the case of Increase Mather, who defined a "particular church" as "a *body-politik* [my italics], or a spiritual corporation, unto which ecclesiastical jurisdiction doth entirely belong,"[108] this authority had met a sharp challenge from the community of rival church leaders, the Brattle Street followers of

Stoddardism. In 1701 they forced him to resign as president of Harvard. After this date the Mathers' progressive decline from a position of power in church and community veered sharply downward. Stoddardism triumphed; the church now had to accommodate the community.

In many ways the Stoddard-Mather controversy resembled a revival movement. Perry Miller called Stoddard "the first great 'revivalist' in New England," the one who "inaugurated the era of revivalism on the American frontier." [109] Walsh corrects Miller's notion that Northampton was a frontier town: it was the Jeremiad (a threatening sermon against backsliding) rather than the frontier, he explains, that accounted for Stoddard's open communion, "which was only part of a larger scheme to Presbyterianize the New England churches." [110] Why did Stoddard advocate open communion? Because he thought the neglect of the sacrament was the cause of "the great Prophaneness & corruption that hath spread over our land." [111] Schafer thinks that Stoddard "saw the special opportunities for conversion that came when numbers of people were being *affected* at the same time," and that therefore "*Evangelism* was the heart of Stoddard's ministry" (my italics). Schafer says that Stoddard himself claimed his system might lead to a revival of religion, because it prevented backsliding. [112] Politically speaking, religious revivalist movements have contributed to the historical spread of democracy.

According to the testimony of Jonathan Edwards, the evangelistic work which his grandfather Stoddard had begun, and which Edwards himself had assisted during the early years of his ministry in Northampton, was continuous with the later revival movement known as the Great Awakening. It is true, of course, that Edwards did ultimately reverse his grandfather's policy of admitting the unconverted to the Lord's supper. Schafer tells us that when this happened "it was the town's memory of the great Stoddard, combined with tensions arising in part from the revival, which brought about Edwards's dismissal from Northampton in 1750." [113]

One important way in which the Great Awakening differed from the earlier revival of Stoddard lay in the stress on conversion. For Stoddard, as we have seen, it was not indispensable for something more than half-way church membership; for Whitefield, the Tennents, and other New Lights during the Great Awakening, conversion was *absolutely indispensable*. Thus we discover Gilbert Tennent preaching a sermon on *The Danger of an Unconverted Ministry* (March 8, 1740). This sermon, which has been called the "manifesto of the revival party," enjoyed a second edition in Philadelphia in 1741, was reprinted in Boston in 1742, and then "enjoyed continuing publication and popularity throughout the century." [114] For at least two reasons this sermon had political importance: 1. It defended the practice of young itinerant Presbyterian preachers (revivalists) who invaded not only so-called "vacant parishes" but also those already served by other Presbyterian ministers. (Needless to say, the invasions of such itinerants were "often without invitation," being prompted only by the zeal of the itinerants, or New Lights.) 2. In the form of an allegory the sermon itself assailed the Old Lights (established ministers), labeling them "Old Pharisee-Teachers," condemning the manner in which such Pharisees "look'd upon others that differed from them, and the common People with an Air of Disdain." [115] Thus the older clergy and the common people were set in opposition with each other. And the boundaries of the parish were no longer inviolable. Tennent saw no reason why congregations should be under "a fatal Necessity" of hearing only their own Parish-Ministers "perpetually, or generally," especially "if the great Ends of Hearing may be attained as well, and better, by Hearing of another Minister than our own." [116]

Other writings that might be singled out as touching on political issues associated with the Great Awakening are those of Ebenezer Kinnersley, Elisha Williams, and Jonathan Mayhew, all of whom were reacting in some degree to the emotional excesses of the New Lights. A scientist friend of Benjamin Franklin, Kinnersley was a Philadelphia Baptist with Deistic predilections. He ran afoul of his fellow Baptists for having attacked in a public sermon—he was not ordained but was permitted to speak from the pulpit—a highly emotionalized sermon of John Rowland, describing it among other things as "unchristian." Kinnersley's defense of himself in *The Right of Private Judgment* was really a plea for toleration—specifically, differences of ideas within sectarian religion. He maintained that private judgment was "sacred and original," that it was "an unalienable Right" of human nature, and that rights of conscience were "sacred and equal in all." [117] A similar line of thought may be observed, Lemay tells us, in Elisha Williams's *The Essential Rights and Liberties of Protestants. A Seasonable Plea for the Liberty of Conscience and the Right of Private Judgment in Matters of Religion* (Boston, 1744). [118] Jonathan Mayhew's sermon *The Right and Duty of Private Judgment*, preached in 1748 at the Boston West-Meeting House and published in Boston, 1749, in a collection entitled *Seven Sermons*, also speaks for every individual man's right to reason for himself. It protests the tyranny of majorities—"the multitude may do evil, and the many judge falsely . . ." —and stakes out a claim for the rights of minorities. "*Truth* and *right* have a real existence in nature, independent of the *sentiments* and *practices* of men," writes Mayhew; "they do not necessarily follow the multitude, or major part. . . ."[119]

What were some of the more important political consequences of the Great Awakening? McLoughlin states them rather succinctly: the creation of "temporary schisms" in almost every denomination in America; vigorous new growth among many churches; the breakdown of denominational barriers; partial unification of the colonies (Whitefield's tour took him from Georgia to New Hampshire); "energetic social and intellectual ferment among the lower classes"; preparation for the separation between church and state that occurred after the American Revolution; "religious activism" and "lay leadership"; "missionary activity, philanthropy, charity, and education"—McLoughlin lists Dartmouth, Princeton, and Brown universities as direct outgrowths of the Awakening.[120] According to Ahlstrom, the Awakening "heightened the back-country opposition to the religious restrictions of the royal government and conduced to a more thorough democratization of society," aroused a critical spirit in people in all walks of life "to question accepted truths of constituted authorities," "intensified the general tendency of the Reformed tradition . . . to set bounds on the will of kings and the arbitrary exercise of government power," and awakened hopes for a second coming of Christ and its realization by a covenanted nation.[121]

Thus far in this chapter we have tried to show a line of increasing democratization (slowly but unmistakably developing from the Half-Way Covenant, through the Stoddard-Mather controversy and the Great Awakening) as it relates to the decline of the theocracy, mainly in New England but also, in the case of the Awakening, elsewhere—in Virginia and the middle colonies of Pennsylvania and New Jersey. We must now backtrack briefly in our chronological presentation—which we have had to violate in order to show this line of logical continuity—to consider a further aspect of the decline of the theocracy, the quarrel between John Wise and the Mathers.

V *John Wise: Morning Star of the American Revolution*

The one person who, with the possible exception of Elisha Cooke, probably contributed more to diminishing the power of the Mathers than any other was John Wise, a minister at Ipswich who had spent three weeks in jail in 1687 for resistance to Andros's arbitrary tax policies. (Two years later, in October 1689, he sued Andros's follower Joseph Dudley for a thousand pounds for having denied him habeas corpus while in jail.) At that time Wise had sided with the Mathers. He also had participated as a chaplain in Sir William Phipps's disastrous expedition against Quebec. In his account of this expedition, written under the date of December 23, 1690, Wise explains what he regarded as the reasons for its failure—the cowardice of Lt. General John Walley, the lack of provisions and ammunition, etc. [122] Another of his early writings was a petition signed by thirty-one members of his congregation in behalf of John and Elizabeth Proctor, his former parishioners, both of whom had been tried for witchcraft. The letter accompanying this petition argued against "spectral evidence" and is supposed to have been written by Wise. [123] In addition, Wise was one of twelve ministers from Essex County who petitioned the general court for resititution of property unjustly taken from persons accused of being witches. (Elizabeth Proctor, for example, had lost all claim to her husband's property, because he had assumed she would be hanged, too, and had left everything to his children. She was saved only when it was discovered that she was pregnant.) [124]

Wise's biography makes fascinating reading; he was a very active man, a wrestler who once threw a challenger over a stone wall. Wise had his finger in many pies. In his correspondence with Samuel Sewall, for example, concerning the contemplated removal of several families from Chebasco, the town in which his church was located, to South Carolina, Wise asks for advice. Sewall rejoiced that "Christ was carrying his trenches so near sin's stronghold," but suggested consulting fellow ministers in the area. [125]

The background of the enmity between Wise and the Mathers goes back to the year 1690, when a ministers' association had been formed. It met every six weeks, at Harvard, according to Cook, from nine to ten o'clock on Monday morning. [126] The purpose of the association was ostensibly to oppose sin and the decay of religion throughout New England. In effect, however, it only succeeded in eventually precipitating a conflict between two factions of the church, those favoring the Presbyterian and the Congregational church governments. The Mathers led the former group, and Benjamin Colman of the Brattle St. Church, as we have seen, argued for the latter group in A Manifesto (1699).

One important issue that arose was the question about who should elect new ministers. The new group contended that "all baptized persons in the church who helped to pay the minister's salary should have a vote in choosing him to office." [127] The older Presbyterians thought that only those who had been admitted to communion should have a vote in this matter. As their spokesman, Cotton Mather drafted a series of *Proposals for the Preservation of Religion in the Churches, by a Due Trial of Them That Stand Candidates of the Ministry* (1702, according to Cook, p. 210). These *Proposals* appeared in print in 1705.

In 1705 the Mather group succeeded in establishing a federated union of churches, which was to have power of selecting ministers for local churches. Wise rose to this challenge with a defense of the autonomy of local churches to hire their ministers—in his two most famous works, *The Churches Quarrel Espoused* (1710) and *A Vindication of the Government of the New-England Churches* (1717).

In *The Churches Quarrel Espoused* Wise attacked the plan of the Presbyterians (or Mathers), using as his text Galatians 5:1, "Stand fast therefore in the Liberties, wherewith Christ has made us free, and be not Intangled again with the Yoke of Bondage." The Epistle Dedicatory of this pamphlet contained an argument in the form of six petitions: in the first of these Wise reminded his readers who they were. "Imagine yourselves to be something more than Ordinary, for Really you be so," he writes. In the second he asks them to esteem church liberties as having the same value as civil liberties in England, recalling the great sacrifices that had been made to purchase these civil liberties. Thirdly, and this was aimed at the ministers' association (the federated union of churches), he urged his readers to honor their pastors, but warned them against "Corrupt and Prejudiced" ministers. Wise says he would be "very loath to share in their [the bad ministers'] triumphs, tho their gains should be seemingly great, and their signals and shouts equal with the Caesars of the World in their going off." Fourthly, he urged the appointment of a ruling elder in each church, arguing that the ruling elder had become "*rara Avis in terra*, like a blak Swan in the Meadow." Fifthly, he called for a new printing of the Cambridge platform (the old Congregational form of government), saying it was "scarce to be found in the hands of one in a Thousand." Finally, he urged a general synod for the purpose of preventing "small Juntos of men, or particular Persons, Member or Members of the Churches

. . . from being so hardy and bold as to Divulge their Pernicious
Doctrines, and seditious Sentiments, with such Presumption, and
such hopes of Impunity, as some of late have done." [128]

The main body of *The Churches Quarrel Espoused* takes up the
Proposals of 1705 (see *supra*). These were sixteen in number and
were presented in the form of a mock trial, which he claimed to
have borrowed from the trial of Sir Walter Raleigh. [129] Wise arraigns
"the Criminal Proposals," as he calls them, with certain "Queries,"
pointing out the inconsistency of Cotton Mather's supporting the
Congregational form of government in his earlier work entitled
Theopolis Americana. Then Wise proceeds to cross-examine the
Proposals. Since Cook's excellent book summarizes in detail the
ridicule of these sixteen proposals (not to be confused, please note,
with the sixteen proposals of the Brattle Street *Manifesto* of 1699) I
will present only one or two samples of the kind of rhetoric Wise
used so effectively against the association and the Mathers. One of
his arguments was directed against the large expense involved in
having the ministers travel to a central place for the meetings of
their association. He proposes setting aside the income from "some
good stout Gold Mine in *Peru*" to defray the costs. Another
example: he attacks the presumption of the proposers' panacea,
saying it reminds him of Epicurus's explanation of the origin of the
world as "a chance coalescence of atoms." The trouble with such a
plan, as well as that of his antagonists, comments Wise, is that it
ignores the Creator. Halfway through the list of proposals, he takes
time out to observe that the association had published them on
November 5, Guy Fawkes Day, "the day of the *Gun-Powder-
Treason*, and a fatal day to Traytors." By such telling blows as these
he undermines the position of his opponents. [130]

In his second major work directed at the Mather ministerial
association and their attempts at controlling the choice of a minister,
Wise turned from satire to more formal argument. The preface to *A
Vindication of the Government of New England Churches* provides
an outline of the book as a whole. Briefly, the vindication, or
justification, of the congregational form of church government
rested on a five-part structure of what Wise called "demonstrations": from Antiquity (especially of the early Christian church);
from Nature; from the Bible; from the constitution of the church
(largely the Cambridge platform); and from "*the* Providence of
GOD *dignifying of it*." Relying on such sources as Grotius, Hobbes,

and Puffendorf—particularly the latter, whom he well-nigh copies word-for-word in some passages—and on allusions to "a formidable array of [other] authors," Wise wrote "for an age fifty years later." [131] It is no accident that both his books, *The Churches Quarrel Espoused* and his *Vindication* were reprinted in the years immediately preceding the Revolutionary War.

Reaction to the *Vindication* during Wise's own day was strong, although nothing really came of such reaction. Cotton Mather, for example, wondered if he "Should not . . . take into Consideration, what may be done for the Service of the Ministry and Religion and the Churches, throughout the Land, that the Poison of Wise's cursed Libel may have an Antidote?" [132] Others wondered, too. But, as Cook says, "No one appeared to confute Wise, and *A Vindication* was not answered until 1774." [133]

The peculiar, one might almost say unique, significance of the book rested in its second part, which presented a highly rationalistic theory of government based on natural rights, explaining how such rights or powers were conveyed to civil rulers and foreshadowing many ideas of such later social contract writers as Rousseau. Wise makes use of the term *immunity*, by which he seems to have meant a special gift of liberty and trust. In this second part he discussed three great immunities of man:

1. The Prime Immunity in Mans State, is that he is most properly the Subject of the Law of Nature. He is the Favorite Animal on Earth; in that this Part of God's Image, *viz.* Reason is congenate with his Nature, wherein by a Law Immutable, Instampt upon his Frame, God has provided a Rule for Men in all their Actions, obliging each one to the performance of that which is Right, not only as to Justice, but likewise as to all other Moral Vertues, the which is nothing but the Dictates of Right Reason founded in the Soul of Man. *Molloy, De Mao, Praef.* That which is to be drawn from Man's Reason, flowing from the true Current of that Faculty, when unperverted, may be said to be the Law of Nature. . . .

2. The second Great Immunity of Man is an Original Liberty Instampt upon his Rational Nature. He that intrudes upon this Liberty, Violates the Law of Nature. . . . [Man's] Liberty under the Conduct of Right Reason, is equal with his trust.

3. The Third Capital Immunity belonging to Man's Nature, is an equality amongst Men; Which is not to be denied by the Law of Nature, till Man has Resigned himself with all his Rights for the sake of the Civil State; and then his Personal liberty and Equality is to be cherished and preserved to the highest degree, as will consist with all just distinctions amongst Men of

Honour, and shall be agreeable with the publick Good. For Man has a high valuation of himself, and the passion seems to lay its first foundation [not in Pride, but] really in the high and admirable Frame and constitution of Humane Nature. The Word Man, says my Author, is thought to carry somewhat of Dignity in its sound. . . .[134]

Each of these immunities deserves some comment. First of all, what did Wise mean by the "Law of Nature"? And what did it mean for man to be subject to it? His emphasis upon reason as relating man directly to God shows that he thought of God as the source for ethical conduct among men. Right, justice, and "all other Moral Vertues," he sees as "nothing but Right Reason founded in the Soul of Man." (He cites Charles Molloy's preface to *De jure maritimo* [1676] at this point.) Thus he implies a close logical connection between the highly respectable Neoclassical concept of reason and the moral virtues, *all of them*. Then he proceeds to identify, at the same time to define, what he calls "the law of Nature" with both reason and all the virtues. If this triple fusion of reason, virtue, and nature strikes the reader as complicated, Wise offers some assistance: "If a Man any ways doubts, whether what he is going to do to another Man be agreeable to the Law of Nature, then let him suppose himself to be in that other Man's Room; And by this Rule effectually Executed" (35). This, of course, clarifies matters considerably; for we now see that for Wise, apparently, "the Law of Nature" is identical with the Golden Rule of the New Testament.

Under the second *immunity*, "an Original Liberty," which must remain forever inviolate, Wise takes up two subpoints—first, an "Internal Native Liberty of Mans Nature" which he defines as the "faculty of Doing or Omitting things according to the Direction of his Judgment," and second, "Mans External Personal Natural Liberty, Antecedent to all Humane parts, or Alliances" (38). The first is mental; the second, external—that is, having to do with physical or bodily freedom of movement. He warns that the first, or mental, kind of liberty "does not consist in a loose and ungovernable Freedom, or in an unbounded License of Acting." Such license would be inconsistent with "the condition and dignity of Man." He quotes Plutarch to the effect that *"Those Persons only who live in Obedience to Reason, are worthy to be accounted free: They alone live as they Will, who have Learnt what they ought to Will"* (38). He also develops and explains the second kind of freedom: ". . . Every Man must be conceived to be perfectly in his own Power and disposal, and not to be controuled by the Authority of any other. And thus every Man, must be acknowledged equal to every Man, since all Subjection and all Command are equally banished on both sides; and considering all Men thus at Liberty, every Man has a Prerogative to Judge for himself, *viz.* What shall be most for his Behoof, Happiness and Well-being" (39).

In Wise's explanation of the third *immunity* we see him moving from a consideration of man in a state of nature (in his second immunity) to man in a civil state—i.e., in a government. But even when he moves into, or under, a government "his Personal Liberty and Equality is to be cherished, and preserved to the highest degree" (39). Later writers on government, such as Paine and Jefferson, explained this principle as the retention of natural rights. A primitive man, for example, on entering into a contractual agreement with a government would give up only *some* of his natural rights—never all of them. He might retain, for instance, the right to dissociate himself from the government if it did not serve his purposes of security, happiness, etc. Too, even the limited degree of personal freedom he might give up, so that he might live in harmony with other citizens in our imagined government, should never (as in a totalitarian state) amount to a total loss of such freedom. In fact, argues Wise, it was incumbent on governments to preserve these natural rights, the personal liberty and equality of their citizens, *"to the highest degree"* (my italics).

Pursuing his view of the progress of man from a natural to a political state, Wise next takes up various matters, such as the reversion of delegated political power to the people on the occasion when a king or other head of government might die, the various ways in which power might validly, or legally, be transferred from people to civil rulers, and various kinds of government (democracy, aristocracy, monarchy, and mixed forms).

It will be easily apparent from this limited presentation of Wise's political ideas that they were of great importance, for they marked a significant turning of attention from church to secular government. Although his purpose was to defend the independence of the congregational church government, he relies heavily in his argument on a broader range of principles than earlier American writers had employed, principles drawn from reason and nature as well as from the authority of Scripture and the practice of the early church. And these were eventually applicable to the year 1772 as well as to

1710 and 1717.[135] It was principles such as these, ringing clearly in the new fresh air of the American Enlightenment that sounded the knell of the old New England theocracy. The Age of Reason was at hand.

CHAPTER 3

The Growth of Antislavery Sentiment

I *Early Objectors: Francis Pastorius* et al., *Cotton Mather, and Samuel Sewall*

ONE of the signs suggesting that the Age of Reason was at hand in the first half of the eighteenth century in the American colonies was the growth of antislavery sentiment. To be sure, faint sparks of enlightenment had already occasionally lit up the general cloud of darkness that seemed to hang over the subject of slavery in the seventeenth century. At the meeting of the general court in Warwick, Rhode Island, in 1652, there had been a Quaker resolution against slavery—a law, in fact, since it stipulated a fine of forty pounds for keeping Negroes in forced servitude for longer than ten years. As Joanne Grant points out, this law represents one of the first steps in America toward racial equality. Had it been enforced, it would have had the effect of putting the Negroes on the same level with white indentured servants.[1]

Then, too, in Germantown, Pennsylvania, on April 18, 1688, Francis Pastorius, Derick and Abram op de Graeff, and Garret Henderich drafted a resolution "to the monthly [Quaker] meeting held at Richard Worrell's," protesting slavery.[2] The resolution is written in a tight style with an interesting argument in almost every sentence. Slavery violated the Golden Rule; it put slave owners on a level with Turks who captured Christians and sold them into slavery; oppression for color of skin (in America) was no better than oppression for cause of conscience (in Europe); slavery was like adultery, since it often separated husbands and wives among the enslaved; slavery ruined the American image abroad, thus interfering with the settlement of America; slavery was a form of hypocrisy and was ruining the good name of Pennsylvania, which had been set up as a haven of freedom for persecuted Quakers; slavery would cause uprisings and possibly civil wars! These were only a few of the points made by these early protesters.

Also, Cotton Mather in his *Life of the Renown'd John Eliot* (1691)

73

had turned his attention to this question, although in that work he seems to have been more interested in it as a theological than a political issue.[3] A few years later, he writes: "The State of your *Negroes* in this world must be low, and mean, and abject; a State of Servitude. No *Great Things* in this World, can be done for them. Something then, let there be done, towards their welfare in the *World to Come.*" This defeatist attitude toward improvement of Negroes' condition in this world may strike us as very harsh and inhuman today, but it is worth remembering that he commended something like this same "other worldiness" to the white Christians enslaved by pirates in Africa.[4]

In *The Negro Christianized* (1706), where he addresses the owners of slaves, he urges them to offer religious instruction to the slaves and to convert them to Christianity:

Be assured, Syrs; Your *Servants* will be the *Better Servants*, for being made *Christian Servants*. . . . Were your *Servants* well tinged with the spirit of *Christianity*, it would render them exceeding *Dutiful* unto their *Masters*, exceeding *Patient* under their *Masters*, exceeding faithful in their Business, and afraid of speaking or doing any thing that may justly displease you. It has been observed, that those *Masters*, who have used their *Negroes* with most of *Humanity*, in allowing them all the Comforts of Life, that are necessary and *Convenient* for them . . . have been better *Serv'd*, had more work done for them, and better done, than those *Inhumane Masters*, who have used their *Negroes* worse than their *Horses*. And those *Masters* doubtless, who use their *Negroes* with most of *Christianity*, and use most pains to inform them in, and conform them to, *Christianity*, will find themselves no losers by it. (21–22)

Pointing out that one entire book in the Bible (*Philemon*) had been written in behalf of Onesimus, who "was doubtless a *Slave*," and who had become more "profitable" as a result of his conversion, Mather entreats the slave owners having difficulty with their charges to examine

Whether Heaven be not chastising of them for their failing in their Duty about their *Negroes*. Had they done more to make their *Negroes* the knowing and willing *Servants* of God, it may be, God would have made their *Negroes* better *Servants* to them. (22)

Mather did not, evidently, view Christianity and paternalistic slavery as incompatible. In this respect he differed markedly from other Puritan writers on this subject—William Ames and Samuel Sewall, for example.[5]

With Sewall's *The Selling of Joseph* (1700) the arguments take a more secular turn. Whereas Mather was interested in spiritual salvation for blacks as well as whites, Sewall seems more interested in human liberty as such; but he is still enough of the older legalistic Calvinist to buttress his essentially humanitarian interests with copious scriptural quotations. Sewall's opening argument, for example, states that since liberty is in value second only to life itself, *"none ought to part with it themselves, or deprive others of it, but upon most mature Consideration."* Accepting prevalent notions of the covenant theology, he argues that through the "Indulgence of God to our First parents after the Fall," this deed of gift (liberty), which he calls "a most beneficial and inviolable Lease," still holds. As equal heirs of Adam, all men must thus remember that "Originally and Naturally" there was "no such thing as Slavery." Consequently the sale of Joseph by his brothers violated this contract (or covenant) of God. According to the law of God, argues Sewall, slavery ranked among "the most atrocious of Capital Crimes," and he quotes from Exodus 21:16 to bolster his position.[6]

After this preliminary orientation, Sewall turns in the second part of his essay to a series of practical considerations among which we find something reminiscent of the earlier argument of the 1652 Quaker resolution: Sewall argues that white servants for a limited term of years "would conduce more to the Welfare of the Province" than "to have [Black] Slaves for Life." Other of his practical considerations have to do with possible misuse of freedom by the slaves once they were freed, with racial intermarriage, with the problem of fornication—between white masters and female slaves. Sewall takes a pragmatic attitude toward these considerations, expressing the opinion that in that time few of the freed slaves used their freedom well.

In the third part of *The Selling of Joseph* he takes up and refutes *four main objections* of his opponents. The *first* of these was to the effect that the descendants of Cham were under the curse of slavery. Since the Bible was still regarded by many of Sewall's contemporaries as the only authoritative revelation of God's word, this objection carried considerable weight. He attacks it in three different ways: First, it was presumptuous, he says, for slave traders to set themselves up as executioners of the "Vindictive Wrath of God; the extent and duration of which is to us uncertain" (2).

Second, it was possible that this sentence, if it ever did exist, might now be out of date. Third, the text was susceptible of more than one interpretation—for example, that the curse applied more to Canaan than to Cham. (Canaan's descendants were not blacks.) Sewall quotes from the Bible in opting for this interpretation.

In the *second* objection, which Sewall says his opponents raised, was the assertion that "the Nigers are brought out of a Pagan Country, into Places where the Gospel is Preached" (2). Sewall answers, "Evil must not be done, that good may come of it. The extraordinary and comprehensive Benefit accruing to the Church of God, and to *Joseph* personally, did not rectify his Brethren's Sale of him" (3).

The *third* objection raised by Sewall's opponents was a species of rationalization: "*The* Africans *have Wars one with another: Our Ships bring lawful Captives taken in those Wars*" (3). This time Sewall delivers his verdict a little more cautiously, and at greater length. "Every War is upon one side unjust," he writes. "An Unlawful War can't make lawful Captives. And by Receiving, we are in danger to promote, and partake in their Barbarous Cruelties." His reasoning may wobble a bit here, but he quickly saves it by resort to an analogy. Imagine, he asks his reader, a boatful of Massachusetts men going fishing, being surprised by a group of pirates, and then sold into slavery. Would not such men regard themselves as "unjustly dealt with"? Then he quotes from Matthew 7:12 to support his position.

The *fourth* objection that Sewall undertakes to refute reads as follows: "Abraham had Servants bought with his Money, and born in his House." Although this objection had a scriptural basis, it could not prevail against Judge Sewall's hard-headed attitude toward the absence of legal evidence. "Until the circumstances of Abraham's purchase be recorded, no Argument can be drawn from it," he maintains, adding, in a manner that weakens his argument, that "in the mean time, Charity obliges us to conclude that He [Abraham] knew it [the purchase] was lawful and good" (3). Sewall concludes with various other biblical citations forbidding the buying and selling of slaves, and he rounds out his conclusion with two paragraphs of Latin quotations.[7]

John Saffin, a wealthy merchant, a rival judge, and something of a poet, but (alas) also a slaveholder, wrote *A Brief and Candid Answer to . . . The Selling of Joseph* (1701). Saffin's reply has recently been reprinted.[8] It is undistinguished, and it concludes with some bad verse, damaging the character of Negroes.

II   *The Quakers: Sandiford, Lay, Woolman, and Benezet*

The Quakers were the single group of eighteenth-century writers who most ardently led the resistance to slavery. As already noted, they were among the first to blaze out in self-critical protest against their own members who by keeping slaves indulged in this most horrible of injustices. In the period 1693–1718 writers like John Farmer, William Southeby, and the followers of the apostate Quaker George Keith were becoming increasingly articulate. From 1714 to 1731 John Hepburn, William Burling, and Elihu Coleman, three other little-known, moderate antislavery writers (Quakers all), continued the good fight.[9] In the half century following the death of Cotton Mather (1728) four other Quakers—Ralph Sandiford, Benjamin Lay, John Woolman, and Anthony Benezet—wrote extensively against this evil. The main concern of this chapter will be with this latter group, all of whom were less theologically minded than Mather and Sewall.

Although his name did not appear on the title page, Benjamin Franklin, then a young Philadelphia printer recently arrived from Boston, was the publisher of Sandiford's *A Brief Examination of the Practices of the Times* (1729). Franklin also published Lay's pamphlet. It is thought that Sandiford brought out his work at his own expense. Apparently, too, he had to distribute it "in the face of threats of prosecution." But he had help in circulating it, for an entry in Franklin's ledger for February 28, 1733, credits Sandiford's account with ten shillings received from Benjamin Lay "for 50 of his [Sandiford's] books which he [Lay] intends to give away."[10] (This note may serve as an effective introduction to the character of Lay, the most histrionic propagandist of the four.)

Sandiford's book begins with a dedication to his friend "Mathew Hughes, Esq., One of the Representatives for the County of Bucks," the dedication being more like a picaresque romance than an introduction to a tract against slavery. Sandiford reminds Hughes of their common experiences on the high seas—after having been robbed by pirates, the sloop in which they were traveling sprang a leak and sank. After various other adventures they finally landed safely in South Carolina. It was while working for a wealthy planter there that he had been sickened by what he saw of both Negro and Indian slavery.

The audience factor is always important in any work of rhetoric or persuasion, and Sandiford makes absolutely clear the general nature of his partly friendly, partly hostile audience on the first page of the main part of his work. He addresses himself disarmingly but firmly to "MY FRIEND, Whomsoever Thou art that deals in Slaves." The nature of his appeals and arguments characterizes this slaveholding audience as one well acquainted with the Bible—a Quaker audience in the main—but one also having an economic interest in slavery. It was, furthermore, an audience that believed in the Devil, an audience that was aware of tendencies to backsliding in religion, an audience that could equate slaveholding with the work of the Devil. Little wonder, then, that Sandiford begins with a statement that the "Principle and Foundation on which this Practice stands . . ." is the Devil himself (1–2). He rehashes the Adam and Eve and Cain and Abel stories, claiming that Cain's real father was the Devil. According to a notion current in Sandiford's day, Cain's race had been destroyed by the deluge. But, argues Sandiford, the "Devil's image and Life remain in all them that Act in the same Principle" (4).

Some of Sandiford's contemporaries regarded slavery as excusable because of a curse which Noah had put on Canaan, the youngest son of Ham (Genesis 9:25). Not so, says Sandiford. This curse is "not so extensive as you would have it" (4). Once the Canaanites had been destroyed, the curse no longer applied (5). Sandiford then argues a later origin for slavery—in the selling of Joseph. He offers two further arguments. First, he states that slavery is the greatest of evils, then asks, "And what greater Unjustice can be Acted, than to Rob a Man of his Liberty, which is more valuable than Life. . . ?" Second, he refers to Acts 17:26, where part of the verse mentions God's having appointed the proper boundaries of man's habitation. In Sandiford's opinion it was therefore a sin against God to take men out of their natural environment and "to remove them, wheresoever Interest shall lead us, to sell them for Slaves, Husband from Wife and Children from both, like Beasts, with all their Increase, to the vilest of Men, and their Offspring after them to all Eternity: Oh! hard Lot! O! Eternal sinking in Iniquity; without Bottom or Bounds . . ." (7). I have quoted this passage at length to give some idea of the quick way in which Sandiford can flame into a passion on this subject.

In the battery of arguments with which Sandiford next explodes he considers the fact that slavery might entail "Sin on our Posterity, *ad Infinitum*" (7). He reminds his reader of Exodus 21:16—probably the most-cited passage in antislavery rhetoric before the invention of the cotton gin—that the penalty for either stealing or *receiving*

men was *Death* (8). He points out that the Quakers were not at war
with the Negroes and that it did not therefore make sense for them
to rationalize their purchases of Negro slaves according to the old
belief that captives in war might be sold as slaves. At that time
slaves caught stealing incurred the death penalty, according to law.
For a white person to steal was not considered a capital crime.
Sandiford says that this double standard of legal administration is
absolutely "contrary to the Law of God" (17).

One of the prime objects of Sandiford's attack was the Quaker
ministers who owned slaves. How, he asks, "can a *Minister of
Christ* own such a Practice, in himself or Flock. . . ?" (52). One of
the principal objections he takes up is that through slavery in
America the African slaves were "brought to the Christian
Religion," which was considered "the greatest of Charity" (63),
apparently, that could be shown them. Sternly he answers that "the
Ground of this Trade had no such Intention" (64). As for the
objection that slavery was necessary because the slaveholders could
not live without them, Sandiford replies that in that case it would be
better for the slaveholders to lose their lives. Thus their chances for
spiritual salvation would be bettered.

In the peroration of his work a powerful image of slavery as "the
Whore" with "all her unrighteous Merchandize" (67) emerges. He
warms to his hortatory conclusion with a warning that slavery
"promotes Idleness in the Rich" and "hinders the Poor from Bread"
(68). With satisfaction he notes that the last meeting of the Quaker
Assembly had "discountnanc'd the Trade, which [he says] has given
them Honour in the Hearts of the Just," etc. (68).

The second edition of Sandiford's *Brief Examination of the
Practice of the Times* was addressed "To the Second Day's Morning
MEETING, and to the Yearly Meeting of *Friends* assembled in
London." [11] The introduction mentions his having been threatened
with jail by "our chief judge, in the face of our annual meeting, for
printing" the first edition (4). Since Sandiford believed that this
opposition to his pamphlet had originated in England, he now
addresses the English annual meeting in London directly (4).

The main body of the text of this second edition (15–89) is
substantially the same as that of the first edition. But the
"POSTSCRIPT," in form of "a LETTER to a Friend" (93–111), is
new. The function of this new postscript was to answer further
objections, one of which was that slavery was simply a symptom of
the times and should be lumped together with various other evils.

Sandiford writes, "Defacing of Dogs and other Creatures," as well as bull and bear baiting and cock fighting were certainly a "Shame to Religion and Government," and tended to the bringing up of our "Youth in Cowardice and Baseness of Spirit: Yet all this is but evading the Matter aimed at, which is the abusing of our selves with this Trading in Mankind, which is pernicious to the Publick . . . " (95). He then repeats his biblical figure of slavery as the whore of Babylon: "*Babylon, who is Harloted from the Truth to feed upon the Flesh, or receive Nourishment from the Blood of the poor Negro or Indian Captive or whomsoever else that ravenous Nature (which is the Beast's Mark) has Power to prey upon*" (96).

His closing appeal stresses the injury slavery does to the commonwealth—it leads to corruption in government, especially in offices of trust. Consequently he maintains that slaveholders should not be admitted to legislatures, "lest we be brought into the same Captivity" as the slave and "lest our liberties and privileges be destroyed" (108).

As a writer Sandiford rambles along and is frequently long winded. His sentences are invariably long. He is not particularly easy reading and the arguments must sometimes be searched for. Although he uses a gently persuasive tone for the most part, he can occasionally lash out fiercely when he warms to his task with a vivid image such as that of slavery as leprosy, or like the whore of Babylon, or his picture of Dives in hell, or that of parasitic slaveholders feeding upon "the Flesh and Blood of Slaves, instead of Christ" (107). His argument as a whole has a theological cast to it, but he was also aware, as already noted, of the civil and political consequences of slavery. Too, he occasionally employs a flash of Swiftian irony and scorn. For instance, he grants to his opponents that the children of slaves cannot live by their own work. And if they steal, "which they cannot avoid, they must be hanged" (104). He then quotes Sir Thomas More to the effect that this is bad pedagogy!

Benjamin Lay's *All Slave-Keepers . . . APOSTATES* (Philadelphia, 1737) added a good deal of oil to the Quaker fire against slavery. Quaker ministers and magistrates, as we have seen, sometimes kept slaves. Thus their own beards were singed by this fire. In this respect Lay caused these two groups no end of public embarrassment, because he insisted on dramatizing his crusade. As one writer describes him, Lay was "of the antique prophetic breed, God-intoxicated and extravagant in his testimonies, implacable, unswervable, explosively imaginative in his propaganda. . . . " [12]

For one of his demonstrations Lay had been publicly disowned by the Yearly Meeting. In 1730 at Burlington, N.J., he is supposed to have risen dramatically in the meeting, thrown off his simple Quaker coat, and appeared in full military regalia with sword in hand. This alone would have been sufficient to shock the peaceable Friends. But Lay carried on. Plunging his sword into "a hollowed-out book, which hid a bladder of red liquid (perhaps pokeberry juice)," he squirted the "blood" over the shocked faces of his auditors at the same time shouting out that the slaveholders might just as well throw off the plain coat (hence unmask their hypocrisy) and thrust a sword into the hearts of their poor slaves.[13]

Lay attacks Quaker slaveholders with extraordinary zeal, proposing to turn them out of the Meeting House, as he himself had been turned out for his demonstrations. The slavery issue was threatening to divide Quaker congregations, and Lay for one thought the departure of the intransigent slaveholders would be good riddance. He further proposes the formation of a list (to be given to certified lay ministers) of persons possibly dangerous because of their proslavery views (26–27).

For Lay slavery was a form of hypocrisy, especially among Quakers, who professed universal brotherhood. It was also a form of piracy, and, as everyone knew, the punishment for piracy was death. Keeping and trading slaves was for him every bit as bad as polygamy, harlotry, concubinage, and other sins mentioned in the Old Testament; quite frequently he holds over the heads of his Quaker reading audience the threat of hellfire and eternal damnation (77, 85, 86). Punishment, at any rate, was certain.

The preface to Lay's book is signed and dated "Abington, Philadelphia *County* in Pennsylvania, the 17th, 9th Mo., 1736."[14] In it he addresses his fellow Quakers and appeals to their love of truth. He claims that his book—it is 271 pages long—was printed at their request. There apparently was no lack of interest in the slavery issue at the time Lay wrote. "Many worthy Men," he says, "have borne Testimony against this foul Sin, Slave-Keeping, by Word and writing . . . but especially *Ralph Sandiford*, amongst many others, has writ excellently well, against that filthy Sin . . . " (18). If for Sandiford slavery had been best represented by the figure of the whore of Babylon, for Lay the practice constituted a "filthy Leprosy and Apostacy" that had all the earmarks of a contagion "spread far and near."[15]

The main part of the book alludes to some observations concerning slave-keeping by William Burling of Long Island (see *supra*) written in 1718 and to the fact that in that same year Lay had been living in Barbados and had there had his eyes opened to the "Hellish Practice" (6.) Addressing the elders of the church, he notes their hypocrisy in refusing to bear "Arms" while at the same time plundering the poor slaves. Quickly rising to a feverish pitch, he asks, "Is this the way to convince the poor Slaves, or our Children, or Neighbours, or the World? Is it not the way rather to encourage and strengthen them in their Infidelity, and Atheism, and their Hellish Practice of Fighting, Murthering, Killing and Robbing one another, to the end of the World?" (11).

Lay had read in Burling of the capture, half a century earlier, of some English and Dutch Christians by Turkish pirates, who had subsequently sold them into slavery—"As our brave Christians so call'd do, and have done for many Years in *Phila.*, and elsewhere in *America*, by the poor Negroes, which is ten times worse in us; all things consider'd. . . ."

. . . What crying, wringing of Hands, what Mourning and Lamentations there was then by their Relations, Wives for their Husbands, parents for their Children, Relations for their Friends, one Neighbor for another! what exclaiming against the *Turk* for his tyranny and oppression, and cruel Dealing and Treatment, towards their Friends, and may be cursing and calling for Damnation to him and his God too.

Well my Friends, consider of it, and make an Application suitable to the circumstance of your own Slaves; for I do not believe in my Soul, the *Turks* are so cruel to their Slaves, as many Christians, so called, are to theirs, by what I have seen and heard of in Barbadoes, and elsewhere; and I give you a reason for it. I was near 18 Months, on board a large Vessel of 400 Tons in a Voyage to *Scanderoon* in *Turky*, with four Men that had been 17 Years Slaves in *Turky*, and I never did understand by them, that they were so badly used as the poor Negroes are by some called Christians. (15–16)

Like Sewall (see *supra*) he presses home to the reader the sense of hypocrisy and injustice, making it vivid and immediate by putting the shoe on the other foot.

Like Sandiford, Lay alludes frequently to the Bible for support of his argument. After citing Mathew 7:17—"*Every good Tree bringeth [forth] good Fruit, but a corrupt Tree bringeth evil Fruit*"—he asks: "Is there any eviler Fruit in the World than Slave-keeping? Any thing more devilish? It is of the very Nature of Hell itself, and is the Belly of Hell" (27). Singling out the slave-keeping ministers for special attention, he asks the reader to observe a modern miracle.

Now, dear Friends, behold a Mystery! These Ministers that be Slave-Keepers, and are in such very great Repute, such eminent Preachers, given to Hospitality, charitable to the Poor, loving to their Neighbors, just in their Dealings, temperate in their Lives, visiting of the Sick, sympathizing with the Afflicted in Body or Mind, very religious seemingly, and extraordinarily devout and demure, and in short strictly exact in all their Decorums, except Slave-Keeping, these, these, be the Men, and the Women, too, for the Devil's purpose, and are the choicest Treasure the Devil can or has to bring out of his Lazaretto, to establish Slave-Keeping. By these Satan works Wonders many ways. (29)

He winds up by comparing them to the Scribes and Pharisees, concluding that a minister who keeps slaves does "more Service for the Devil, and Hurt in the Church . . . than twenty Publicans and Harlots . . ." (30). Then, systematically he plows through chapters twelve and thirteen of the Book of Revelation and through verses nine and ten of chapter fourteen, explicating these passages in terms of condemnation of the slave trade (101–17).

As for his arguments, beyond what has already been said, Lay has a tendency to use a shock technique, as one might expect. In reporting sailors' use of female Negroes for sexual purposes, for instance, he cites the case of a ship captain who had "6 to 10 of 'em in the Cabbin [*sic*] and Sailors as many as they pleased; with much more too foul for me to mention, or for chaste Ears to hear" (77). A few pages later, however, he does mention it—his opinion that slavery "is as great a cause of the Sins of *Sodom*, as any thing is or ever was in the whole World" (88). He then calculates the total population of slaves during the past half century and asks, "Is not this ten times worse than the Sins of *Sodom* and *Egypt*, *Turk*, *Jew* or *Infidel*?" (89).

Lay also occasionally displayed unusual invention in refuting objections of his opponents. For example, in answer to certain slaveholders who had considered a rather postponed form of freeing their slaves, he writes: It won't do to free one's slaves after one's own death; that will not "salve the Sore." "It is too deep and rotten, God will not be mocked so, nor Wise Men either; they rather think of the old Proverb . . .

When the Devil was Sick, the Devil a Monk would be, But when the Devil was well, the Devil a Monk was he." (87)

While one might object that an argument against precisely this same principle of postponing good actions until after one's death can be found in Montaigne's *Essais* (Bk. 1, chap. 7), it is highly unlikely that Lay, an "illiterate" man, found it there. Rather, his hitting on this device seems a singular mark of his independent thinking, his agility at invention.

Toward the end of the book Lay asks the reader to overlook errors and to "remember that it [the book] was written by one that was a poor common Sailor, and an illiterate Man" (271). But for an "illiterate man" Lay could sometimes show astonishing sophistication.

The work of John Woolman, the third writer in this Quaker galaxy, is better known to the general public than that of Sandiford or Lay, particularly through recent books by Paul Rosenblatt and Edwin H. Cady, who have described his antislavery writings and analyzed the main arguments.[16] With Woolman freedom for the slaves became a real crusade; he devoted a large part of the last twenty years of his life to it.

Woolman's main writings on slavery consist of four separate works: the essay entitled *Some Considerations on the Keeping of Negroes* (part 1) published in 1754; part two, published in 1762; the *Epistle of Caution and Advice Concerning the Buying and Keeping of Slaves* (formerly attributed to Anthony Benezet), which was circulated (1753–54) to various Yearly Meetings of Friends all along the eastern seacoast (from Maine to Georgia) as well as in London and Dublin; and the essay "On the Slave Trade," written during the last four months of his life, in England.[17]

Rosenblatt differentiates between the two parts of *Some Considerations*, saying that "in Part I, Woolman had argued for the 'freedom' of the children of the slaveowner. Much of Part II is concerned with a plea for the freedom from slavery of the children of slaves. The text is '*The son shall not bear the iniquity of the father.*' "[18] Some passages from both parts of *Some Considerations* crop out in the *Epistle of Caution and Advice*, and the final "On the Slave Trade" repeats many of Woolman's earlier ideas on slavery. Rosenblatt finds the latter document "a personal, deeply felt statement of a man at the end of his years who has devoted a lifetime to the abolition of slavery."[19] In two other of Woolman's works, his well-known one entitled "A Plea for the Poor" and his superbly written *Journal*, further views and experiences relating to the slavery question may be found.

Woolman is important in the history of antislavery writing because his *Considerations* (1754) was distributed by the Overseers of the Quaker press in Philadelphia "to every Yearly Meeting in America." [20] According to Drake, "no one anti-slavery document had hitherto received such extensive circulation in any language anywhere." [21] Moreover, Woolman was, as we shall see, the best of the Quakers *as a writer*. The tone of his writings differed radically from the spread-eagle ranting of such predecessors as Lay and Sandiford; Woolman appealed quietly and calmly to Reason. His controlled style persuaded more effectively than their bombast. Morevoer, his life itself—the epitome of quiet dignity, simplicity, and Christian brotherhood—made him a kind of walking instance of his writing, the best of all possible ethical proof. His wide-ranging travels, in which he covered thousands of miles, not only gave him a broad first-hand acquaintance with slavery but also enabled him to spread his antislavery protest in England as well as in America. Woolman typifies in a rather wonderful way the remarkable power of the nonviolent but dedicated individualists—like Thoreau, Gandhi, and Martin Luther King, Jr.—who in the eminence of their personality work effective and far-reaching changes, whole revolutions, sometimes, in the political structure of their own times or in the lives of those who come after them.

As a Quaker antislavery writer, Woolman's basic premise in *Considerations*, part I, is that all men are brothers. Quoting the Bible—"All Nations are of one Blood" (Gen. 3:20)—he asserts that "in this World we are but Sojourners," subject to similar afflictions, temptations, death, and judgment—"the All wise Being is Judge and Lord over us all" (2). Thus the essential difference between slave and slave owner is for him merely that of different gifts or different "circumstances." Given this assumption, he then argues that the gifted and those in strong or favored circumstances owe an obligation to the less gifted, the weak, those in less favorable situations. Warning that misuse of such gifts can lead to God's displeasure, he reminds us that God's judgments are "just and equal" and that He "exalts and humbles to the dust as he seeth meet" (4). Furthermore, highly "favored" men "have been apt to err in their Opinions concerning others." (He cites the "holier than thou" attitude of the children of Israel in Isaiah 65:5.) In sharp departure from the old Covenant theology of Winthrop, Cotton, and the Mathers as well as the "national covenant" concept of Stoddard, Woolman states that "to think Favours are peculiar to one Nation, and exclude others, plainly supposes a Darkness in the Understanding: For as God's love is universal, so where the Mind is sufficiently influenced by it, it begets a Likeness of itself, and the Heart is enlarged towards all Men" (6).

Accordingly, he suggests we put ourselves in the slave's place, "make their Case ours," sketching at length the misery of their situation—the constant servitude, suffering, lack of training in reading and writing, etc. Then he asks, "Should we, in that Case, be less abject than they now are?" Antislavery argument based on the Golden Rule soon became common enough in the eighteenth century. Less common, however, was Woolman's addition to the Golden Rule, his recourse to the Old Testament idea of *hospitality*: "If a Stranger sojourn with thee in your Land, ye shall not vex him; but the Stranger that dwelleth with you, shall be as One born amongst you, and thou shalt love him as thyself" (Lev. 19: 33, 34) (10). If the idea of treating the slave with *hospitality* (ancient or modern) had been considered before Woolman, it certainly had not been expressed in print!

To the economic objection of the slave owners that there was "Cost of Purchase," and risk of life to "them who possess 'em [slaves]," Woolman replies, "In a Practice just and reasonable, such Objections may have Weight; but *if the Work be wrong from the Beginning*, there's little or no Force in them" (11). "If I purchase a Man who hath never forfeited his Liberty, the *natural Right of Freedom* is in him; and shall I keep him and his Posterity in Servitude and Ignorance? 'How should I approve of this Conduct, were I in his Circumstances, and he in mine?' " (11, my italics.) Here again, as in the above instance, Woolman couples something new to the commonplace Golden Rule—the eighteenth-century idea of the social contract, the idea that every man born on the face of the earth possessed certain inalienable rights.[22]

Another objection, or rather practice, of the slave owners concerned their desire to pass on to their children a comfortable material inheritance. That such a legacy depended very largely on slave labor was glossed over, while the owners maintained their role as unselfish parents intent only on providing for their offspring. Woolman begins by pointing out that "wise Instructions, a good Example, and the Knowledge of some honest Employment" are far more important to such offspring than "laying up Treasures," which, he says, "are often rather a Snare, than any real Benefit" (13).

. . . If Children are not only educated in the way of so great Temptation [as slavery], but have also the Opportunity of lording it over their Fellow Creatures, and being Masters of Men in their Childhood, how can we hope otherwise than that their tender Minds will be possessed with Thoughts too high for them? Which, by Continuance, gaining Strength will prove, like a slow Current, gradually separating them from . . . that Humility and Meekness in which alone lasting Happiness can be enjoyed. (15)

True happiness, according to Woolman, might be achieved by a relatively modest recipe—"A Supply to Nature's lawful Wants, joined with a peaceful humble Mind . . . and if here we arrive to this, and remain to walk in the Path of the Just, our Case will be truly happy" (13). To which he adds:

Man is born to labour, and Experience abundantly sheweth that it is for our Good: but where the Powerful lay the Burthen on the Inferiour, without affording a Christian Education, and suitable Opportunity of Improving the Mind, and a Treatment which we, in their Case, should approve, that themselves may live at Ease, and fare sumptuously, and lay up Riches for their Posterity, this seems to contradict the Design of Providence, and, I doubt, is sometimes *the Effect of a perverted Mind*: For while the Life of one is made grievous by the Rigour of another, it entails Misery on both. (15–16, my italics)

Thus the unselfish desire of the owners to provide for their children is reduced to absurdity; seen in the brighter, inner light of Woolman's vision, it amounts to no real argument or reasoning, but only to "a perverted Mind." More than any previous antislavery writer, Woolman emphasizes the *psychological* effects of slavery, especially *on children*, whereby we see his magnanimous concern for posterity—his feeling for *the great family of man* instead of merely for one's own immediate family.

As Rosenblatt says, in part II of *Considerations* Woolman takes up the effect of slavery, not this time on the slave owner's children, but on the *slave's* children. Admitting for the purpose of the argument that some Negroes might be imported "who, for their Cruelty to their Countrymen, and the evil Disposition of their Minds" might be unfit to be at liberty, he writes, "yet the innocent Children ought not to be made Slaves, because their Parents sinned" (9–10).

When the Awl was bored through the Ear of the *Hebrew* Servant, the Text saith, *He shall serve for ever*; yet we do not suppose that by the Word *for ever*, it was intended that none of his Posterity should afterwards be free. (17)

Much is written today of the political, religious, and economic rights of all kinds of people; surely Woolman was one of the first American writers to champion the political rights of children.

Custom in Woolman's view played an important part in slavery. Here again, as he had done in part I of his *Considerations*, he analyzes an important psychological cause,

. . . owing chiefly to the Idea of Slavery being connected with the Black Colour, and Liberty with the White: . . . where false Ideas are twisted into our Minds, it is with Difficulty we get fairly disentangled. (29)

In "Matters of Right and Equity," he writes: "The Colour of a Man avails nothing" (30). Here, too, he repeats the idea in part I that slave owners are less happy, less "calm," because they have left "the true Use of Things" ordained by the Creator (32). It is impossible, therefore, to be involved in the slave trade and retain one's innocence (42–43).

Two important terms in the second part of *Considerations* are *Guilt* and *Luxury*. It is these, he argues, that were poisoning the minds of the slave owners; the genteel purchaser was equally guilty with the brutal slave trader (45). Slavery depraves the mind of the slave owner (51). The desire for luxury results from the fact that the owners have left "the true Use of Things," which he claims is the simple way of life. Luxury is potentially dangerous, not only morally but politically, he reasons, since, joined with *Oppression* (his third important term in this section), it leads to "War and Desolation" (34). Thus Woolman's significance may be said to rest partly in his role as an early prophet of the Civil War. He foresaw that the political consequences of continued slavery would eventuate in war, because of the conflict between Gain and Equity:

. . . Wherever Gain is preferred to Equity and wrong Things publickly encouraged to that Degree, that Wickedness takes Root, and spreads wide amongst the Inhabitants of a Country, there is real Cause for Sorrow to all such, whose Love to Mankind stands on a true Principle. . . (52)

The conflict between Gain and Equity saddened Woolman to the extent that he carried his antislavery crusade to England.[23] What had begun as an attempt to root out slavery among Quakers in America had now spread to international dimension. While it is true that Woolman resembled in some ways a kind of traveling revivalist and that he addressed mainly Quaker meeting audiences in his speeches and his writings in England and America, his English tour nevertheless represented a very significant spread of antislavery sentiment among the members of this sect. The Quakers were geographically widespread both in America and in England, and since Woolman traveled so extensively among them, his influence and power as an individual cannot be overestimated. His literary skill, his tact, his success in Quaker politics, his integrity and broad rational faith in the brotherhood of man facilitated the great work of his life—the consolidation of Quaker sentiment for emancipation.[24]

A brief recapitulation may clarify one or two points with respect to the larger picture of these three Middle Atlantic Quaker writers—Sandiford, Lay, and Woolman—and their differences from Mather and Sewall. Sandiford differed from these two New England writers in putting more stress on the public rather than the theological aspects of slavery—its bad effect on commonwealth government, specifically the weakening of a legislature composed of slave owners, but also on all offices of public trust. Mather was primarily interested in the spiritual salvation of Negro servants and not a little worried about fulfilling the moral obligations of catechetical instruction, although he was also pragmatic enough to say that Negroes who received religious instruction would make better servants than those who had not. Judge Sewall took the viewpoint of his profession, considering the lack of legal evidence in connection with the slave's loss of freedom. But like Mather, he was a proper Calvinist who relied on the authority of the Bible for justification of his arguments. Benjamin Lay, in the manner of a hell-fire preacher, played on the fear of spiritual damnation awaiting owners of slaves, especially emphasizing the hypocrisy of Quaker ministers who kept slaves. More or less implicit in the Quaker writings was an idea that Woolman made very explicit—*the guilt of the purchaser of the slave*, the owner's role as accomplice in the crime. This was the important basic premise that supported many of Benezet's arguments as well as those of other writers we have yet to consider.

Anthony Benezet, the last of these four Quaker writers, was probably the most prolific and widely published among eighteenth-century American antislavery writers. His devotion to the antislavery crusade spanned nearly half a century. His *Observations on the Inslaving, Importing and Purchasing of Negroes* underwent two editions, as did his work entitled *A Short Account of that Part of Africa, Inhabited by the Negroes . . .*, which was also later translated into German in Philadelphia and then later reprinted in a third edition (in English) in London.[25] His *Caution and Warning to Great Britain and her Colonies, in a Short Representation of the Calamitous State of the Enslaved Negroes in the British Dominion . . .* was printed twice in Philadelphia (1766 and 1767) and twice in London (1767 and 1784).[26] Prior to the Revolutionary War he brought out *Some Historical Account of Guiana . . . With an Inquiry into the Rise and Progress of the Slave-Trade, its Nature and Lamentable Effects.*[7] During the war (in 1778) he published *Serious Considerations on Several Important Subjects; viz. on War and its Inconsistency with the Gospel; Observations on Slavery . . . etc.*[28] Other works by other writers on slavery, both before and after the war, have been erroneously attributed to him.[29]

Benezet's *Observations on the Inslaving, Importing and Purchasing of Negroes* is an eleven-page pamphlet which begins by sketching the history of slavery, noting especially that it had arisen in ancient times from the need to defray expenses of war. But modern slavery more often than not dispensed with such preliminaries as war. The purchasers of slaves were the guilty ones, according to Benezet, and he threatened them with the judgment of God: "Without Purchasers, there would be no Trade; and consequently every Purchaser as he encouraged the Trade becomes partaker in the Guilt of it" (4).

In the remainder of the pamphlet Benezet follows his usual method of anthologizing quotations from other writers, "Persons of Note, who have been long employed in the African Trade, and whose Situation and Office in the Factories will not admit any to question the truth of what they relate" (4). Thus he quotes one William Bosman, "Factor for the Dutch *African* Company, at the Factory at *Delmina*, who wrote an Account of that Country, now more than fifty Years past . . . [saying]

'That the Booty which the Negro Soldiers aim at in their Wars, are Ornaments of Gold and Prisoners of War, in Order to sell them for Slaves at Pleasure, that many of the Inhabitants depend on Plunder and the Slave-Trade; and that when Vessels arrive, if they have no Stock of Slaves, the Factors trust the Inhabitants with Goods for the Value of one or two

Hundred Slaves, which they send into the inland Country in Order to buy Slaves at all Markets, even sometimes two Hundred Miles deep in the Country, where Markets of Men were kept in the same Manner as those of Beasts with us.' " (4–5)

Thus, too, he quotes from one John Barbot, "Agent General of the French Royal African Company," who "in his Acc[ount] printed 1732" had written that "those Slaves sold by the Negroes, are for the most Part Prisoners of War, taken either in fight or pursuit, or in the incursions they make into their Enemies Territories; others are stolen away by their own Country-Men, and some there are who will sell their own Children, Kindred or Neighbours" (5). Benezet also quotes from Joseph Randal's account of the "*Guinea* Trade," in the latter's *Book of Geography* (1744), to the effect that children there sometimes sold "their Fathers and Mothers" into slavery (7).

In summary, Benezet sees "the Trade as inconsistent with the Gospel of Christ, contrary to natural Justice, and the common feelings of Humanity, and productive of infinite Calamities to many Thousand Families, nay to many Nations, and consequently offensive to God the Father of all Mankind" (9). He admits that some slave owners (who may have acquired slaves by inheritance, etc.) might care for them in a benevolent manner. But the "Trade" itself was "destructive of the Welfare of human Society, and inconsistent with the Peace and Prosperity of a Country: as by it the number of the natural Enemies must be encreased." Moreover, he continues, "I might shew from innumerable Examples how it introduces Idleness, discourages Marriage, corrupts the Youth and ruins and debauches Morals" (9). After refuting objections by defenders of slavery, whose "true Motive" he attributes to "selfish Avarice" (9), he concludes with another quotation—the ever-reliable Exodus 21:16—"*He that stealeth a Man and selleth him, or if he be found in his Hands, he shall surely be put to death.*" [30]

Benezet's *A Short Account of that Part of Africa, Inhabited by the Negroes* is a longer pamphlet (eighty pages). Although the title might give the impression of a general descriptive work, the subtitle makes clear that it concerns the slave trade and that here again Benezet is employing his usual technique of anthologizing. The subtitle mentions "Quotations from the Writings of several Persons of Note, *viz.* GEORGE WALLIS, FRANCIS HUTCHESON, and JAMES FOSTER, and a large Extract from a Pamphlet, lately published in *London*, on the Subject of the SLAVE TRADE." [31]

In the body of the text the author takes up such topics as the area
from which the slaves were obtained, their good disposition (a moot
point among authorities of that time—see pp. 15n and 18), their
civil government (99f), and matters of justice among the Hottentots
(21). Of the latter he says that they constitute the "only *Negro*
Nation that we know of, that are not engaged in making and selling
Slaves." Here, as elsewhere in his pamphlets, Benezet bases his
principal arguments on the authority of the Christian gospel. And
he attacks the hypocrisy of so-called Christian slave dealers and
owners. But if these so-called Christians were hypocritical, so also
were the African kings, who sometimes sold their own subjects into
slavery. (Benezet explains that this practice was regarded as
exceptional, only being carried out when the kings were short of a
saleable commodity of prisoners of war.)

Among the authors Benezet quotes in *A Short Account* are
Francis Hutcheson, an eminent professor of moral philosophy and
aesthetics at the University of Glasgow, and George Wallis, a
Scottish lawyer.[32] This time the arguments rest on the well-known
natural-right theory of eighteenth-century political theorists: "He
who detains another by Force in Slavery, is always bound to prove
his Title" (34). "The violent Possessor must in all Cases shew his
Title, especially where the old Proprietor is well known. In this
Case each man is the original Proprietor of his own Liberty" (34).
Slavery is "a *criminal* and outrageous Violation of the natural Right
of Mankind" (35). (This last quotation comes from James Foster's
Discourses on Natural Religion and Social Virtue.)

After quoting from Hutcheson, Wallis, and Foster, Benezet next
gives us the "large Extract" from the pamphlet mentioned in the
subtitle as "lately published in *London*." This pamphlet, *Two
Dialogues on the Man-Trade* (1760) by F. Philmore, occupies pp.
37–63 of Benezet's anthology. Briefly summarized, the passages
Benezet quotes from Philmore argue a common species or descent
of Negroes and whites (38), their both being under the same moral
law—"the eternal Law of Reason," "which God had written upon
the Table of Man's Heart" (39); [33] their common society (39); the
obligations Christians owe non-Christians (39–41); the sufferings of
Negroes on slave ships (48–49), during and after the "seasoning"
process, and on plantations (55n); the perverted role of government
in not effecting a cure of slavery (60); and an attack on the idea that
the sugar and tobacco trades might suffer if slavery were abolished
(60–61).

Benezet also includes the peroration of Philmore's *Two Dialogues*—some rather impassioned rhetoric in the form of an *"Address to the Guinea Merchants in England,"* in which Philmore asks the dealers to consider how they will "come off in the great and awful Day of Account" (61). In his own peroration, which immediately follows, Benezet by contrast employs a calm and dispassionate tone. He first defends the authorities he has cited (65), although his defense is really more of an explanation as to why the Negroes sometimes were thought to submit to slavery without vocal complaint.[34] He then suggests various practical remedies (69 ff), refutes the idea that the African Negroes lived "in the same unsettled Manner as the American Indians" (72), and describes the free Negroes living off the west coast of Africa as exhibiting a high degree of innocence and moral virtue—specifically charity, humility, hospitality, and reverence for age (78). He closes with an appeal for *"Love, Meekness and Charity, which is the unchangeable Nature and Glory of Christianity"* (80). This pamphlet was addressed to a wide reading audience, not limited to Quakers. In the last resort Benezet appealed not only to the consciences of the slave dealers and owners but also "to every honest and unprejudiced Reader" (78).

Four years later, in 1766, Benezet published a third pamphlet attacking slavery, *A Caution and Warning to Great-Britain, and her Colonies, In a Short Representation of the Calamitous State of the Enslaved Negroes in the British Dominions.*[35] In this work he makes a three-pronged onslaught on slavery as "inconsistent with the plainest Precepts of the Gospel, the Dictates of Reason, and every common Sentiment of Humanity" (4). This pamphlet is yet another of Benezet's anthologies, running to forty-eight pages, in which he quotes from many authors in several different countries. Among these George Whitefield occupies a prominent position. (Whitefield had warned against slavery in his *Letter from Georgia, to the Inhabitants of Maryland, Virginia, North and South Carolina, printed in the Year 1739.)* [36]

Benezet's longest work, *Some Historical Account of Guinea* (Philadelphia, 1771), was in part "a Republication of the Sentiments of Several Authors of Note . . . , particularly an extract of a Treatise written by Granville Sharp." [37] Brookes points out that this work of Benezet's contains much the same material as is found in *A Caution and Warning to Great Britain*, including Benezet's plan for abolishing slavery. Briefly, this plan urged stopping the importation of slaves, freeing those already in America (after a certain period of service), and settling them on lands west of the Alleghenies.[38]

During the Revolution, Benezet persistently crusaded against slavery, continuing to wage relentless war on this and other evils. He reprinted his *Serious Considerations on Several Important Subjects* (Philadelphia, 1778), which had first appeared in 1769.[39] This work treats three chief topics—war, slavery, and alcoholism— all of which Benezet ardently opposed. In his "Observations on Slavery" (pp. 27–40) Benezet follows a slightly different line of argument, pointing out the inconsistency of the continuation of slavery with the recently published Declaration of Independence and the resolution against slavery by the Virginia Convention. (In this he anticipated most of the post-Revolutionary antislavery writers.) But he sounds more like a Puritan than a Quaker in the way he describes slavery as "one of the principal causes of those heavy judgments, which are now so sensibly displayed over the Colonies" (29). [40] In the middle part of this essay Benezet addresses progressively three large groups involved in slavery (captains, merchants, and slave owners), threatening each with eternal punishment. Against an imagined captain of a slave ship his rhetoric rises most sharply:

What is your heart made of? Is there no such principle as compassion there? Do you never feel another's pain? Have you no sympathy? No sense of human woe? No pity for the miserable? When you saw the flowing eyes, the heaving breast, or the bleeding sides and tortured limbs of your fellow creatures. Was [sic] you a stone or a brute? Did you look upon them with the eyes of a tiger? When you squeezed the agonizing creatures down in the ship, or when you threw their poor mangled remains into the sea, had you no relenting? Did not one tear drop from your eye, one sigh escape from your breast? Do you feel no relenting now? If you do not, you must go on until the measure of your iniquities is full. Then will the great God deal with you, as you have dealt with them. . . . (36)

He urges the captain to "immediately quit the horrid trade" and "be an honest man" (36). The same line of suasion is taken with the merchants and the owners of slaves, although with less zeal. Nevertheless he accuses the accomplice slaveholders of fraud, robbery, and murder.

Benezet covered such a wide variety of topics and arguments that it is difficult to keep them all in mind. Like Sandiford, he considered the effect of slavery on the community—not only its corrupting effect on morals generally (especially those of the youth) but the fact that it also made the state or community more vulnerable by increasing the number of its enemies. Other points he called attention to were these: the hypocrisy of the so-called Christian slave dealers, the violation of the natural-rights theory, the inconsistency of slavery with the Gospel, with reason, and with humanity, the certain guilt of the purchasers at the Day of Judgment, and—during the Revolutionary War—the inconsistency with the Declaration of Independence and his interpretation of the war itself as God's just punishment upon the colonists for continuing the practice of slavery. More positively, he advocated stopping importation, freeing present slaves (after a certain period), and settling them on land west of the Alleghenies.

In attempting to assess Benezet's importance as a rhetorical writer, Drake concludes that, considering the wide circulation of his pamphlets among Quakers and others "in the colonies, in England, and on the Continent," it is no exaggeration to call him "the foremost propagandist against the slave trade and slavery in the later eighteenth century."[41] Finally, it should be noticed that Benezet also influenced his friends and followers to write against slavery, people like William Dillwyn, John Wesley, and Dr. Benjamin Rush.[42]

III   *Other Pre-Revolutionary Writers*

A. *Benjamin Rush*

Probably the most important single antislavery work in the pre-Revolutionary period—beyond those already discussed—was *An Address to the Inhabitants of the British Settlements in America, upon Slave-Keeping* (Philadelphia, 1773). Its author was Dr. Benjamin Rush, a Philadelphia physician.

Rush refused to accept the proposition that blacks did not possess as much intellectual capacity as whites. Allowing "for the diversity of temper and genius which is occasioned by climate," he writes, "the Intellects of Negroes" as well as "their capacities for virtue and happiness" are equal to those of Europeans (2). And he refers to Phyllis Wheatley, a free Negro girl in Boston, "whose singular genius [at Neoclassical verse] and accomplishments are such as not only to do honour to her sex, but to human nature." Rush admitted, however, that slavery itself was "so foreign to the human mind, that the moral faculties, as well as those of the understanding" were "debased, and rendered torpid by it" (2).

Taking a detached, scientific viewpoint, he attacks the curious idea that the black color of the skin qualified the Negro for slavery. (He footnotes this false theory with a long quotation from Montesquieu's *Spirit of Laws*, Bk. 15, chap. 5, where the idea is ridiculed.) The Negroes' dark color of skin qualifies them not for slavery, but for life in that "part of the Globe in which providence has placed them," he contends, adding his opinion that they are less susceptible to the ravages of "heat, diseases and time" than white people (4).

For purely enlightened argument on social and political matters, however, Rush cannot be beaten. With him the Age of Reason comes into full bloom, albeit with a considerable amount of passion. To the objection that Negro slavery was necessary for carrying on the manufacture of sugar, rice, and indigo, he simply answers, "No manufactury can be of consequence enough to society, to admit the least violation of the Laws of justice or humanity" (5). On the authority of one M. Le Poivre, the French ambassador to China, he then argues that sugar is more efficiently, more advantageously, cultivated by freemen (in China) than by slaves in the West Indies (5-6).

In the main, Rush's position is that slavery not only violates the laws of nature but also those of religion. Consequently he spends a good deal of time refuting proslavery arguments drawn from the Bible. In fact, the purpose of his whole pamphlet is largely refutative, as he explains in his statement on the first page. (Unlike many other antislavery writers of the period, he skips the history of slavery, which so often served as a prelude to the reasoned part of the discourse.)

But like Benezet he also had a constructive program. "The first step to be taken . . . [was] to leave off importing slaves" (21). "For this purpose let our assemblies unite in petitioning the king and parliament to dissolve the African company." (A footnote explains that the Virginia Assembly had already so petitioned—see 21n.) Secondly, he proposed emancipation of young Negro slaves, but not of old ones (who he thought might be "unfit to set at liberty"— because of vices acquired during slavery) (22). Third, he advocated education—reading, writing, and job training for those to be set free. Fourth, he suggested a time limit on all other servitude. Finally, he pointed out that in some of the Spanish colonies it was customary to award the Negroes one free day a week on which they might work for pay and thus earn money to buy other free days, eventually to free themselves by their own efforts (22–23n).

Despite the fact that Rush was a physician, he manifests little scientific detachment in his impassioned peroration, which rises sharply to a powerful climax and which is too long to quote in entirety:

> . . . Let us . . . see the various modes of arbitrary punishments inflicted upon them by their masters. Behold one covered with stripes, into which melted wax is poured—another tied down to a block or a stake—a third suspended in the air by his thumbs—a fourth obliged to set or stand upon red hot iron—a fifth—I cannot relate it. ———Where now is Law or Justice? Let us fly to them to step in for their relief. ———Alas!———The one is silent, and the other denounces more terrible punishments upon them. Let us attend the place appointed for inflicting the penalties of the law. See here one without a limb, whose only crime was an attempt to regain his Liberty—another led to the Gallows for eating a morsel of Bread, to which his labor gave him a better title than his master—a third famishing on the gibbet—a fourth in a flame of Fire!—his shrieks pierce the very heavens.———O! God! Where is thy Vengeance!—O! Humanity—Justice—Liberty—Religion!—Where,—where are ye fled. ——— ———
> ——— This is no exaggeration Picture. It is taken from real life. (24–26)

In his conclusion Rush exhorts various classes of his countrymen to help him abolish slavery—magistrates, legislatures, "men of Sense and Virtue—Yes ADVOCATES for American Liberty [since the Revolution was already in the air] but chiefly—ye MINISTERS OF THE GOSPEL," to whom he goes on to address another long, eloquent plea (29).

Rush did not always know when to stop, and his well-reasoned arguments sometimes veered perilously close to bathos, as Professor David Freeman Hawke says. Yet Hawke concludes (and we concur) that in this *Address* Rush had produced "a remarkable pamphlet, one that appealed both to the mind and to the heart, and [that] for a half century few attacks on slavery surpassed the power of its emotional appeal and logic." [43]

Rush's *Address* was challenged by Richard Nesbit, a former West-Indian planter then living in Philadelphia. [44] The title of Nesbit's pamphlet—*Slavery Not Forbidden by Scripture; Or a Defense of the West-India Planters from the Aspersions thrown out against them by the Author of A Pamphlet Entitled "An Address"*— is self-explanatory, at least with respect to its author's general position. Nesbit claimed that Rush's account of cruelty to Negroes was exaggerated, that his condemnation of slavery was "Utopian," and that Negroes were an inferior race. Rush answered all three of these claims of Nesbit in a *Vindication* of his *Address*. Both the *Address* and his fifty-four-page *Vindication* appeared together in the second edition, apparently published on September 15, 1775, according to the one-page preface, or "Advertisement" to this edition. As at the conclusion of the *Address* so near the end of the *Vindication* Rush again rises to an emotional climax. With a brilliant and passionate recapitulation of Nesbit's arguments, Rush overwhelms the reader, and turning the tide in his favor becomes prosecutor instead of vindicator. With burning eloquence he presses home his advantage over Nesbit for having dared to defend slavery:

You have called in question the Justice and goodness of the Supreme Being. You have charged the FATHER of Mankind with being the Author of the greatest Evils to his Children. You have aimed to establish Principles, which justify the most expensive and cruel Depredations which have been made by Conquerors and Tyrants, upon the Liberties and Lives of Mankind, and which at the same time condemn those glorious Events, and illustrious Men, that Britain and her Colonies, are indebted to for their Liberty and Prosperity. You have misrepresented the true Interests of our Mother Country. You have attempted to palliate Crimes which are founded on a Pride and Depravity of Soul, unavoidable in Masters and Slaves in the West-Indies. You have thrown a Veil over the true Causes which destroy so many Thousands of your fellow Creatures every year. You have (to use your own Words) "unworthily traduced" not "many of my valuable Friends" but the *whole* of your own Brethren—the poor Africans. You have attempted to sink Creatures, formed like yourself, in the image of God, and equally capable of Happiness both here and hereafter, *below* the rank of "Monsters and Barbarians" or even Brutes themselves. You have——but I forbear to add to the Reproaches to which you have exposed yourself——. "As a Person cannot err so grossly as not to be able to make Atonement" I hope you will not fail immediately to ask forgiveness of your Maker, and your Country, for the Attack you have made upon the Rights of Mankind. (51–53) [45]

Had Rush ended his *Vindication* here, it would have packed a wonderful climactic effect. Unfortunately, he continued for two more pages, affirming all the while that his descriptions of the tortures of slavery rested on facts and on good authorities, but admitting that the inhuman practices described in his *Address* did not apply to all West-Indian planters. Consequently he fades away with a conciliatory tone and a watered-down conclusion that is considerably less powerful. While it may be argued that he thus wins some amount of credence for his argument, yet the sudden descent of the tone is so observable as to mar the power of the ending.

Rush was paid off for these two antislavery tracts in unpopularity among his Philadelphia townsmen, and evidence exists to support the theory that his medical practice suffered, at least temporarily.[46] But he soon recovered from this little setback.

Like his friend Benezet, Rush continued his interest in the slavery issue after the Revolution. In Mathew Carey's *American Museum* (July 1788) he published "An Account of the DISEASES peculiar to the negroes in the West Indies, and which are produced by slavery." [47] Along with Tench Coxe, Rush was one of the secretaries of the Pennsylvania abolition society which Franklin presided over, and he is supposed to have "had a hand in the petition condemning slavery which was sent to the Constitutional Convention . . . calling for an end to the slave trade after twenty years." [48]

B. *Jefferson, Henry, Paine, Franklin, Hopkins,* et al.

Among the remaining writers who treated slavery before the Revolution almost all, with the possible exception of Samuel Hopkins, handled it cursorily, both in the North and in the South. Southern as well as northern writers tended to oppose slavery in this period. There were, of course, one or two exceptions. Robert Beverley, for instance, wrote in *The History and Present State of Virginia* (1705) that slaves in that colony were not "worked near so hard nor so many hours in a day as the husbandmen and day laborers in England." [49] Too, a group of Georgia landowners, temporarily lodged in Charleston, S.C.—Pat Tailfer, Hugh Anderson, David Douglas, *et al.*—argued in *A True and Historical Narrative of the Colony of Georgia* (Charleston, 1741) that General Oglethorpe's policies in denying them the use of slaves to till their land had resulted in a state of extreme poverty closely resembling slavery![50] The Reverend Samuel Davies, on the other hand, condemned "Negro slavery as contrary to God's law" during the Great Awakening.[51] Arthur Lee published in London (1764) *An Essay in Vindication of the Continental Colonies of America, from a Censure of Mr. Adam Smith, in His Theory of Moral Sentiments.*

With some reflections on slavery in general. Lee opposed slavery as "absolutely repugnant to justice" and "highly inconsistent with civil policy; first [,] as it tends to suppress all improvements in arts and sciences. . . . Secondly, as it may deprave the minds of the freemen. . . . And, lastly, as it endangers the community by the destructive effects of civil commotions," to which he adds "that it is shocking to humanity, violative of every generous sentiment, abhorrent utterly from [to?] the Christian religion." [52]

Thomas Jefferson struck at slavery in a work that brought him to the attention of his fellow Americans, *A Summary of the Rights of British America* (1774), although his more detailed discussion did not appear until later (*Notes on Virginia*, 1784). In the *Summary*, which included Jefferson's instructions to the Virginia delegates to the Continental Congress, he wrote:

The abolition of domestic slavery is the great object of desire in those colonies where it was unhappily introduced in their infant state. But previous to the infranchisement of the slaves we have, it is necessary to exclude all further importations from Africa. Yet our repeated attempts to effect this by prohibitions, and by imposing duties which might amount to a prohibition, have been hitherto defeated by his majesty's negative: thus preferring the advantages of a few British corsairs to the lasting interests of the American states, and to the rights of human nature deeply wounded by this infamous practice. [53]

It is interesting to see Jefferson here pinning the blame for the continuation of slavery in America on the British king!

Patrick Henry, in a letter dated Hanover, January 18, 1773, to Robert Pleasants, a Virginia Quaker abolitionist, thanks him for the receipt of a book by Anthony Benezet and asks:

Is it not amazing, that at a time, when ye Rights of Humanity are defined & understood with precision, in a Country above all others fond of Liberty, that in such an Age, & such a Country we find Men, professing a Religion ye most humane, mild, meek, gentle & generous; adopting a Principle repugnant to humanity as it is inconsistent [*sic*] with the Bible and destructive to Liberty[?] [54]

In this same letter Henry confesses that he himself is an owner of slaves and is "drawn along by ye general inconvenience of living without them," however culpable such conduct may be. But he believes that "a time will come when an opp[ortunity] will be offered to abolish this lamentable Evil." Meanwhile, everything that one could do to alleviate the distress of the slaves should be done. He closes by remarking, "I could say many things on this Subject; a serious view of which gives a gloomy perspective to future times."[55]

In the 1770s, before the Revolutionary War, Tom Paine and Benjamin Franklin turned their serious attention to the problem. Neither of these two great propagandists for freedom created any considerable body of antislavery writings, either before or after the war, but both were very much aware of the issue and gave it serious consideration in this time of approaching crisis.

Paine supposedly wrote his short essay on slavery at the end of 1774, but it was not printed until March 8, 1775, in the *Pennsylvania Journal and Weekly Advertiser*.[56] With characteristic directness it is addressed "To Americans" and argues that slavery is "unnatural" as well as a violation of principles of "justice and humanity." After refuting a few of the more common proslavery arguments and noting that many eminent men, including Locke and Montesquieu, had already attacked slavery, Paine presents five central points: 1. The inconsistency of the Americans' crying out against English attempts to enslave them (politically), while they (the Americans) were holding "many hundred thousands in [domestic] slavery" (18). 2. The threat of punishment from an angry providence—conceivably a reference to the approaching war.[57] 3. The possibility of a social, economic, and religious boycott against dealers in slaves (18–19). 4. Practical measures for those already enslaved. "To turn the old and infirm free, would be injustice and cruelty. . . . Perhaps some could give them lands upon reasonable rent. . . . Perhaps they might form useful barrier settlements on the frontiers," etc. (19). 5. Reparation for injuries to slaves as a Christian duty, possibly in the form of religious education or other instruction (19).

In an even shorter piece—a two-paragraph notice of about 400 words—which appeared in the *Pennsylvania Journal* (October 18, 1775), Paine reflects on "the horrid cruelties exercised by Britain in the East Indies" and on the Indians in America. Coupling his animosity against the political tyranny of the mother country with his indignation at slavery, he writes,

. . . Ever since the discovery of America she has employed herself in the most horrid of all traffics, that of human flesh, unknown to the most savage nations, has yearly (without provocation and in cold blood) ravaged the hapless shores of Africa, robbing it of its unoffending inhabitants to cultivate her stolen dominions in the West—When I reflect on these, I hesitate not for a moment to believe that the Almighty will finally separate America from Britain. . . .

And when the Almighty shall have blest us, and made us a people *dependent only upon Him*, then may our first gratitude be shown by an act of continental legislation which shall put a stop to the importation of Negroes for sale, soften the hard fate of those already here, and in time procure their freedom.
Humanus (20)

Five years later, when he was Clerk of the Pennsylvania Assembly, Paine wrote "The first legislative measure for the emancipation of Negro slaves in America" (21). [58]

Before the year 1770, according to Paul W. Conner, Benjamin Franklin was lukewarmish toward the whole problem of Negro slavery and its abolition. But, like Paine, in the early 1770s Franklin "finally translated his theoretical aversion to slavery and the slave trade into abolitionist activity. . . ." [59] His letter in the *London Public Advertiser* (January 30, 1770), entitled "A Conversation between an ENGLISHMAN, a SCOTCHMAN, and an AMERICAN, on the Subject of SLAVERY," extends the debate on slavery into areas other than Negro servitude.[60] Although approving Granville Sharp's book on slavery, the AMERICAN takes exception to Sharp's statement that slavery was widespread in the colonies, saying that only about one family in a hundred had a Negro slave. "Many Thousands there [in America] abhor the Slave Trade as much as Mr. Sharp can do," says the AMERICAN, and then asks if it is "right to stigmatize us all" with the crime of slavery? (188). He continues: "Of those who keep Slaves, all are not Tyrants and Oppressors" (188). Many, he argues, treat their slaves with "great Humanity" and "provide full as well for them in Sickness and in Health, as your labouring People in England are provided for." From this point on Franklin expands the discussion to attack harsh treatment of poor workers in great Britain. But at the same time he blames the English for beginning the slave trade and for dumping them and convicts from English jails in the American colonies.

You bring the Slaves to us, and tempt us to purchase them. I do not justify our falling into Temptation. To be sure, if you have stolen Men to sell to us, and we buy them, you may urge against us the old and true saying, that *the Receiver is as bad as the Thief*. This Maxim was probably made for those who needed the Information, as being perhaps ignorant that *receiving* was in its Nature as bad as *stealing*; but the Reverse of the Position was never thought necessary to be formed into a Maxim, nobody ever doubted that *the Thief is as bad as the Receiver*. This you have not only done and continue to do, but several Laws heretofore made in our Colonies, to discourage the Importation of Slaves, by laying a heavy Duty, payable by the Importer, have been disapproved and repealed by your Government here [in England], as being prejudicial, forsooth, to the Interest of the African Company. (188)

Then, after remonstrating against slavery of workers in British coal mines, the AMERICAN sets up an elongated definition of a slave, which for purposes of discussion the ENGLISHMAN agrees to accept. The ENGLISHMAN insists, however, that there are no such slaves in England. But the AMERICAN effectively demonstrates that the definition fits the soldiers and the sailors forced into British military service. And the AMERICAN also gets in the last word by pointing out that English slavery, in the armed forces, actually goes beyond slavery of Negroes and indentured servants in America (192).

In his personal letters of the period as well as in this satiric dialogue, Franklin shows unmistakably his committed opposition to slavery. Writing to Benezet from London on August 22, 1772, he says,

Dear Friend,
I made a little extract from yours of April 27, of the number of slaves imported and perishing, with some close remarks on the Improving of this country, which encourages such a detestable commerce by laws for promoting the Guinea trade; while it piqued itself on its virtue, love of liberty, and the equity of its courts, in setting free a single negro. This was inserted in the London Chronicle of the 20th of June last.
I thank you for the Virginia address, which I shall also publish with some remarks. I am glad to hear that the disposition against negroes grows more general in North America. Several pieces have been lately printed here against this practice and I hope in time it will be taken into consideration and suppressed by the legislature. Your labours have already been attended with great effects. I hope, therefore, you and your friends will be encouraged to proceed. My hearty wishes of success attend you, being ever, my dear friend, yours affectionately,

B. Franklin [61]

This letter speaks for itself, as does the following excerpt from another to his friend Dean Woodward, dated London, April 10, 1773:

I have had the Satisfaction to learn that a Disposition to abolish Slavery prevails in North America, that many of the Pennsylvanians have set their Slaves at Liberty, and that even the Virginia Assembly have petitioned the King for Permission to make a Law for preventing the Importation of more into that Colony. This request, however, will probably not be granted, as their former Laws of that kind have always been repealed, and as the Interest of a few Merchants here [in London] has more weight with Government, than that of Thousands at a Distance.[62]

On the eve of the Revolutionary War, Samuel Hopkins, a friend and disciple of Jonathan Edwards, brought out *A Dialogue Concerning the Slavery of the Africans*, dedicated to the Continental Congress.[63] In this dialogue, which takes place between *A* (a slaveholder) and *B* (an advocate of immediate total abolition), *A* begins by asking *B* what he thinks of a recent move "to free all our African slaves." "They say," continues *A*, "that our holding these blacks in slavery, as we do, is an open violation of God, and is so great an instance of unrighteousness and cruelty, that we cannot expect deliverance from present calamities, and success in our struggle for liberty in the American colonies, until we repent and make all the restitution possible." *A* thinks the proponents of this movement "carry things too far on this head" and that "this is not a proper time to attend to" freeing the slaves "while we are in such a state of war and distress, and affairs of much greater importance demand all our attention. . ." (11).

B agrees with the proposition that slavery is wrong, that "it is a very great and public sin," and also with the idea that God is punishing this sin by sending the "present calamities." Consequently, he says, slavery "must be reformed before we can reasonably expect deliverance." "It would be worse than madness then, to put off attention to this matter, under the notion of attending to more important affairs. This is acting like the mariner, who, when his ship is filling with water, neglects to stop the leak or ply the pump, that he may mend his sails" (11–12). Calculating that there are about 800,000 slaves "in British America, including the *West-India* islands," although few of these were in New England, *B* considers the failure to emancipate in the light of the public guilt of all white Americans.

We have no way to exculpate ourselves from the guilt of the whole . . . but by freeing all our slaves. Surely then, this matter admits of no delay; but demands our first, and most serious attention, and speedy reformation. (12)

From this sample the pattern of the work as a whole is obvious—it consists again and again of an objection by A followed by a corresponding refutation by B. (I cannot resist another example, because it is timely.) A wishes modern ministers of the gospel would be a little more discreet, saying that the apostles, by contrast, had not meddled "with the affair of slavery." In general, he objects to public discussion of such matters, particularly in the presence of the slaves themselves. B answers that the slaves don't need to be told they are in slavery; they know it. He then asks, "Would you desire they should be held in ignorance, that you should exercise your tyranny, without opposition or trouble from any quarter?" (36). And he goes on as follows:

It has always been the way of tyrants to take great pains to keep their vassals in ignorance, especially to hide from them the tyranny and oppression of which they are the subjects. And for this reason they are enemies to the liberty of the press, and are greatly provoked when their conduct is set in a true light before the public, and the unrighteousness they practice, properly exposed. (36)

Then he asks, "Why should the ministers of the gospel hold their peace, and not testify against this great public iniquity, which we have reason to think, is one great cause of the public calamities we are now under?" (38).

With equal skill abolitionist B answers numerous other objections of slaveholder A—*viz.*, that slaves represent an economic interest, that they are more expensive than they are worth, that some slaveholders treat their slaves kindly, that the slaves have no desire to be free, that freeing them would be to put them in a worse plight, etc. In all this argumentation Hopkins shows himself an inventive and exhaustive thinker, remarkably like Jonathan Edwards in some ways. Occasionally his style is a bit wordy or he may permit his persona B to digress momentarily, but he speedily comes back to the point at issue and always overcomes A's objections. Invariably this is accomplished with superior logic, moral force, and persuasiveness.

Francis Hopkinson is a writer not usually connected with abolitionist sentiment. Yet one of his best satires, his *Translation of a Letter Written by a Foreigner on His Travels*, first published in

1776, touches on the subject of slavery and employs a method similar to that we have already seen in Franklin and Jefferson.[64] Hopkinson attacks the national character of the English in a letter from an imaginary visitor to London writing to a count. The visitor complains that the character of the English is "the most fantastic and absurd that ever fell to the lot of any known nation. . . . They are made up of contradictions. . ." (99).

An Englishman will treat his enemy with great generosity, and his friends with ingratitude and inhumanity. (98–99)

Slavery is cited as one example of the inherently contradictory nature of the English.

The English assume to themselves the character of being the most just, generous, and humane nation in the world, and yet they encourage the *African trade*—a trade attended with circumstances of injustice, cruelty, and horror, that disgrace human nature; whereby they fasten for life, the chains of servitude the most abject, and misery the most complete, on many hundred of their fellow creatures every year. (100)

What Hopkinson is doing here is rather subtle. We might state his argument this way: The English are not only *contradictory* in treating their enemies with "great generosity" and their friends (the American colonies) "with ingratitude and inhumanity," but they are also *contradictory* in assuming that they are humane when they are actually perpetrating "injustice, cruelty, and horror," etc., by encouraging the African slave trade. Implied is the proposition that such a people deserves armed resistance, before they extend their tyranny further. Also implied, since the argument is in the nature of an enthymeme, is this premise, that such a people (the English) can be defeated by another people (the Americans) who are of an opposite nature—i.e, justice-loving, truly humane, etc., since those who support good causes will, *with the help of Providence*, inevitably win. This seems to be the conclusion that Hopkinson would insinuate to his audience of despairing Americans. That this line of argument resembles that of Paine in the first *Crisis* paper and also that of Freneau's satire "George the Third's Soliloquy" is quite obvious. Like Franklin and Jefferson, too, Hopkinson strengthens his attack on domestic slavery by combining it with political slavery and by blaming the British for both.

IV   *Post-Revolutionary Writers*

After the Revolutionary War, and especially after the Constitutional Convention, antislavery writings appeared more frequently. Limited space does not permit even listing the great number of these writers, let alone examining the arguments.

As one might expect, many of the writers during this period drew attention to the inconsistency of fighting for political freedom and failing to emancipate the Negro slaves in the new republic. Because of the Declaration of Independence it was easier to write on this issue after the war than before. However, the whole temper of the slavery controversy was to be changed as a result of the invention of the cotton gin in 1793.

A.   *Crèvecoeur*

Everyone who has ever taken a course in American literature is probably acquainted with the ninth chapter of Hector St. John de Crèvecoeur's *Letters from an American Farmer* (1782).[65] The chapter, or letter, comprises a description of Charleston, an attack on slavery (which is related to Crèvecoeur's Deistic views on nature and man), and a "Melancholy Scene," a vivid, "horrid treatment of a Negro slave," shackled and hung in a well-opened cage in a tree so as to be blinded and pecked at by birds. Thomas Philbrick summarizes the argument of this letter and discusses it in connection with Crèvecoeur's experience—for example, the fact that Crèvecoeur may never have visited Charleston.[66] But while these *Letters*, as Philbrick states, are related to the promotional tract literature of the late sixteenth and early seventeenth centuries, they are also related to the cult of sensibility of Rousseau—his romantic fervor, his lack of restraint, his *enthusiasm* (to use an eighteenth-century word of derogation)—as the following passage illustrates:

The chosen race eat, drink, and live happy, while the unfortunate one grubs up the ground, raises indigo, or husks the rice; exposed to a sun full as scorching as their native one; without the support of good food, without the cordials of any cheering liquor. This great contrast has often afforded me subjects of the most conflicting meditation. On one side, behold a people enjoying all that life affords most bewitching and pleasurable without labour, without fatigue, hardly subjected to the trouble of wishing. With gold dug from Peruvian mountains, they order vessels to the coasts of

Guinea; by virtue of that gold, wars, murders, and devastations are committed in some harmless and peaceable African neighborhood, where dwelt innocent people, who even knew not but that all men were black. The daughter torn from her weeping mother, the child from the wretched parents, the wife from the loving husband; whole families swept away and brought through storms and tempests to this rich metropolis [Charleston]! There, arranged like horses at a fair, they are branded like cattle, and then driven to toil, to starve, and to languish for years on the different plantations of these citizens. And for whom must they work? For persons they know not, and who have no other power over them than that of violence, no other right than what this accursed metal has given them! Strange order of things! Oh, Nature, where art thou?—Are not these blacks thy children as well as we? . . . Day after day they drudge on without any prospect of ever reaping for themselves; they are obliged to devote their lives, their limbs, their will, and every vital exertion to swell the wealth of masters; who look upon them with half the kindness and affection with which they consider their dogs and horses. (160–61)

Exclamatory sentences, rhetorical questions, and balanced phrases produce a very powerful emotional effect in this passage.

B. *Jefferson*

Like Crèvecour's *Letters*, Jefferson's *Notes on Virginia* (1784) [67] has received considerable attention elsewhere. It is probably the chief source for documenting Jefferson's very complicated attitudes toward slavery, an adequate statement of which would have to include his strange mixture of prejudice, legalism, and humanitarianism. Like Franklin and others of his time, he was greatly concerned about population figures and the effects of the increasing importation of slaves on the new nation. He writes:

In the very first session held under the [new] republican government, the assembly passed a law for the perpetual prohibition of the importation of slaves. This will in some measure stop the increase of this great political and moral evil, while the minds of our citizens may be ripening for a complete emancipation of human nature. (129)

Like Franklin again, he considers the question of black slavery along with bad treatment of the Indians. Since black slaves before the Revolution were regarded as part of the land, they were inherited with the land as real property. But, Jefferson points out, by an act of the first republican assembly this kind of entail was abolished (194). The Indians, although badly treated, were slightly better off, since as original proprietors of the land they could sell it. Toward the end of his book (in Query XVIII) Jefferson writes:

I think a change already perceptible, since the origin of the present revolution. The spirit of the master is abating, that of the slave arising from the dust, his condition mollifying, the way I hope preparing, under the auspices of heaven, for a total emancipation, and that this is disposed, in the order of events, to be with the consent of the masters, rather than by their extirpation. (238)

C. Black Writers

Among the black writers who in some fashion criticized slavery in the post-Revolutionary period, several achieved some prominence. The astronomer Benjamin Banneker, for example, wrote a by now famous letter to Jefferson, which was later published in the form of a fifteen-page pamphlet embodying Jefferson's answer. Banneker's *Copy of a Letter from Benjamin Banneker To the Secretary Of State [Jefferson], With His Answer* (Philadelphia, 1792) is a very skillful piece of persuasion. The modest, indeed humble and ingratiating tone that Banneker takes with Jefferson is irresistible. Specifically, however, he singles out Jefferson's statement in *Notes on Virginia* that the latter considered Negroes inferior to whites in mind. He softens up his audience (Jefferson) by praising him. Reports have reached Banneker, he says, that Jefferson is "a man far less inflexible in sentiments of this nature than many others; that you are measurably friendly, and well disposed towards us; and that you are willing and ready to lend your aid and assistance to our relief, from those many distresses, and numerous calamities, to which we are reduced" (4).

Banneker himself was a free Negro—in full possession of his rights, as he emphasizes in this letter. He reminds Jefferson of what he had written in the *Declaration of Independence*—"that all men are created equal; that they are endowed by their Creator with unalienable rights, and that among these are life, liberty, and the pursuit of happiness" (7). "But, Sir," he goes on,

how pitiable is it to reflect, that although you were so fully convinced of the benevolence of the Father of Mankind and his equal and impartial distribution of the rights and privileges, which [he conferred on all men] . . . you should at the same time counteract his mercies, in detaining by fraud and violence so numerous a part of my brethren, under groaning captivity and cruel oppression, that you should at the same time be found guilty of that most criminal act, which you professedly detested in others [the British] with respect to yourselves. (8)

The remedy? He quotes from the book of Job—"put your soul in their souls' stead." Doing this would take care of the problem.

Banneker ends briefly and effectively by saying it had not been his original plan to write about this matter, but rather to present Jefferson with a copy of an astronomical Almanac which he had calculated for the succeeding year. In a letter dated Philadelphia, August 30, 1791, Jefferson thanked Banneker for the almanac and mentions his having forwarded it to M. de Condorcet, the Secretary of the "Academy of Science at Paris," "because I considered it as a document, to which your whole color had a right for their justification, against the doubts which have been entertained of them" (12). Jefferson had the magnanimity to admit he was wrong once the evidence was at hand, as in this case it was.

Jupiter Hammon, unlike Banneker, was a slave. His twenty-page pamphlet, *An Address to the Negroes in the State of New York* (1787), resembles in style and tone an epistle of the apostle Paul.

Respecting obedience to masters, Now whether it is right, and lawful, in the sight of God, for them to make slaves of us or not, I am certain that while we are slaves, it is our duty to obey our masters, in all their commands, and mind them unless we are bid to do that we know to be sin, or forbidden in God's word. (7)

Although he sounds suspiciously like a modern "Uncle Tom," Hammon was no fool. He did insist on the slave's sovereignty in moral matters. As one advances toward the end of his pamphlet, the impression grows on the reader that Hammon had probably made a very realistic appraisal of his own relatively hopeless state. In his conclusion he urges Negroes already freed to be of exemplary conduct, so as not to hurt the chances of the unfreed ones by giving slaveholders opportunity to point to them as living examples of the old argument that the Negro could not care for himself if left to his own devices. Hammon closes with a benediction.

Gustavus Vassa differed from Hammon in having bought his freedom in 1766—with money he himself had earned. Although Vassa lectured in England against slavery, his book—*The Interesting Narrative of the Life of Olaudah Equiane, or Gustavus Vassa, the African* (1789)—was more of "a highly readable travel book," than a work of antislavery rhetoric. It was a best-seller of its day.[68]

In one or two memorable passages, however, it touches on slavery. For example, Vassa compares slavery in Africa with that in the West Indies, exclaiming, "How different was their condition from that of the slaves in the West Indies!" [69]

During the yellow fever epidemic of 1793 in Philadelphia, two Negroes, Absalom Jones and Richard Allen, answered an appeal in the public papers promising freedom to those of their race who would come forward to assist in the relief of the sick and dying, it being thought by Dr. Rush and others at that time that Negroes were immune to the fever. Later, these two and other blacks who had performed heroically during this terrible plague were accused by Mathew Carey of looting. Jones and Allen answered this charge very ably in a work entitled *A Narrative of the Proceedings of the Black People, During the Late Awful Calamity in Philadelphia, in the Year, 1793* (London, 1794). [70] Besides a testimonial in their defense by Matthew Clarkson, the mayor of Philadelphia, this pamphlet also contained three other short works by Jones and Allen: 1. "An Address to those who keep Slaves, and approve the Practice." 2. "To the People of Colour." 3. "A Short Address to the Friends of Him who hath no Helper." The first of these argued, among other things, that Negro children "were not inferior [to white children] in mental endowments" (19–20). The other two presented fewer specific arguments but more sympathy for the slaves in their sufferings.

D. *Federalist Writers* et al.

In the last decade of the eighteenth century several writers contributed importantly to the growing power of the early gradual-abolitionist movement. These writers were not all Federalists, although some were—such figures as Timothy Dwight and Noah Webster, for example. Jonathan Edwards, Jr., also wrote an extensive work, a sermon developed into a book, under the title of *The Injustice and Impolicy of the Slave-Trade, and of Slavery of the Africans* (Providence, 1792). These writers used a variety of rhetorical genres—sermons, orations, satires, tracts, anonymous and pseudonymous letters and essays, dissertations, etc.

One of the most interesting of the writers during this decade was Gilbert Imlay. In the ninth and part of the tenth letters of *A Topographical Description of the Western Territory of North America*, vol. I (New York, 1793), Imlay takes issue with Jefferson's deportation plan for Negroes. He proposes in its place a system of gradual emancipation, such as had been employed in Pennsylvania.

He also suggests a land reclamation project, turning areas wasted by tobacco culture in Virginia into small farms for Negroes in process of gradual emancipation.

Interracial marriage offered no obstacle to Imlay:

It will, doubtless, require a length of time to generalize marriages between the whites and blacks; but that would not prove a material disadvantage to the State [Virginia]. There would always be some whites who would marry blacks for the sake of property; and, no doubt, when prejudices are worn away, they would unite from more tender and delicate sentiments. (178–79)

Racial intermarriage would, in time, clear up the whole matter of skin complexion, he argues (179).[71]

At the conclusion of his ninth letter Imlay takes Jefferson to task very severely indeed:

You see, my dear friend, how powerful is the effect of habit and prejudice; that with ideas and principles founded in reason and truth, sufficient to demonstrate that slavery destroys the energy of the human mind, and with a heart which does honour to Mr. Jefferson as a man, his mind is so warped by education, and the habit of thinking, that he has attempted to make it appear that the African is a being between the human species and the oran outang; and ridiculously suffered his imagination to be carried away with the idle tales of that animal's embracing the negro women, in preference to the females of its own species.

Great God! how long is the world to be tantalized with such paltry sophistry and nonsense! (188)

The first five paragraphs of Imlay's tenth letter (190–91) continue his attack on slavery, commending this English correspondent for giving up sugar in protest to West-Indian slavery, but fearing that this act of a lone individual protestor would hardly compel Parliament to "abolish the slave trade upon the principle of policy" (190). Imlay looks forward, nevertheless, to the time when "the odious mask" which for so long had obscured "the face of reason" would be torn off (191).

E. *Forgotten White Voices from the South*

It is easy to forget today that Southern writers ever did anything except defend slavery. In addition to Jefferson and one or two others already mentioned, three who wrote very sizable antislavery tracts during the 1790s were David Rice, George Buchanan, and St. George Tucker.

David Rice was a Presbyterian minister who urged adoption of an antislavery resolution in the Kentucky constitutional convention. This resolution was unfortunately defeated. But the survival of the work defending his position before this convention reveals him as a rhetorician of considerable ability. Rice's *Slavery Inconsistent with Justice and Good Policy* (Lexington, Kentucky, 1792), which he wrote under the pseudonym of Philanthropos, offered a definition of slavery and then argued that slavery violated natural rights and amounted to a sin against God. One of the greatest of the many injustices connected with slavery, according to Rice, was the fact that a virtuous female slave might have no power over her chastity. Consequently he revises his definition to cover this case: "A Slave is a free moral agent legally deprived of free agency, and obliged to act according to the will of another free agent of the same species; and yet he is accountable to his creator for the use he makes of his own free agency" (7). Obviously this put the slave in a very tight spot indeed, for it made him accountable for a moral freedom which had been taken from him and which he no longer possessed. Rice argues, further, that the masters "designedly keep their Slaves in ignorance," and that thus religious privileges and "rights of conscience" etc., are stolen from them (10).

Having proved in the first part of his document that slavery is inconsistent with *justice*, Rice then proceeds to argue that it is also inconsistent with "good policy."

For who would venture to assert, that it would be good policy, for us to erect a public monument of our injustices, and that injustice is necessary for our prosperity and happiness? That old proverb that honesty is the best policy ought not to be despised for its age. (12)

Rice's next step is to revise still further his original definition:

A Slave is a member of civil society, bound to obey the law of the land; to which laws he never consented; which partially and feebly protect his person; which allow him no property; from which he can receive no advantage; and which chiefly, as they relate to him, were made to punish him. (12–13)

From this point it is an easy, logical move to a slight revision of his earlier statement that the master was the slave's enemy and was actually carrying on war against the slave. "Properly speaking," Rice now says, the slave is "in a state of war" not only with his master but also with "his civil rulers, and every member of that society" (13).

Then he raises the question whether it is good policy to keep such "a numerous body of people among us, who add no strength to us in time of war" (13–14). Like other writers of that time he sees slavery as the great American *inconsistency*, in view of the principles the Revolutionary War was fought for, and thinks it saps confidence in government. After refuting objections, he calls for an unconditional end to slavery in Kentucky. In his recapitulation he stresses the advantages of abolition to white children of slave owners—the fact that they would have to be better educated and would probably have their wealth on a sounder basis, the fact that the children of slaves would become more useful citizens (a source of strength instead of weakness during war time), and the fact that peaceful emancipation would prevent a future struggle by force (42).

Five years later, Rice again appeared in print, this time with a series of five letters in the first two volumes of *The American Universal Magazine* (February 6 to May 1, 1797) published in Philadelphia by Richard Lee. These *Letters on Liberty and Slavery: In Answer to a Pamphlet, Entitled, "Negro Slavery Defended by the Word of God"* were ostensibly written from various significant places and were signed "PHILANTHROPOS." In these letters Rice refutes the "diabolical reasoning" of a certain Mr. John Laurence of South Quay, Virginia.

Turning from David Rice to George Buchanan, a Maryland doctor and a member of the American Philosophical Society, we encounter a Fourth of July speech against slavery—*An Oration Upon the Moral and Political Evil of Slavery* (Baltimore, 1793). Buchanan reminds his auditors that the fall of ancient civilizations—he mentions Egypt, Greece, and Rome—was due to their use of slavery. Although he blames mainly the Portuguese, French, and British for the present state of slavery, he also attacks American inconsistency, quoting passages relevant to natural rights from the *Declaration of Independence*. The rapid progress of slavery in America, as he saw it, threatened the destruction of the entire country.

St. George Tucker was a "Professor of Law in the University of William and Mary, and one of the Judges of the General Court, in Virginia," according to the title page of *A Dissertation on Slavery: With a Proposal for the Gradual Abolition of It in the State of Virginia* (1796). The preface to this dissertation explains that this document was "part of a course of Lectures on Law and Policy" delivered at William and Mary. Tucker regarded the abolition of slavery as necessary "not only to our moral character and domestic peace, but even to our political salvation." After sketching the history of slavery from 1620, including various plans for emancipation, he offers an eight-point program for the gradual abolition of slavery, to be stretched out over a period of forty years. Although Tucker's dissertation is one of the longest of such tracts, it is well organized, well written, and well argued from the realistic position of a person who, no matter what one may think of his somewhat prejudiced and unduly elongated emancipationist program, probably represented a sincere interest in the long-range good of his state and nation.

To recapitulate the long and complex growth of antislavery sentiment before the year 1800 in America is no easy task. But let us try to indicate a few main lines.

We have seen the manner in which the Calvinist preoccupation with theological aspects of slavery differed from the Quaker concern for its incriminating effect on the individual purchaser and on the community or state as a whole, whose government and public offices, Sandiford thought, it often weakened. Latter day Calvinists like Samuel Hopkins and Jonathan Edwards, Jr., in stressing *public* or *corporate guilt*, actually resembled Quakers more than their Puritan predecessors like Mather and Sewall. Hopkins raised and gave an affirmative answer to the question—still moot in some regions—of the minister's right to discuss political matters (like slavery) in the pulpit. As a group the Deists—Paine, Franklin, Jefferson, and Crèvecoeur—tended to stress the broad principle of violation of natural rights and, in the case of Crèvecoeur, the narrower one of *economic injustice*. Franklin, Jefferson, and Paine—Deists involved in international politics—blamed the British for failure to stop importation, as did other founding fathers such as Francis Hopkinson. Like the Deists, Banneker, a black writer, considered the violation of natural rights, but he also attacked Jefferson's theory of the mental inferiority of the Negro. (Rush, a white physician, took the same stand as Banneker on these two points.) Hammon, another black, challenged the hitherto absolute power of master over slave by asserting the right of the slave to disobey his master—in a matter of morality. During the Revolutionary War period and afterward the "inconsistency" theory—that slavery contradicted the principles of the Declaration of Independence—appeared in many a pamphlet, as did the proposition that the war was a just punishment inflicted by a Calvinistic deity for the failure of his chosen but erring people to eliminate slavery, an idea which occurred in the writings of Quaker Benezet and Deist Paine. Both New England Federalists and Southerners agreed in espousing the notion of gradual emancipation during the 1790s. In this latter group Rice, Buchanan, and Tucker all agreed on three principal arguments: slavery violated natural rights; it constituted bad policy (Rice and Buchanan thought the presence of large numbers of slaves in a state made it vulnerable to external enemies); and it was inconsistent with the principles of the Declaration of Independence.

By meandering paths, sometimes retracing each other's steps, Calvinists, Quakers, Deists and founding fathers, blacks, New England Federalists, and Southerners advanced toward the ground upon which various constructive plans for large-scale political action—gradual emancipation and the end of importation—eventually took shape.[72]

CHAPTER 4

The Period of Protest: The Stamp Act and Other Taxes

I *Jonathan Mayhew's Four Sermons*

THE preceding chapter dealt with the century-long growth of feeling against domestic slavery. The next two chapters will treat the reaction and resistance to another kind—political slavery. The early light of this resistance, as we have already seen, may be traced back to the writings of John Wise, the morning star of the Revolution. But on January 30, 1750, a young minister continued Wise's basic argument, standing up in the West Church at Boston and speaking to this effect:

Tyranny brings ignorance and brutality along with it. It degrades men from their just rank, into the class of brutes. It damps their spirits. It suppresses arts. It extinguishes every spark of noble ardor and generosity in the breasts of those who are enslaved by it. It makes naturally-strong and great minds feeble and little; and triumphs over the ruins of virtue and humanity. This is true of tyranny in every shape. There can be nothing great and good, where its influence reaches. For which reason it becomes every friend to truth and human kind; every lover of God and the Christian religion, to bear a part in opposing this hateful monster.[1]

The speaker on this occasion was Jonathan Mayhew. The date was the anniversary of the execution of Charles I, who had by this time come to be regarded as a martyr and saint in the Anglican church, a church, incidentally, which at this time in America was enjoying such a phenomenal growth in membership that Jonathan Edwards protested against it.[2] On this day it had become the custom for Anglican orators to revive the divine-right-of-kings theory despite the fact that it had been generally discredited in the Glorious Revolution of 1688, when James II was deposed.[3]

Mayhew was not an Anglican, and the growing power of this

church bothered him as much as it worried Jonathan Edwards. Although he was a Calvinist, Mayhew was not especially popular with his own people. His ordination had been boycotted, and a story was current about young Paul Revere, who had been whipped for listening to Mayhew preach.[4] Bernard Bailyn presents Mayhew as a radical, liberal thinker who enjoyed the support of various British rationalists, among them the Bishop of Winchester, Benjamin Hoadley, and Dr. Benjamin Avery, a leading nonconformist and activist in politics. Mayhew's *Seven Sermons* (1749), published in England, had been well received in the mother country and had secured him an honorary doctorate from the University of Aberdeen in April 1750.[5] But it was his *Discourse Concerning Unlimited Submission* that made him famous.

As Mayhew explains in the preface to this *Discourse* he planned to treat—upon the authority of the "holy apostles"—both civil and ecclesiastical tyranny.

A spirit of domination is always to be guarded against both in church and state, even in times of greatest security. . . . Civil tyranny is usually small in its beginning, like "the drop of a bucket," till at length, like a mighty torrent, or the raging waves of the sea, it bears down all before it, and deluges whole countries and empires. Thus it is as to ecclesiastical tyranny also,—the most cruel, intolerable and impious, of any. From small beginnings, "it exalts itself above all that is called GOD and that is worshipped." People have no security against being unmercifully priest-ridden, but by keeping all imperious BISHOPS, and other CLERGYMEN who love to "lord it over God's heritage," from getting their foot into the stirrup at all. Let them be once fairly mounted, and their "beasts, the laiety," may prance and flounce about to no purpose: And they will, at length, be so jaded and hack'd by these revered jockies, that they will not even have spirits enough to complain, that their backs are galled; or like Balaam's ass, to "rebuke the madness of the prophet."[6]

Taking his text from Romans 13:1–8, Mayhew argues from the authority of the apostle Paul that "it is the duty of *Christian* magistrates to inform themselves what it is which their religion teaches concerning the nature and design of their office. And it is equally the duty of all Christian people to inform themselves what it is which their religion teaches concerning that subjection which they owe to *the higher powers*" (2). With respect to the first verse of this text, enjoining obedience to the "higher powers" as ordained by God, he expains that the Roman Christians, to whom Paul was writing, had "seditiously disclaimed *all* subjection to civil authority; refusing to pay taxes," etc. (3),. Thus, according to the apostle, *such* disobedience to civil rulers, as Mayhew puts it, amounted to "not merely a *political sin*, but an heinous *offence* against God and *religion*" (10). Still, Mayhew would raise the question as to the *extent* of subjection the dutiful Christian citizen owed the civil powers.

Some have thought it warrantable to disobey the civil powers in certain circumstances; and, in cases of very great general oppression, when humble remonstrances fail of having any effect; and when the public welfare cannot be otherwise provided for and secured, to rise unanimously even against the sovereign himself, in order to redress their grievances; to vindicate their nature and legal rights: to break the yoke of tyranny, and free themselves and posterity from inglorious servitude and ruin. (12)

On this principle, he continues, Tarquin was expelled from Rome, Caesar was assassinated, Charles I was beheaded, and James II "was made to fly that country which he aim'd at enslaving" (13). Although some might object that, in general, the Scripture "makes all resistance to princes a crime, in any case whatever," Mayhew questions whether a prince "had God's authority to bear him out in the worst of crimes"—"whether we are obliged to yield such an absolute submission to our prince" (13). This, he says, "is the inquiry which is the main design of the present discourse" (13).

Then, resting his case on the fact that the rulers Paul was discussing were *good* rulers—*politically good*, as he explains in a footnote—(20), he argues that "rulers have no authority from God to do mischief " (23).

It is blasphemy to call tyrants and oppressors, *God's ministers*. They are more properly *the messengers of Satan to buffet us*. No rulers are properly God's ministers, but such as are *just, ruling in the fear of God*. When once magistrates act contrary to their office, and the end of their institution; when they rob and ruin the public, instead of being guardians of its peace and welfare; they immediately cease to be the *ordinance* and ministers of God; and no more deserve that glorious character than common *pirates* and *highwaymen*. (24)

Following this point, which is really the thesis of his entire sermon, he examines carefully and in detail "the apostle's reasoning in favor of submission" (24–28), concluding that Paul approved *only* submission "*to such rulers as he himself describes*; i.e., such as rule for the good of society, which is the only end of their institution" (28–29). "Common tyrants," on the other hand, "and public oppressors, are not intitled to obedience from their subjects, by virtue of any thing here laid down by the inspired apostle" (29).

In the eighteenth century it was common to combine appeals to the Bible with Reason, or common sense. Mayhew consequently proceeds to strengthen his position by an argument drawn from common sense.

If we calmly consider the nature of the thing itself, nothing can well be imagined more directly contrary to common sense, than to suppose that *millions* of people should be subjected to the arbitrary, precarious pleasure of *one single man*; (who has *naturally* no superiority over them in point of authority) so that their estates, and every thing that is valuable in life, and even their lives also, shall be absolutely at his disposal, if he happens to be wanton and capricious enough to demand them. What unprejudiced man can think, that God made ALL to be thus subservient to the lawless pleasure and phrenzy of ONE, so that it shall always be a sin to resist him! (34–35)

To his opponents' objection that this proposition would tend "to the total dissolution of civil government," Mayhew replies:

. . . Similar difficulties may be raised with respect to almost every duty of natural and revealed religion. . . . It is unquestionably the duty of children to submit to their parents; and of servants, to their masters. But no one asserts, that it is their duty to obey, and submit to them, in all supposeable cases; or universally a sin to resist them. Now does this tend to subvert the just authority of parents and masters? Or to introduce confusion and anarchy into private families? No. How then does the same principle tend to unhinge the government of that larger family, the body politic? (36)

In the concluding part of his sermon Mayhew raises the question as to how the anniversary of Charles I's death came to be celebrated as a day of public fasting and humiliation. His answer is that the fast "was instituted by way of *court* and *complement* to king Charles II, upon the restoration. . . . To effect this, they [the Anglicans] ran into the most extravagant professions of affection and loyalty to him, insomuch that he himself said, that it was a *mad* and *hair brain'd* loyalty which they professed" (48). Mainly this section discredits the charter of Charles I, whom Mayhew calls "a man black with guilt and *laden with iniquity*. . . . He liv'd a tyrant; and it was the oppression and violence of his reign, that brought him to his untimely and violent end at last. Now what of saintship or martyrdom is there in all this!" (49).

It is easy to see why Bailyn calls this sermon the most famous one preached in pre-Revolutionary America.[7] It provoked widespread reaction, particularly from the Anglicans, and it was reprinted several times before the Revolution. Englishmen read extracts from it in the *Gentleman's Magazine* as the French Revolution was beginning in 1789.[8] The sermon laid a solid foundation not only for the protests against the injustices in the eighteenth century but also for such mid-nineteenth-century documents as Thoreau's *Civil Disobedience* (1849) as well as for twentieth-century protests such as those of Gandhi and the late Dr. Martin Luther King, Jr.

Three other of Mayhew's published sermons are worthy of attention in any consideration of the resistance during this period to the British system of taxation. The first of these, *A Sermon Preached in the Audience of his Excellency William Shirley* (Boston, 1754), is less a protest than an outline of Mayhew's theory of government. Perry Miller once made the statement that the election sermon was "the most important single form of publication concerned with the theory of society" during the colonial period, since political and social issues were often discussed during these discourses delivered on the date of annual elections, whether of artillery officers or members of the governor's council.[9] Mayhew does not discuss issues so much as he outlines a theory of government that was to serve as the basis for protest during the next two decades.

As for the source and origin of civil power, Mayhew finds it "ultimately derived from God, whose 'kingdom ruleth over all' " (3). The end, or purpose, of government "can be no other than the good of man, the common benefit of society" (6). He sees government as "instituted for the preservation of mens persons, properties & various rights, against fraud and lawless violence; and that by means of it, we may both procure, and quietly enjoy, those numerous blessings and advantages, which are unattainable out of society . . ." (7). In the last analysis the voters are responsible for the kind of rulers they delegate their power to by means of an election.

In his two sermons more directly concerned with the Stamp Act, Mayhew played a more important role. The first, delivered on the day before Lt. Governor Hutchinson's house was looted by a mob, protesting the stamp tax, led to Mayhew's being accused of provoking this action.[10] The second, preached on Friday, May 23,

1766, on the occasion of the repeal of the Stamp Act, was more of a
paean of thanksgiving and a pious hope for a peaceful future than a
voice of protest. Entitled *The Snare Broken* (Boston, 1766), it was
published six days after its delivery. Although several hundred
other American sermons celebrated this same event, Mayhew's
was, according to Akers, the one most widely circulated and read.[11]
It is filled with warm rhetoric and leaves little doubt that Mayhew
was one of the greatest orators America ever produced.

II Stephen Hopkins, Martin Howard, Jr., and James Otis

While Mayhew was creating thunder in the pulpit and sending
out wave after wave of lightning in his published sermons against
civil and ecclesiastical tyranny, protesting the Stamp Tax and
celebrating its repeal, three more secular colonists in (respectively)
Providence, Newport, and Boston were firing away at similar topics
in a raging paper war. In later life one of these, Stephen Hopkins, a
friend of Benjamin Franklin, was a signer of the Declaration of
Independence; a second, Martin Howard, Jr., turned Tory and fled
to England, dying there in 1781; the third, James Otis, a prominent
Boston lawyer, unfortunately had his brilliant career cut short in
1769—by a whack on the head (from the sword in the hand of an
irate political opponent), a blow that, according to some, caused his
subsequent insanity. The political significance of these three
writers, especially that of Otis, lay not only in their differing
attitudes toward the Stamp Act, the Sugar Act, and the tax policies
of the British Parliament generally—from which the principle of no
taxation without representation arose—but also in the fact that out
of their paper war came the first sharp separation between Loyalists
(or Tories) and the Sons of Liberty.

Stephen Hopkins was a descendant of Thomas Hopkins, an
associate of Roger Williams, who had settled at Providence in 1638.
Stephen Hopkins gained the post of Chief Justice of the Rhode
Island Superior Court in 1751, becoming governor of that state in
1755. He attended the Albany Congress (1754) and later (1774)
called for "powder and ball" to decide the issue at the First
Continental Congress. Today he is often remembered as the first
chancellor of Brown University. More to our immediate purpose,
however, he helped found the *Providence Gazette* (1762), a populist
journal that opposed the Loyalist *Newport Mercury* and printed
many of his writings, including probably his most important one,
The Rights of the Colonies Examined (December 22, 1764).[12]

Hopkins was one of the first to protest the tax policies of the Grenville administration, when it tried to raise money for the British government to recoup its debts from the Seven Years War. In October 1763, he had published in various newspapers "An Essay on the Trade of the Northern Colonies of Great Britain in North America," resisting the proposed Sugar Act, a tax on sugar, molasses, and rum from the West Indies. (The Sugar Act proposed revival of the Molasses Act of 1733, which had never been enforced.) [13] In *Considerations Upon the Act of Parliament* Hopkins argued that the proposed Sugar Act would adversely affect the fish and lumber industries—fish were fed to West-Indian slaves, since it was cheaper than Irish beef—[14] and the whale industry, not only in the American colonies but also in the West Indies and in Great Britain. He argued, further, that the deleterious effects on shipping would reduce the power of the British navy, putting it at the mercy of their enemies, the French.

When the Stamp Act further threatened the economic existence of merchants in Newport, Rhode Island, and elsewhere, Hopkins again responded. This time the matter was more complicated, for the government over which Hopkins presided was now beset with a local faction of Loyalists, Anglican Lawyers, etc., who were intent on revoking the democratic charter under which Rhode Island had so long flourished. James Otis referred to this Newport faction as a "dirty, drinking, drabbing, contaminated knot of thieves, beggars and transports." [15] This faction caused a great deal of trouble, and it was with the wholehearted approval of the legislature that Hopkins finally wrote from Providence on November 30, 1764, *The Rights of Colonies Examined.*

In *The Rights* Hopkins sets up an analogy between the British colonial system and that of the Greeks and Romans, arguing that the colonists of these ancient empires had equal privileges and rights with those who remained at home—in Athens or Rome. After a brief historical survey of colonial government, he concludes that "colonies in general, both ancient and modern, have always enjoyed as much freedom as the mother state from which they went out. And will any one suppose that *Brit.* colonies in *America*, are an exception to this general rule?" (8). In the past, writes Hopkins, the colonists had always been ready and obedient to the British demands for "men and money" (9). But the scene was changing. And he immediately voices what was to be the main objection to the Stamp Act—taxation without representation. The stamp tax, according to Hopkins, was an *internal* tax; Parliament had "little [direct] knowledge" of internal or local affairs in the colonies. As he himself sees it, the three pence per gallon tax on molasses would put a total stop to the exporting of "lumber, horses, flour, and fish to the French and Dutch sugar colonies" (12). Distilleries would be hurt, as would also "the rum trade to the coast of *Africa*" (12). Since Rhode Island alone at that time imported annually more than a million gallons of molasses, he argues, that colony *would have little money left*—after paying the stamp duties—*to buy British goods.* This would hurt the economy of the mother country.

Hopkins raises other objections. Under the provisions of the Stamp Act the Courts of Vice-Admiralty in the colonies—with whom Hopkins had already had difficulties—were to be enlarged.[16] (This meant that goods could be seized in Georgia and the trial held in Halifax.) Too, he objects to the statement that Parliament had the right to tax the colonists at pleasure. He writes: "It must be absurd to suppose, that the common people of *Great Britain* have a sovereign and absolute authority over their fellow-subjects in *America*, or even any sort of power whatsoever over them; but it will be more absurd that they can give a power to their representatives, which they have not themselves" (20). Finally, he objects that if Great Britain sends all its money out of the country (never to return), it will be exhausted within three years. The same situation would hold for the colonies, he says, were they forced to such an expedient (23). He closes by reminding the reader of the colonists' previous record of good conduct and obedience to king and mother country.

One of the leading members of the Newport faction of Grenville sympathizers which opposed Hopkins was Martin Howard, Jr., Hopkins' corepresentative at the Albany Congress in 1754.[17] Howard's faction expressed its views in the *Newport Mercury* and Hopkins's group retaliated in the *Providence Gazette*. One of the chief productions of this paper war was Howard's *A Letter From a Gentlemen at Halifax to his Friend in Rhode Island* (Newport, 1765), written in answer to Hopkins's *Rights Of the Colonies Examined.*

Howard insists upon what he regards as an important distinction—the difference between *personal* rights and *political* rights. Personal rights (such as life, liberty, and property—which were secured by *common law*) were held in common by every Englishman, whether born in England or the colonies. Political rights, on the other hand, were "more limited" and depended upon "the patent or charter which first created and instituted them" (9). In addition, both political rights and personal rights sprang from a common source—the common law or "constitution" of Britain. Any political rights which the colonists might trace to their charters could not contradict or invalidate the jurisdiction of parliament over the colonies. For, says Howard, the jurisdiction of parliament over the colonies is *also* established in the common law.

For Hopkins *personal rights* seem to have been equated with *natural rights*, and for him natural rights were consequently more basic, more valuable, than political rights. For Howard, on the other hand, personal rights were derived from the same source as were political rights—"from the constitution of England" rather than from *nature*. Since England had no written constitution, the "constitution" was for all intents and purposes the *common law*.

Bailyn tells us that the supporters of Hopkins in the Rhode Island General Assembly tried to suppress Howard's *Letter*, to have it declared a libel and burned by the public hangman.[18] Several replies to Howard were published in the *Providence Gazette*, none of which was as extensive, however, as Hopkins's own reply, "A Vindication of a Late Pamphlet," which appeared in three different issues of this paper.[19] Although Hopkins wrote a second reply, *Letter to the Author of the Halifax Letter . . .* ([Newport], 1765), it was the work of a spirited friend that was to supply a more definitive answer with *A Vindication of the British Colonies, against the Aspersions of the Halifax Gentleman, in His Letter to a Rhode Island Friend* (Boston, 1765).

On June 17, 1775, an old man who four years earlier had been declared *non compos mentis* borrowed a gun and rushed into the Battle of Bunker Hill. As luck would have it, he emerged unscathed. At the end of the war, however, this man met death under unusual circumstances. Writes Samuel Eliot Morison:

Only fire from heaven could release his fiery soul; death came, as he had always wished it to come, by a stroke of lightning, as he was watching a summer thunderstorm in the Isaac Osgood farmhouse at Andover on May 23, 1783.[20]

Twenty years before this date, in a fiery speech at Faneuil Hall this same man, James Otis, had declared, "Every British Subject in

America is . . . entitled to all the essential Privileges of Britons." [21] Although the vehemence of his language often distressed
his auditors, continues Morison, "Friends and foes alike agreed that
from 1761 to 1769 Otis was the political leader of Massachusetts
Bay, although Samuel Adams was more popular in Boston." [22] In
1760 Otis had resigned his lucrative post as king's advocate general
of the vice-admiralty court in Boston and undertaken to defend his
fellow Bostonians against the "writs of assistance" (search warrants)
which Pitt had issued by way of enforcing the old Molasses Act of
1733. At the ensuing trial in the Old State House at Boston
(February, 1761) Otis and Oxenbridge Thacher argued the writs
were *illegal*. On this occasion John Adams wrote:

Otis was a flame of fire! . . . He hurried away every thing before him.
American independence was then and there born; the seeds of patriots and
heroes were then and there sown. . . . [23]

Otis's argument during this trial turned on the principle that
natural law was superior to the acts of Parliament, a principle that
during the next twenty-five years finally resulted in "the American
doctrine of judicial supremacy." [24] During the period 1761-69 Otis
contributed numerous signed and unsigned articles to the *Boston
Gazette*. During the years 1766-68 he often prepared the rough
drafts which Sam Adams smoothed up and revised, expressing the
majority opinion of the Massachusetts House of Representatives.
He and Sam Adams wrote the Massachusetts circular letter that was
adopted on February 11, 1768, a call for resistance which, according
to Morison, "did more to unite the colonies than any measure since
the Stamp Act." [25] Previous to this important work, however, Otis
had undertaken another very serious effort with his pen—the
defense of his friend Stephen Hopkins.

Otis's taking up arms in behalf of Hopkins was not an entirely
disinterested action. Martin Howard had referred in his *Letter
from . . . Halifax* to Otis as "misled by popular ideas," etc.[26] Otis
therefore now took the occasion not only to defend Hopkins but also
to defend himself, more specifically his earlier work entitled *The
Rights of the British Colonies Asserted and Proved* (Boston, 1764).

In this eighty-page pamphlet, *The Rights*, Otis had presented a
four-part consideration of political theory that had aroused much
pro and con discussion:[27] 1. "Of the Origin of Government"; 2. "Of
Colonies in General"; 3. "Of the Natural Rights of Colonists"; 4. "Of

the Political and Civil Rights of the British Colonies." Under the first heading, the origin of government, he takes up four theories— that it was founded on *Grace*, on *force* or mere *power*, on a *contract*, or on *property*. He finds each of these unsatisfactory in one way or another.

The first of these opinions is so absurd, and the world has paid so very dear for embracing it, especially under the administration of the *roman pontiffs*, that mankind seem at this day to be in a great measure cured of their madness in this particular; and the notion is pretty generally exploded, and hiss'd off the stage. (3)

To those who lay the foundation of government in force and meer *brutal power*, it is objected; that, their system destroys all distinction between right and wrong; that it overturns all morality, and leaves it to every man to do what is right in his own eyes; that it leads directly to *skepticism*, and ends in *atheism*. When a man's will and pleasure is his only rule and guide, what safety can there be either for him or against him but in the point of a sword? (3)

Those who favor the "original compact" theory "have been often told that *their* system is chimerical and unsupported by reason or experience" (4). Otis raises a whole pageful of questions implying objections and concludes:

I hope the reader will consider that I am at present only mentioning such questions as have been put by high-flyers & others in church and state, who would exclude all compact between a Sovereign and his people, without offering my own sentiments upon them; this however I presume I may be allowed hereafter to do without offence. Those who want a full answer to them may consult Mr. Locke's discourses on government, M. De Vattel's law of nature and nations, and their own consciences. (5)

With regard to the fourth opinion, that *dominion is founded in property*, Otis asks, "What is it but playing with words?" (7). Here Otis argues that since one end of government is the protection of property, property cannot at the same time be the foundation of government, for the *end* cannot both be *end* and *origin* at the same time—a logical absurdity.

Finally, he concludes that government is "founded on the necessity of our natures." "I say this supreme absolute power is *originally* and *ultimately* in the people; and they never did in fact *freely*, nor can they *rightfully* make an absolute, unlimited renunciation of this divine right" (9). "Government is . . . most evidently founded *on the necessities of our nature.* It is by no means an *arbitrary* thing, depending merely on *compact* or *human will* for its existence" (8). The end of government is "the good of *the whole.*" "*Salus populi suprema lex esto* [Let the welfare of the people be the supreme law], is of the law of nature, and part of that grand charter, given the human race (tho' too many are afraid to assert it,) by the only monarch in the universe, who has a clear and *absolute* power; because he is the *only* ONE who is *omniscient* as well as *omnipotent*" (10).

Otis is so full of principles that have become accepted as an integral part of the American political tradition that he makes good reading today—and indeed in any time of political crisis. The duty of government, he tells us, is "to provide for the security, and happy enjoyment of life, liberty, and property." Government should advance "the security, tranquility and prosperity of the people" (10). "Men cannot live apart or independent of each other" (11). Hence government is founded "immediately on the necessities of human nature" but "ultimately on the will of God, the author of nature . . ." (11).[28] Isolation from the species endangers self-preservation. But every individual has the right to choose "what society he will continue to belong to," and "they may alter it from a simple democracy, or government of all over all, to any other form they please" (11).

Such alteration may and ought to be made by express compact. But how seldom this right has been asserted, history will abundantly show. For once that it has been fairly settled by compact, *fraud, force,* or *accident* have determined it an hundred times. As the people have gained upon tyrants, these have been obliged to relax *only* till a fairer opportunity has put it in their power to encroach again. (11–12)

"The wiser and more virtuous states, have always provided that the representation of the people should be numerous" (14). "Nothing but life and liberty are *naturally* hereditable." Space does not permit detailed consideration of the three other main divisions of this important pamphlet, but I shall try to outline briefly the main function of each.

The second of these, "Of Colonies in General," is the briefest (24–25). In this section Otis protests mistreatment of the colonists and the British attitude toward the colonies as "little insignificant conquered islands" (24). (He cites the instance of a former British "secretary of state, during whose *wonderful* conduct of national affairs, without knowing whether *Jamaica* lay in the Mediterranean, the Baltic, or in the Moon," had directed letters "to the Governor of the *island* of New-England" 24–25.) With characteristic rhetoric he defines "*modern* colonists" as "*noble discoverers and settlers of a new world,*" etc. In his definition of a "plantation or colony," which follows, Otis states that "the colonists are entitled to as *ample* rights, liberties, and privileges as the subjects of the mother country are, and in some respects *more*" (25).

The third division (25–31), dealing with the "Natural Rights of Colonists," begins by criticizing Grotius and Puffendorf, two of the best-known contemporary authorities on international law, as unsatisfactory on this subject and by commending Locke.[29] He also criticizes a certain Dr. Strahan for saying that there was "an affinity" between the British and the Spanish colonial systems—with regard to proprietary government and feudal tenure. "With submission," writes Otis, "to so great an authority as Dr. Strahan, 'tis humbly hoped that the British colonists do not hold their lands as well as liberties by so slippery a tenure as do the Spaniards and the French" (27). In this division, too, Otis argues during two whole pages for equality of blacks and whites—all men being by the law of nature born with equal rights (29–30). "It is a clear truth," he says, "that those who every day barter away other men's liberty will soon care little for their own" (29).

In the fourth and last division, "Of the Political and Civil Rights of the British Colonists," Otis argues strongly for colonial representation in Parliament, against arbitrary legislatures, against racial discrimination, and for equal rights with other Englishmen.

Otis's second major contribution to the Stamp Act literature, *A Vindication of the British Colonies against The Aspersions of the Halifax Gentleman*, is less important as a statement of his political principles, since it is, as already mentioned, an answer to Martin Howard's *Letter* attacking Stephen Hopkins.[30] But it is still interesting to watch him at work.

Of course Otis challenges Howard's statement that the Stamp Act was reasonable and equitable. He ridicules Howard's comparison between the Roman and British colonial systems. He denies that American merchants are the only class profiting from smuggling, as Howard had charged. He defends Hopkins against Howard's allegation that he had denied the jurisdiction of Parliament over the colonies. And he quotes at length several passages from his own *Rights of the British Colonies Asserted and Proved* to prove that he himself had not denied this jurisdiction. Finally, he takes offense at Howard's threat of violence against the colonies and, referring to Lord Peter's method of reasoning by force (in Swift's *A Tale of a Tub*), he suggests that such a policy, if put into operation, would be the equivalent of expulsion from the British commonwealth.[31]

This controversy continued. Howard replied in kind with *A Defence of the Letter from a Gentleman at Halifax* (Newport, 1765), published only one month later. He congratulated Otis on having betrayed a friend (Hopkins) and on having recanted from his old position in favor of a new faith in Parliament. Angered by this sarcasm, as well as by the passage of the Stamp Act, Otis swung back wildly at Howard with *Brief Remarks on the Defence of the Halifax Libel on the British-American-Colonies*. Nor was this the end. Driven once more to vindicate his position, he brought out *Considerations on Behalf of the Colonists in a Letter to a Noble Lord* (London, 1765), which had first appeared as a series of articles in the *Boston Gazette*.[32]

III   Daniel Dulany, Jr.

Our scene now shifts from New England cities—Providence, Newport, and Boston—(where, respectively, Hopkins, Howard, and Otis had published their most important works) to Annapolis, Maryland, where there first appeared in 1765 a not very well written pamphlet entitled *Considerations on the Propriety of Imposing Taxes in the British Colonies, For the Purpose of Raising a Revenue, by Act of Parliament*. The author of this document was Daniel Dulany, Jr., a wealthy lawyer who had been educated at Eton and Cambridge and admitted to the Inns of Court, and who at the time was Secretary of the Colony and a member of the Governor's Council.[33]

Dulany wrote in response to a whole flurry of activity by apologists for the stamp tax—such skillful writers as Thomas Pownall, Soame Jenyns, Thomas Whately (Grenville's secretary and chief draftsman of the tax), and William Knox.[34] Despite his lack of skill as a writer, Dulany nevertheless managed to score one or two important points in this controversy. He successfully attacked the notion of the apologists that the colonists had "*virtual*" representation in parliament, saying that this was "a mere cob-web, spread to catch the unwary, and intangle the weak" (6). He refuted their notion that if Parliament could not tax the colonies then the colonies were not dependent on Great Britain, arguing that the colonists had the right (from their original charters) to tax themselves, a right which the British ministers and Parliament had recognized. "May not then the line be distinctly and justly drawn between such acts as are necessary, or proper, for preserving the dependence of the colonies, and such as are not necessary or proper for that very important purpose?" he asks (15). Admitting that the king had the right to levy "men and money" (16), he argued in the following little allegory that the Stamp Act was not a disinterested levy:

When an house is in flames, and the next neighbor is extremely active, and exerts his endeavors to extinguish the fire, which, if not conquered, would catch, and consume his own dwelling, I don'[t] say, that if the owner of the house which had been in flames, should, after the fire subdued, complaisantly thank his neighbor generally for his services, he would be absurdly ceremonious; but, if the assistant should afterwards boast of his great generosity, and claim a right to the furniture of the house which he had assisted in saving, upon the merit of his zeal and activity, he would deserve to be put in mind of the motive of his service. (17–18)*

Dulany also argued that the stamp duties were disproportionate to *"their* circumstances from whom it is exacted" (24). But mainly he argued that only representative bodies could impose taxation and that the colonial assemblies were the only representative bodies in America.[35] Willingly he acknowledged, in his conclusion, dependence on Great Britain; but he could perceive, he says, "a degree of it without slavery," and he disowned all other (48). Bailyn states the really important issue when he writes that Dulany disproved the "virtual" representation theory by demonstrating that the close interdependence of interests between members of parliament and their English constituents who had only "virtual" representation did not exist for the colonists—because of the great geographical distance separating the colonists from parliament.[36]

Alden considers Dulany's *Considerations* "undoubtedly the most significant and influential" "of all the controversial writings provoked in the American colonies by the passage of the Stamp Act." [37]

---

*The "house in flames" was the American colonies, beset by the French and Indians; the "neighbour" or "assistant," clearly Great Britain.

This may be true. Dulany's later reputation suffered, however, because of his espousal of the proprietary interest of Lord Baltimore. In his paper war with Charles Carroll of Carrollton (in the *Maryland Gazette*) on whether the Assembly or the proprietor should control certain fees (in 1773) he backed the proprietary interest and was labeled an "enemy to his country." His neutral position during the Revolution hurt him beyond repair.[38]

IV   John Dickinson and Richard Bland

John Dickinson was also the son of a wealthy Maryland landowner, and like Dulany he had been educated for the law in England. Like Dulany, too, he defended the wealthy proprietary interest—in Pennsylvania rather than in Maryland. His defense of this interest brought him into opposition with Benjamin Franklin, who led the populist, antiproprietary group. It was quite natural, considering his background, for Dickinson to develop into a rather cautious and conservative kind of thinker. Nevertheless, Dickinson was a "radical" in some respects.[39] He helped draft the Declaration of the Stamp Act Congress. And he also contributed importantly to the opposition to the Stamp Act with *The Late Regulations Respecting the British Colonies . . . Considered, In a Letter from a Gentleman in PHILADELPHIA to his Friend in LONDON* (Philadelphia, 1765).

This thirty-six-page pamphlet—thirty-eight pages, if one counts the postscript—differs from some of the other literature on this issue in directing its arguments to "strictly economic grounds," more specifically, "grounds of material self-interest narrowly defined." [40] Dickinson argues that the Stamp Act would hurt the *"merchants* and the *lower ranks of people*," argues, in fact, that the colonies were already in a desperate economic condition and that the act would only aggravate this condition.

Trade is decaying . . . credit is expiring. Money is becoming so extremely scarce, that reputable freeholders find it impossible to pay debts which are trifling in comparison to their estates. . . . The debtors are ruined. The creditors get but part of their debts, and that ruins them. Thus the consumers break the shop-keepers; they break the merchants; and the shock must be felt as far as *London.* (18–19)

"Thus drained," as he describes the colonists' economy, they were being asked "to take up and to totter under the additional burthen of the STAMP ACT." (8).

One argument urged by the British government in favor of the Stamp Act had been that "our islands ought to be encouraged." Dickinson answers:

They ought to be: But should the interest of one colony be preferred to that of another? Should the welfare of millions be sacrificed to the magnificence of a few? If the exorbitant profits of one colony must arise from the depression of another, should not such injustice be redressed? (12)

And he provides lengthy statistical comparisons between the "Northern Colonies" and the "West-India Islands" to justify his contention (12n–13n).[41]

In England, argues Dickinson, money was easier to acquire. Merchants in the colonies, however, had sunk more capital in their business than had their counterparts in England, and they were thus less capable of bearing up under the Stamp Act. As a general policy, the wealthy "undoubtedly ought to pay the most towards the public charges." But the Stamp Act imposed the "whole weight" of such charges upon "the necessitous and industrious, who most of all require relief and encouragement" (21–22).

Nor was this the only difference between the economy of the colonies and that of the mother country. England was a very rich and populous country, where the manufacturers and landholders made pressing demands upon the merchants; America was a poorer and less populous country, composed mainly of small farmers. Thus he refutes the argument (of some British theorists) that American merchants would not really be affected by the Stamp Act because they could circumvent its bad effects by raising prices so that ultimately all taxes would "arise from lands" (22). A nation consisting principally of farmers would obviously not appreciate a heavy tax passed on to those who worked the land. Pushed far enough by exacerbations of this kind, the colonial farmers might eventually be forced to develop their own economy by promoting their own manufactures "and thereby remove the necessity we are now under of being supplied by *Great-Britain*" (25).

In one of his most novel propositions, or arguments in reverse, Dickinson argues that, generally speaking, all colonies tended to enrich their mother countries "without laying taxes upon *them*" (my italics). Mother countries were thus *expensive* to colonies, rather than vice versa. His argument culminates in his statement that "THE FOUNDATIONS OF THE POWER AND GLORY OF GREAT BRITAIN ARE LAID IN AMERICA" (sic, 31). Notwithstanding these justifiable causes for independence, Dickinson describes the colonists' feelings as "but the resentment of dutiful children, who have received unmerited blows from a beloved parent." And he ends with a hope for an "everlasting union" between England and her colonies (36). In the postscript he points out that the American colonists were receiving less material advantage from Florida under British rule than when it was owned by the Spanish (37–38).

If, for Bailyn, John Dickinson was something of a "radical," Richard Bland (1710–1776) was, for Rossiter, "the very model of the American Whig." [42] This is all the more surprising, since at first view Bland seems cut from much the same cloth as Dulany and Dickinson. [43]

Bland was the author of an important pamphlet entitled An Enquiry Into the Rights of the British Colonies (Williamsburg, 1766). [44] Like Dickinson, Bland conceived his purpose as being to answer those who had argued that Parliament had a legal right to tax the colonies. Bland's work is actually an answer to another pamphlet—"The Regulations Lately Made Concerning the Colonies, and the Taxes Upon Them Considered." He accuses the author of this pamphlet of endeavoring "to fix shackles upon the American colonies" (5). He argues against taxation without representation and for the natural rights theory, tracing the connection of the colonies to the crown and Parliament from the time of the Raleigh expedition to the present (10–16). Referring to the first settlement in North America, he says:

America was no part of the kingdom of England; it was possessed by a savage people, scattered through the country, who were not subject to the English dominion, nor owed obedience to its laws. This independent country was settled by Englishmen at their own expence, under particular stipulations with the crown. (16)

Although he had heard it argued that no power could abridge the authority of Parliament, Bland rests his case with the prerogative of the king. He writes: "May not the king have prerogatives, which he has a right to exercise, without the consent of parliament? If he has, perhaps that of granting licence to his subjects to remove into a *new* country, and to settle therein upon particular conditions, may be one" (16).

Toward the end of the decade, however, John Dickinson eclipsed the fame not only of Bland but of almost all other writers of "protest" literature with his series of twelve *Letters from a Farmer in Pennsylvania To the Inhabitants of the British Colonies.* These had begun in William Goddard's *Pennsylvania Chronicle* (in December, 1767) and then spread to nearly thirty other papers in most of the other colonies. (These letters were provoked by the Townshend Acts of 1767, which placed new taxes on tea, paper, paint, glass, and lead.) By March they had appeared in pamphlet form (Boston, 1768). Besides seven American editions, other editions appeared in London and on the continent.[45]

The letters are addressed to the Farmer's "Beloved Countrymen" and object to various matters. The first letter concerns an act of Parliament suspending the legislature of New York, an act which Dickinson regarded "as injurious in its principle to the liberties of these colonies, as the Stamp Act" (7). In this letter Dickinson argues that the cause of one is the cause of all. If Parliament can deprive New York of its rights, it may deprive other colonies as well. The second letter argued that duties on paper were unconstitutional, as were similar taxes on glass, iron, and steel. The third letter shows Dickinson's purpose in the whole series—to seek redress of grievances but not to separate from the mother country—especially not by force of arms.

Reflecting upon the twelve letters as a whole, if one were asked to express their single purpose, he would probably have to state it in terms of a warning against British incursions upon American liberty, and the need for resistance to such incursions. At the end of the last letter the following italicized paragraph is added:

Is there not the greatest reason to hope, if the universal sense of the colonies is immediately exprest, by resolves of the assemblies, in support of their rights; by instructions to their agents on the subject; and by petitions to the crown and parliament for redress; that these measures will have the same success now that they had in the time of the Stamp-act.

This paragraph seems a succinct statement of Dickinson's purpose in the entire series.

V *Other Protesters*

There were, of course, many, many writers other than those presented thus far in this chapter who raised their voices and set pen to paper against the Stamp Act and other taxes during this period. Among the clergy, besides Mayhew the name of the Rev. Dr. Samuel Cooper (1725–1783) should certainly be mentioned. Cooper wrote a pamphlet called *The Crisis* (1754), which resisted British tax policies. Cooper was the minister of the Brattle Square Church in Boston and was a friend of Franklin and John Adams.[46] Stephen Johnson, another clergyman, delivered a long sermon on the occasion of a public fast day (December 18, 1765). The sermon was later published in the form of a sixty-one-page pamphlet, *Some Important Observations* (Newport, 1766). In this sermon Johnson paraphrases John Locke to this effect:

The best writers upon government, tell us, that when the authority of a free government invade [*sic*] the liberties of the people, and endeavor [*sic*] arbitrarily to take away their properties, and reduce them to slavery under arbitrary power; that such slavish endeavours dissolve the government, and the subjects ['] obligation of obedience;—yea, constitutes a state of war with the people, in which the latter may resume their natural rights, and defend themselves with all the power which God has given them; and that they may use this power in way of prevention, before actually reduced to bondage. (23)

Toward the end of his sermon Johnson warned his auditors (and readers) against the tyranny of the British, asking, "Will not posterity applaud, and all impartial, good patriots, and good friends to the British interest, rejoice in the noble stand made by the colonies (in this day of trial) for the liberty and welfare of their country, as an essential and very important service to Great-Britain, as well as the colonies?" (51).

Among Southern orators and writers Patrick Henry occupies a unique place not only because of his famous "Give me liberty or give me death" speech but also because of his brilliant speech and resolutions against the Stamp Act.[47] Arthur Lee (1740–1792) penned a series of ten letters (*The Monitor's Letters*) which first appeared in Rind's *Virginia Gazette* (February 25 to April 28, 1768). These letters resembled Dickinson's *Farmer's Letters* and were actually published along with them.[48] As indicated on the last page of his last letter, Lee's purpose in resisting the Stamp Tax and some of the measures which followed it was quite similar to Dickinson's:

. . . to show the nature and excellence of liberty, the vices, the miseries and abasement which slavery produces, to develop the artful design of our enemies, the arbitrary tendency of their late conduct in Britain, the fatal consequences that must inevitably follow our acquiescence under the rights lately assumed and exercised over us, by the *British* Parliament; and the necessity of an unanimous and determined opposition to the meditated subversion of our constitutional freedom and happiness. (97)

Lee displays an extensive knowledge of the classics in these letters, and every page is heavily ballasted with footnotes. At one point he recommends the study of Greek and Roman history—especially of Plutarch's *Lives*—to his "younger" countrymen—in order "to secure this blessing of liberty" (67). Henry Laurens of South Carolina is another Southern writer who should not be overlooked. He opposed the Townshend Acts with *Some General Observations on American Custom House Officers and Courts of Vice-Admiralty* (1769).

Figures like Franklin and Galloway have already been covered by other writers.[49] Nothing would be gained by repeating their work. Samuel Adams will be treated at greater length in the chapter following. But the Massachusetts Circular Letter (usually attributed to him, James Otis, and Joseph Hawley) was important in the reaction to the Townshend Acts and also in crystalizing sentiment (in other colonies as well as in Massachusetts) *for taxation only by colonial assemblies*.

As we cast our eye back over the prolific reaction of colonial writers against the policies of the British government during the period 1750–1770, we sense a unification of a large amount of public opinion. The American nation was being conceived.

CHAPTER 5

The Revolution, 1769–1783

"**I** am sorry to inform your Lordship that a great Riot has
happened in this Town last Evening." The time was June 11,
1768, the town was Boston, and the author of this regrettable piece
of information, Francis Bernard, the royal governor of Massachusetts. Bernard's correspondent was the British Minister, the
Earl of Hillsborough. The riot itself was a reaction to the seizure,
because its owners had not paid the tax, of a ship bearing a cargo of
wine. Bernard's letter continues, "And now the Terror of the Night
is over, it is said to be only a Prelude to further Mischiefs, the
Threats against the Commissioners and all the Officers of the Board
being renewed with as great Malice as ever." [1]

Two days later Bernard was compelled to report a further piece of
regrettable information. His tax commissioners along with their
families had been forced to remove to the safety of the warship
Romney. He writes: "This Morning a Paper was found stuck upon a
Liberty-Tree, inviting all the Sons of Liberty to meet at 6 o'clock, to
clear the Land of the Vermin, which are come to devour them &c.
&c. I have been in Council all this Morning to consider of
preventing an Insurrection To-night." [2] Less than a fortnight later
Bernard reported that the faction which had been opposing him in
the assembly had moved *for the third time* to impeach him. [3] The
"Mischiefs" were indeed beginning. The Revolution, in fact, had
begun.

I *Samuel Adams*

One of the first manifestations of this new trend of events was the
printing of an anonymous work with a dramatic title, *An Appeal to
the World*, which Bailyn ascribes to Samuel Adams. [4] The *Appeal*
was a "VINDICATION of the Town of Boston," and it answered
"Many false and malicious Aspersions" contained in Bernard's and
others' letters to the British ministry. [5]

The *Appeal* falls into six well-marked divisions: pages 4–14 refute Governor Bernard's report to the Earl of Shelburne, in which (according to the author's rhetoric) he had imagined the citizens of Boston virtually in a state of insurrection, particularly in their opposition to the tax commissioners. The report is described as "groundless" and as supplied by Bernard's "own pimps" (11). Pages 14–32 take note of the account of the riot in Bernard's letter of June 11, 1768, to the Earl of Hillsborough. Pursuing the same kind of clever rhetoric which permeates this entire pamphlet, the author blames the riot on the commissioners and claims it was "far from being so great as the Governor represents it to be." He also denies that it was a "numerous mob," nor was it of "long continuance, neither was there much mischief done" (14). He blames Bernard himself as the source of "*frequent rumours* of an insurrection" and for misrepresenting "the whole continent as ripe for revolt" (18). Continuing the attack on Bernard, he says,

The Governor has often been observed to discover an aversion to free assemblies; no wonder then that he should be so particularly disgusted at a legal meeting of the town of Boston, where a noble freedom of speech is ever expected and maintained; an assembly, of which it may be justly said . . . they think as they please, and speak as they think.—Such an assembly has ever been the dread—often the scourge [—] of tyrants. (29)

Pages 32–38 recount Bernard's accusation that the Sons of Liberty had attempted to capture him and had plundered his fruit trees when they failed in this attempt. The author (surely it must have been Sam Adams) answers,

This is a very solemn account indeed; but he [Bernard] never laid this "manoevre of the sons of liberty," *extraordinary* as it was, before the Council, while he never failed to do [so] on like occasion; thinking possibly, that respectable body might be of [the] opinion, that a gentleman of any political party may be supposed to have had his orchard robbed by *liquorish boys*, without making a formal representation before his Majesty's first ministers of state. (33)

Pages 38–53 cover Bernard's letters of September 16 and September 12 (in this order), ridiculing Bernard's fear that the two regiments of General Gage called in to quiet the uproar might not be sufficient (48–49). In this section the author's tone becomes warmer and he pours scorn and ridicule on Bernard. He waxes downright militant in his demands:

. . . the grievances which lie heavily upon us, we shall never think redressed, till *every act*, passed by the British Parliament for the express purpose of raising a revenue upon us without our consent, is repealed; till the American board of Commissioners of the Customs is dissolved; the troops recalled, and things are restored to the state they were in before the late extraordinary measures of administration took place. (53)

Pages 53–55 take up letters of General Gage and Commodore Hood. But the main attack is on Gage, who, according to the author, had written "in such a positive strain, as must unavoidably give high disgust to every reader of candor and impartiality" (53). He accuses Gage of being prejudiced against a town which had up to that time been favorably disposed toward him. Pages 56–58 include the Resolutions of the Town of Boston in view of all the foregoing circumstances. Briefly put, these comprised votes of censure against Bernard, Gage, and Hood and affirmed a petition of the Massachusetts House of Representatives for the removal of Bernard as governor.[6]

Behind the clever rhetoric of Adams's *Appeal*, the caustic *ad hominem* onslaught aimed at Governor Bernard whereby Adams redirected upon the governor and his associates any possible guilt of his fellow townsmen for the Boston disturbances, some important political principles lay. In essence the *Appeal* defended the right of freedom of assembly and of the "noble freedom of speech" maintained at Boston town meetings. In calling for Bernard's removal, it asserted the right to impeach a tyrannical ruler. In demanding redress of grievances and repeal of *"every Act"* for raising revenue upon the colonists without their consent, it claimed "equal rights with Britons," which Otis had championed in the making of tax laws. Furthermore, it protested the quartering of troops attendant on attempts to enforce the Townshend tax on glass, lead, paint, tea, and paper. It declared the intended partial repeal of this tax unsatisfactory. Finally, it accused Bernard of attempting to slander not only Boston and Massachusetts but the whole British-American continent, and (in its title) it antedated Jefferson's famous appeal to a world court of public opinion.

II   *Benjamin Franklin*

During the 1770s Franklin in London was addressing a predominantly English court of public opinion with brilliant criticism of the same British colonial policies that Sam Adams, Otis, and their fellow Bostonians had resisted so eloquently. In the year 1773, for example, Franklin produced two of his very best satires—*Rules by Which a Great Empire May be Reduced to a Small One* and *An Edict by the King of Prussia*—both of which appeared anonymously in the *London Public Advertiser*. Franklin himself considered the *Rules* his best satire.[7] It attacked the policies of the Earl of Hillsborough, listing twenty rules, or grievances, by which the British empire might, like a large cake, be first diminished at the edges and finally ultimately reduced to practically nothing. Each of the rules is an argument and contains Franklin's spirited (often highly indignant) comment—usually in the form of a sudden turn of the tone from lightness to seriousness, from ironic humor and hoax to severe warning and actual threat. The *Edict*, on the other hand, restricts itself to a smaller number of arguments—five, to be exact—each of which was highly important to the colonists. Principally, it protested the 4.5 percent *ad valorem* tax, but it also protested the prohibition of iron manufactures in the colonies, the prohibition of woolen manufactures, the restrictions on the manufacture of hats, and, finally—another sore point—the dumping of convicts from British jails in the colonies. During the war Franklin lashed out against the use of German mercenaries in *The Sale of Hessians* (1777).[8]

A brief analysis of the *Rules* may help us understand the issues with which Franklin was involved. In this vitriolic satire he suggests that the administrative policies of the first Earl of Hillsborough and the second Earl of Dartmouth—who during the period 1768–1773 were largely responsible for American affairs—were actually leading not only to secession of the American colonies but to the complete dissolution of the entire British empire! (One or two of these policies antedated these administrations.) Specifically these policies or grievances concerned: the inequality of rights that Adams and Otis had objected to, the disregard for the hardships of the early settlers and their later costly participation in the wars against the English and the French, the quartering of troops during peace time, the bad selection of governors and judges—who held office "*during pleasure*," the dilatory methods of handling the colonists' complaints, the rewarding of tyrannical governors who had been driven from the colonies, the harassment of the colonies with a great variety of taxes and the misapplication of such tax money, the Declaratory Act of 1766 (which stated that "King, Lords, and

Commons had . . . full power and authority . . . to bind the unrepresented [American] provinces IN ALL CASES WHAT-SOEVER"), the dissolution of the Massachusetts House of Representatives following their refusal to rescind the circular letter sent to other colonial assemblies, the failure to redress grievances, the handling of the Castle William affair, and the maldistribution of troops on the frontier. Many of these policies or grievances which Franklin lists as "rules whereby the great British empire may be reduced to a small one" were, of course, repeated by Jefferson in the *Declaration of Independence*. The tone of savage indignation that Franklin employs in this satire is that of an *ultimatum*. Essentially that is what the *Rules* was. It heralded the forthcoming war.

During the war Franklin performed with *The Sale of the Hessians* (1777) a service similar to that of Tom Paine in the *American Crisis* papers. *The Sale* was intended as a morale builder for the colonists' cause. In many ways it resembled pure propaganda. (So far as we know, it first appeared anonymously in Paris.) [9] It implied cowardice on the part of the English in hiring Hessians to do the dirty work they themselves feared to do; it presented the Hessians as being decimated by the Americans; it showed the mercenaries under the control of a moral monster—one Count de Schaumberg—who urged the commanding Hessian general in America to kill ever more of his troops, since the more killed the greater the profit—for the count! To be sure, the latter was reduced to sending boys instead of men from Germany; but the more he sent, the more he was paid! From reading such propaganda, French sympathizers with the colonists might assume the Americans were winning the war, might feel a justifiable moral superiority, and take new heart to support their long, hard fight. In reality, the Americans were having a hard time of it in 1777 and needed every possible encouragement that Franklin and his French sympathizers and Paine could give.

III   *Thomas Jefferson*

Prior to the *Declaration of Independence* Jefferson's best-known work was *A Summary View of the Rights of British America* (Williamsburg, 1774). Before leaving to attend the Virginia State Convention of 1774 (at which delegates to Congress were to be chosen), he had prepared some "Instructions" for the delegates. Since he suffered an attack of dysentery at the time, these instructions were sent on to the convention, which thought them too strong for adoption. They were printed, however, under the above title; and, as Padover says, they exploded like a bombshell on the Anglo-American world.[10] Reprinted several times in London, they were used by Edmund Burke, friend of the colonies, and eventually proscribed by an act of Parliament.[11]

The *Summary View* is essentially a petition for redress of grievances. Addressed directly to King George III, it notes the violation of natural rights and previous unsuccessful attempts at redress by the individual states. It states flatly that the colonists are asking rights, not favors, and tells the king that "he is no more than the chief officer of the people, appointed by the laws, and circumscribed with definite powers, to assist in working the great machine of government, erected for their [the people's] use, and, consequently, subject to their superintendence. . . ."[12]

After this blunt beginning, Jefferson proposes a sketch of the origin and first settlement of the colonies "in order that these, our rights, as well as the invasions of them, may be laid more fully before his Majesty" (186). His introductory argument in this sketch very much resembles Franklin's reasoning in *An Edict of the King of Prussia*. (It is quite possible that Jefferson had read this work, since it was published a year before his *Summary View*.) According to this argument, the Saxons who had migrated from Germany to England had never been subject to claims from, or taxes imposed by, the mother country, such migration being considered a natural right. Jefferson also stresses the fact that America was settled "at the expense of individuals, and not of the British public" (187). The colonies had never received as much as a shilling, he asserts, "from the public treasures of his Majesty, or his ancestors, for their assistance, till of very late times . . . " (187). Jefferson does not deny the help supplied by England during the French and Indian War, but he argues that "often before" England had done as much for Portugal "and other allied states." "Yet these states never supposed that by calling in her [English] aid, they thereby submitted themselves to her sovereignty" (187). Grateful as the colonists were for such assistance against the French and the Indians, writes Jefferson, they did not believe that such aid gave parliament a right to set up "exclusive privileges in trade" for Great Britain.

Other grievances related to the Tea Act of 1772 (which provoked the famous Boston Tea Party of December 1773) and the infamous "Intolerable Acts" of the summer of 1774—the Boston Port Bill, the Massachusetts Government Act, the Quartering Act, and the

Administration of Justice Act.[13] Still another grievance concerned what Jefferson calls "an error in the nature of our land holdings" (190). Here he refers to the introduction by William the Conqueror of the feudal system in England, which postdated the old Saxon system of "absolute dominion." "America," explains Jefferson, "was not conquered by William the Norman, nor its lands surrendered to him or any of his successors" (191). Since the early settlers in America had been laborers rather than lawyers, continues Jefferson, they were easily misled, being imposed upon by this error that they held their land (by feudal tenure) from the British king rather than by "absolute dominion," or independent ownership. "It is time, therefore," he writes, "for us to lay this matter before his Majesty, and to declare that he has no right to grant land himself " (192).

In his wonderful exhortation to the king at the close of this work Jefferson reveals his splendid magnanimity:

Open your breast, Sire, to liberal and expanded thought. Let not the name of George the Third be a blot on the page of history. You are surrounded by British counsellors, but remember that they are parties. You have no ministers for American affairs, because you have none taken from among us, nor amenable to the laws on which they are to give you advice. It behooves you, therefore, to think and to act for yourself and your people. The great principles of right and wrong are legible to every reader; to pursue them, requires not the aid of many counsellors. The whole art of government consists in the art of being honest. (192)

Thus urging the king no longer to sacrifice "the rights of one part of the empire to the inordinate desires of another," but to "deal out to all equal and impartial right," he concludes with his plea for redress of "these our great grievances" (192, 193).

In the *Declaration of Independence* itself Jefferson again showed his great skill as a writer. The structure of this document deserves a little analysis.

The first paragraph makes an announcement—the dissevering of political ties of America with Great Britain—which makes necessary a statement of the causes for the separation. This paragraph also makes clear the nature of the audience addressed—a court of world opinion. The next paragraph states the "self-evident" truths (or natural rights) the violation of which has caused the separation. Following this statement of Jefferson's political philosophy comes a more extended third part—the list of grievances, the function of which is to prove that the natural rights (or self-evident truths) have been violated. (Jefferson was a lawyer, and he here presents legal evidence.) The list is a long one, containing approximately twenty-odd grievances (a curious coincidence with Franklin's *Rules*), and it proceeds from the general to the specific and from the less flagrant to the more flagrant acts of injustice. Jefferson's handling of tone progresses from a relatively calm opening to a highly inflammatory climax. The fourth part follows logically on the third, describing the colonists' repeatedly unsuccessful attempts at securing redress of these grievances, and their remarkable patience notwithstanding this lack of success. Finally, since every effort to obtain redress has failed, Jefferson presents the actual declaration, characterized by appropriate solemnity of tone and legal diction, and concluding with the climactic pledge or oath.

A proper assessment of the *Declaration of Independence* is virtually impossible. For it has been "construed as everything from a bid for foreign aid to a précis of John Locke's *Essay Concerning the True Original, Extent and End of Civil Government.*" [14] One interpreter has viewed it as an antislavery tract—in its original version. [15] Carl Becker refers to it as "a literary as well as a political classic." [16] To William Jennings Bryan it meant that "all men stand equal before the law." [17] One group of writers sees it as justifying revolution when there are repeated violations of these principles which make a free, ideal society: "equal rights derived from the laws of nature," "popular sovereignty," and "limited government." [18] As we have already seen, Jefferson himself subscribed to these principles in his *Summary View*, where he describes the English king as "no more than the chief officer of the people . . . circumscribed with definite powers . . . and . . . subject to their superintendence. . . ." Thus the importance of these two documents by Jefferson is intimately related to these principles, which they make explicit. Collectively the documents say that the failure of a government to redress long-standing grievances (violations of natural rights) inevitably culminates in an action damaging to that government. Like other revolutions the colonists' separation from England had ultimately to depend on force of arms, but it was unique in that it rested on the rational, well-defined, clearly expressed, and previously announced philosophy of government found in Jefferson's *Summary View* and in his eloquent *Declaration*.

IV   *James Wilson*

In the summer of 1774—that busy summer for Jefferson and other patriots—James Wilson, a Scottish-born and Scottish-educated lawyer who later had read law with John Dickinson, produced an important contribution to the thinking of the time on government theory.[19] Wilson's *Considerations on the Nature and Extent of the Legislative Authority of the British Parliament* (1774) takes up the problem of the origin of the so-called unlimited power Parliament assumed it held over the colonies.[20] He asks:

But from what source does this mighty, this uncontrolled authority of the House of Commons flow? From the collective body of the commons [the people] of Great Britain. This authority must, therefore, originally reside in them; for whatever they convey to their representatives must ultimately be in themselves. And have those, whom we have hitherto been accustomed to consider as our fellow-subjects, an absolute and unlimited power over us? (105)

Wilson had a masterful way with rhetorical questions. He was also singularly proficient at quoting legal precedents. Citing a judgment in the second year of Richard III's reign in which it was determined that Ireland was not bound by the statutes of the British Parliament (since the Irish had their own parliament) but were still considered under the jurisdiction of the British king, Wilson argues that "if the inhabitants of Ireland are not bound by Acts of Parliament made in England, *a fortiori*, the inhabitants of the American colonies are not bound by them" (108). (Wilson's reasoning here rests on the fact that the Irish were subject to the British law courts but that the American colonies were not.)

Wilson cites as inapplicable to the American colonies Blackstone's definition of *dependence* as "an obligation to conform to the will or law of that superior person or state, upon which the inferior depends" (Blackstone's quotation, 110). In the American case, argues Wilson, the settlement of the British had not conquered the colonists. He therefore concludes that there exists no legal precedent for "the superiority of Great Britain over the American colonies" (110). Hence, since the English people had no right of dominion over the colonists, they could not confer any "right to their delegates [in Parliament] to bind those equals and fellow-subjects by law" (111). The only dependency the colonists owed was to the King of England (113). (In this instance Wilson cites *Calvin's Case* (1608) from Coke and Bacon—to the effect that subjects of the king are not necessarily subjects of Parliament.) [21]

In an important footnote Wilson goes even further, carefully defining what was meant by the king's power to regulate trade. Many legal authorities, Wilson finds, agreed that the king's regulation of trade was a very limited kind of power and did not extend to laying of impost duties (115n–116n).

These distinctions, precedents, and careful definitions on which Wilson based his case against Parliament helped the colonists to clarify their thinking.

V John Dickinson

As one would expect, several other writers were at work during this hectic period of 1774—James Iredell, for example, whose *Address to the Inhabitants of Great Britain* anticipated the modern system of "several *distinct* and *independent* legislatures each engaged within a *separate* scale and employed about *different* objects." [22] John Dickinson was at work, too, arguing that the exercise of unlimited power was neither *legal* nor *rightful.* His *Essay on the Constitutional Power of Great Britain over the Colonies in America* (Philadelphia, 1774) has been described as follows: "A remarkable compendium of quotations loosely attached to a brief text; the text itself is submerged for pages, as footnotes and then footnotes on footnotes pile up." [23] While this is true, it is also worth noting that Dickinson's "brief text" remonstrated against the Declaratory Act, the claim of Parliament to bind the colonies "IN ALL CASES WHATSOEVER" (13), and against the punitive "Intolerable" Acts (26) following the Boston Tea Party. It also called for a Continental Congress (26–27) and stated that the issue of trade regulations should be settled by mutual consent (27). In addition, it asked for redress of grievances and even suggested making the Continental Congress "PERMANENT" (*sic,* 28–29). The text took the form of a set of resolutions with Dickinson, Joseph Read, and Charles Thomson designated as a committee to "write to the neighbouring colonies, and communicate to them the resolves and instructions" (31). The resolutions were passed by a large committee of the Pennsylvania Assembly with two or three representatives from each county, and the "Instructions" (9–31) explained the above-mentioned points. After the "Resolves" and the "Instructions," the footnotes, as Bailyn says, begin for the next sixty pages "to pile up." In what remains of the text Dickinson attempts to trace the line between the rights of the colonies and those of the mother country, accomplishing his task by numerous appeals to legal precedents in his footnotes.

Like James Wilson, Dickinson tackles the concept of colonial *dependency* on Great Britain at one point, saying:

A DEPENDANCE [*sic*] on the crown and PARLIAMENT of *Great-Britain*, is a novelty—a dreadful novelty. It may be compared to the engine invented by the *Greeks* for the destruction of *Troy*. It is full of armed enemies, and the walls of the constitution must be thrown down, before it can be introduced among us. (94)

The word *dependence* is a relatively new one, he argues, having been introduced into British legal usage by the Commonwealth Act of 1650. "A 'dependance on parliament' is still more modern. A people cannot be too cautious in guarding against such innovations" (94).

But it is well to remember that Dickinson's *tone*, particularly in the "Instructions," the earlier part of this essay on British constitutional power, was definitely conciliatory. His use of such phrases as "tender concern," "a sense of duty to our soverign, and of esteem for our mother country," "the pleasures of gratitude and love, as well as advantages from that connexion [*sic*]" are not ironical but sincere (19–20). He even goes so far as to say that "we now think we ought to contribute more than we do to the alleviation of her burdens" (20). In return for redress of grievances he promises that the Americans will obey not only the "acts of navigation" but "every other act of parliament declared to have force, at this time, in the colonies except those above-mentioned." (The exceptions were the assumed power to tax the colonies and regulate their trade without representation, the power to quarter troops at the colonists' expense, and the bill closing the port at Boston—in short, the Intolerable Acts and the Declaratory Act.) According to these terms, the colonists were to "settle a certain revenue on his majesty, his heirs and successors, subject to the control of parliament, and to satisfy all damages of the *East-India* company." Thus, he writes, "We shall contentedly labour for her, as affectionate *friends*, in time of tranquillity; and cheerfully spend for her, as dutiful *children*, our treasure and blood, in time of war" (21).

Although Dickinson's purpose was conciliatory and he was doing his best to work out a compromise and to avoid war, the significance of this *Essay* lies both in his protest against grievances and in his careful definition of the limits of parliamentary power—Parliament did not, for example, have the right to "unlimited" legislation (84).

Nevertheless, at least one of his arguments hinted in its logical inference that the next step following any British claim to *unlimited power* over the colonies might well be separation from the mother country—in other words, *no power* of England over the colonies:

. . . a power of government, in its nature tending to the misery of the people, as a power that is *unlimited*, or in other words, a power *in which the people have no share*, is proved to be by reason and the experience of all ages and countries, cannot be a *rightful* or *legal* power. For, as an excellent Bishop of the Church of *England* argues, "the *ends of government* cannot be answered by a total dissolution of all happiness at present, and of all hopes for the future. The just inference therefore would be an exclusion of *any* power of parliament over these colonies, rather than the admission of *unbounded* power." (45–48) [24]

Accordingly, in 1775, after the battles of Lexington and Concord, Dickinson helped draft for the Continental Congress a fifteen-page pamphlet that more clearly spelled out the possibility of such exclusion of parliamentary power, indicating that war might be inevitable.

Thomas Jefferson assisted in the composition, but Dickinson probably wrote most of the work entitled *A Declaration by the Representatives of the United Colonies of North-America Now Met in General Congress at Philadelphia, Setting Forth the Causes and Necessity of their taking up ARMS.*[25] This *Declaration* fills in the historical background of the colonies, including the Seven Years War (1756–1763), and concludes with sharp irony that "the new ministry [of Grenville] finding the brave foes of Britain, though frequently defeated, yet still contending, took up the unfortunate idea of granting them a hasty peace, and then subduing her faithful friends." Dickinson goes on with irony to say,

These devoted colonies were judged to be in such a state, as to present victories without bloodshed, and all the easy emoluments of statuteable plunder. (7)

The *Declaration* then repeats the by now familiar list of grievances and asks, "But why should we enumerate our injuries in detail? By one statute it is declared that parliament can 'of right make laws to bind us in ALL CASES WHATSOEVER' " (8). Following this answered question, Dickinson sketches the more recent history of the long dispute—General Gage's arrival and the battles of

Lexington and Concord, saying, "His troops have butchered our countrymen; have wantonly burnt Charles-Town, besides a considerable number of houses in other places; our ships and vessels are seized; the necessary supplies of provisions are intercepted, and he is exerting his utmost power to preach destruction and devastation around him" (12–13).[26]

In the middle of page 13 there is a decided break in the style, and Morison attributes the remainder of the document to Jefferson. Consider the following passage, for example, which has a decidedly Jeffersonian ring: "Our cause is just. Our union is perfect. Our internal resources are great, and if necessary, foreign assistance is undoubtedly attainable" (13). But the last three paragraphs (14–15)—the gist of which is that the colonists disclaimed separation from Great Britain, still hoped for reconciliation with her, and thought of this highly defensive act as something to which they had been driven by "Necessity" (14), in short, as a kind of prelude to "the calamities of civil war" (14)—sound like Dickinson's earlier attempts at conciliation, at least in thought if not in style. This document is signed by John Hancock and Charles Thomson and dated "Philadelphia, July 6th, 1775" (15).[27]

VI   John Adams

The *Novanglus* papers of John Adams appeared weekly in the *Boston Gazette* from January 23 to April 17, 1775. They answered another series of letters, published by Daniel Leonard, a Tory, under the pseudonym of *Massachusettensis*, which first appeared on December 12, 1774, in the *Massachusetts Gazette and Post-Boy* and continued until April 3, 1775, the date of Leonard's final letter. The Battle of Lexington (April 19, 1775) terminated this paper war. In this paper war the battle lines between patriot Whigs and Loyalist Tories now became clearly visible. The most important of these letters, arranged in alternating order, so that the arguments can be easily compared, are available in an inexpensive reprint.[28] Consequently I shall limit my discussion to a few remarks about the two series as wholes.

As a writer Leonard had greater fluency but less solidity than Adams. He had facility at handling rhetorical questions and the tone of his letters often rises to the level of eloquent pleading. Less legalistic than Adams, he uses fewer quotations of legal precedent. He mentions *Novanglus* far less frequently than Adams mentions

Massachusettensis. He appears, in fact, barely to notice *Novanglus*, almost ignoring him by name in contrast to Adams's constant mention and blame of him. In general, Leonard's tone is more impersonal. Here is a sample of his style, as he gives his reaction to the Boston Tea Party:

. . . the British lion was roused [on hearing that 10,000 pounds Sterling of tea had been destroyed]. The crown lawyers were called upon for the law; they answered, high Treason. Had a Cromwell, whom some amongst us deify and imitate in all his imitable perfections, had the guidance of the national ire, unless compensation had been made to the sufferers immediately upon its being demanded, your proud capital had been levelled with the dust; not content with that, rivers of blood would have been shed to make atonement for the injured honor of the nation. It was debated whether to attaint the principals of treason. We have a gracious king upon the throne; he felt the resentment of a man, softened by the relentings of a parent. The bowels of our mother yearned toward her refractory, obstinate child.

It was determined to consider the offence in a milder light. . . . (164) [29]

Adams's reaction to this same subject in his letter of February 27, 1775, contrasts sharply both in style and substance. He argues in the first place that "there are tumults, seditions, popular commotions, insurrections and civil wars, upon just occasions, as well as unjust," defending this statement with a quotation from Grotius—*viz.*, "that some sort of private war may be lawfully waged—It is not repugnant to the law of nature, for any one to repel injuries by force." He also quotes from Algernon Sidney to the effect that one tries in vain to seek a government entirely free of tumults and seditions, since these may arise from "just occasions or unjust" (62). This thought leads him into a discussion of the magistrate's role in putting down such dissensions. *"The magistrate,"* he writes, *"is comprehended under both* [God's ordinance (that men should live justly with one another) as well as the civil law], *and subject to both, as well as private men"* (63). Further quotations from Puffendorf, Barbeyrac, Locke, and LeClark help Adams support his position until he says, "If there is any thing in these quotations which is applicable to the destruction of tea, or any other branch of our subject, it is not my fault; I did not make it" (66). Then, weighing these widely accepted authorities against "the mercenary scribblers in New York and Boston, who have the unexampled impudence and folly, to call these . . . revolution[ary] principles in question, and to

ground their arguments upon passive obedience as a corner stone,"
he says that the "mercenary scribblers" overestimate the value of
Bute, Mansfield, and Lord North (66).

In his account of the Boston Tea Party Adams calls it a
"ministerial tea" (67), "an oblation to Neptune" (68), and describes
it at great length. Yet he takes time out occasionally to vilify
Massachusettensis, caustically referring to "the wit and beauty of his
style," which he says "seem to have quite enraptured the lively
imagination of this writer" (69). Adams writes:

Our acute logician . . . undertakes to prove the destruction of the tea
unjustifiable, even upon the principle of the Whigs, that the duty was
unconstitutional. The only argument he uses is this: that "unless we
purchase the tea, we shall never pay the duty." This argument is so
frivolous, and has been so often confuted and exposed, that if the party had
any other, I think they would relinquish this. Where will it carry us? If a
duty was laid upon our horses, we may walk;—if upon our butcher's meat,
we may live upon the produce of the dairy;—and if that should be taxed, we
may subsist as well as our fellow slaves in Ireland upon Spanish potatoes
and cold water. If a thousand pounds was laid upon the birth of every child,
if children are not begotten, none will be born;—if, upon every marriage,
no duties will be paid, if all the young gentlemen and ladies agree to live
batchelors and maidens. (70)

. . . .

But most people in America now think, the destruction of the Boston tea
was absolutely necessary, and therefore right and just. (70)

The letter of March 6, 1775, is probably crucial to the main issue
debated in this series.[30] In it Novanglus quotes Massachusettsensis
as saying, "If we are a part of the British empire, we must be subject
to the supreme power of the state which is vested in the estates in
parliament. . . ." Novanglus denies that the British system is an
empire, comparing it to a "limited monarchy," arguing that it was
"even more like a republic according to Aristotle, Livy, and
Harrington" (83–84). He concludes that the colonies are not a part of
the British empire and that the provincial legislatures of America
were the only supreme authorities. The colonies did not owe
allegiance to any "imperial crown," but only to the *person* of the
king (93). Also, in the last paragraph of this letter Adams very clearly
intimates that failure to provide a colony adequate representation in
government will "infallibly" lead to armed resistance from that
colony (94).[31]

Politically speaking, this interchange of letters between Leonard and Adams was important in defining the deep rift between Loyalist (Tory) and Whig sentiment in American public opinion. Leonard, an extremely wealthy man who had been driven from his comfortable country home by patriots who objected to his support of the crown, had taken refuge in Boston. His letters established the Tory view, submission to the crown and avoidance of the dangers of rebellion.[32] Hornberger notes that Adams's letters, on the other hand, were "typical of the great mass of Whig writing" and that being reprinted almost at once in Boston, New York, and London, they "contributed mightily to the determination of the patriots to resist the encroachment on their liberties." [33] Adams's argument that the colonies owed allegiance only to the person of the king (in the manner of a twentieth-century commonwealth) and that the provincial legislatures in the colonies were their only supreme authorities showed clearly how far the disruption between Britain and America had gone.

VII *Alexander Hamilton*

In 1774–1775 Alexander Hamilton was a student at Kings College (now Columbia University). At the age of seventeen he was not too young to be already taking an active part in politics. The colony of New York had at this time begun to take sides on the decision of the new Continental Congress to have no commercial relations with Great Britain. Protesting this no-trade policy, which amounted to a boycott, Tory Samuel Seabury had produced *Free Thoughts on the Proceedings of the Continental Congress*. Hamilton's two works *A Full Vindication of the Measures of Congress* (1774) and *The Farmer Refuted* (1775) answered Seabury's *Free Thoughts*, which had been written under the pseudonym of a Westchester Farmer.

In his role as "Defender of Congress" Hamilton wrote in his *Vindication* that "all men have one common original; they participate in one common nature, and consequently have one common right. . . . The pretensions of Parliament are contradictory to the law of nature, subversive to the British Constitution, and destructive of the faith of the most solemn compacts." Anticipating his later *Report on Manufactures* (1791), he argued that American manufactures, once established and extended, would pave the way "to the future grandeur and glory of America." He also thought that a lessened "need for external commerce" would render the colonies "still securer against the encroachments of tyranny." [34]

In *The Farmer Refuted* (February 5, 1775) Hamilton attacked

Seabury for his enmity to and ignorance of the natural rights of mankind, recommending that he study Grotius, Puffendorf, Locke, Montesquieu, and Burlemaqui and pointing out an inconsistency with Hobbes, whom in other respects Seabury greatly resembled. Although Hobbes felt that man in a state of nature was "perfectly free from all restraint of *law* and *government*," he did not believe in the existence of God. Since Seabury had invoked the name of the deity in his *Free Thoughts*, Hamilton presumed him a believer. But Hamilton was quick to point out the inconsistency between the idea of a deity who regulates the actions of human beings and the idea that human beings in a state of nature are absolutely free of such regulation. Quoting Blackstone, Hamilton then defines natural rights and human law as derivative from the law of God. "Hence, in a state of nature, no man had any *moral* power to deprive another of his life, limbs, property, or liberty; nor the least authority to command or exact obedience from him, except that which arose from the ties of consanguinity" (5). In his indictment Hamilton consequently accuses Parliament not only of subverting the natural liberty of the colonies, by assuming authority over them to which they had not assented, but also of divesting the colonies "of that *moral security* for our lives and properties, which we are entitled to, and which is the primary end of society to bestow" (6).[35]

In his statement of his theory of human nature (on which his whole later system of government depends) Hamilton quotes extensively from Hume:

". . . in contriving any system of government, and fixing the several checks and controls of the constitution, *every man* ought to be supposed a *knave*, and to have no other end, in all his actions, but *private interest*. By this interest we must govern him, and by means of it *make him co-operate to public good*, notwithstanding his insatiable avarice and ambition. Without this we shall in vain boast of the advantages of *any constitution*, and shall find, in the end, that we have no security for our liberties and possessions except the *good-will* of our rulers; that is, we should have *no security at all*." (8)

Besides *The Farmer Refuted* Hamilton wrote toward the end of the Revolutionary War a series of six papers entitled *The Continentalist* (1781).[36] In these he advocated (for the colonies) a more powerful central government by way of taxing and regulating trade. In 1783 he penned a second *Vindication of Congress*.

The significance of the *Continentalist* papers rests in the fact that they reveal young Hamilton's already fixed belief that the only safety lay in a strong central government, a government that had, in his words, "power of purse." For, as he remarks in *Continentalist* No. 4, "Power without revenue . . . is a [mere] name." According to Prescott, by 1781 Hamilton was no longer appealing to the abstract arguments of the "natural right" doctrine he had written about in his first *Vindication* of Congress. Rather, by 1781 Hamilton had permanently shaped his political system into an unalterable mold—these principles might develop, as Prescott says, "but they do not change." By the end of the war in 1783 in his second *Vindication* we shall find Hamilton arguing for a powerful and efficient central government, a government with *power of purse*, in order to correct the all-pervasive anarchy and bankruptcy that was then threatening to destroy the country.[37] But in the mid-1770s, as we have seen, Hamilton was defending the patriot position with arguments not too dissimilar to those of the writer we shall next consider.

VIII   *Thomas Paine*

The cause of America is in a great measure the cause of all mankind. Many circumstances have, and will arise, which are not local, but universal, and through which the principles of all lovers of mankind are affected, and in the event of which their affections are interested. The laying a country desolate with fire and sword, declaring war against the natural rights of all mankind, and extirpating the defenders thereof from the face of the earth, is the concern of every man to whom nature hath given the power of feeling; of which class, regardless of party censure, is

THE AUTHOR.[38]

With these ringing words Tom Paine introduces what one writer has called "the first open appeal for a declaration of independence." [39]

Common Sense was published in Philadelphia in January 1776. It sold 125,000 copies in the first three months, according to Hornberger, and "appeared in fifteen or more editions" before the end of the year.[40] Measured by its rhetorical aim, it was eminently successful; for it created, probably more than any other single factor, a tide of public opinion that swept everything else before it and made Jefferson's *Declaration of Independence* a logical and appropriate expression of the feelings of the American people.

In the "Introduction" to *Common Sense* Paine states his intention of inquiring into the pretensions of both king and parliament and of rejecting the usurpation of either. Accordingly, in the first part of his discourse he speedily goes to work investigating the "Origin and Design of Government in General, With Concise Remarks on the English Constitution." First, he defines *government*, by comparing it with *society*.

Society is produced by our wants and government by our wickedness; the former promotes our happiness positively by uniting our affections, the latter negatively by restraining our vices. The one encourages intercourse, the other creates distinctions. The first is a patron, the last a punisher.

Society in every state is a blessing, but government, even in its best state, is but a necessary evil, in its worst state an intolerable one. . . . (4)

The "true design and end of government," according to Paine, is security (4). Government is necessary—"to supply the defect of moral virtue" (5). "Here then is the origin and rise of government; namely, a mode rendered necessary by the inability of moral virtue to govern the world; here too is the design and end of government, viz. freedom and security" (6).

After this definition of government and the brief illustrative historical sketch whereby man proceeds from a state of nature into a state of government (in which he recommends frequent elections), he launches his attack on the British constitution. He lays down a general principle—"a principle in nature which no art can over-turn"—upon which he says he has formed his idea of government: "that the more simple any thing is, the less liable it is to be disordered, and the easier repaired when disordered" (6). Absolute governments, which Paine regards as "the disgrace of human nature," have at least the advantage of simplicity: if the people suffer, they know the remedy. "But the Constitution of England is so exceedingly complex, that the nation may suffer for years together without being able to discover in which part the fault lies; some will say in one and some in another, and every political physician will advise a different medicine" (7).

In his examination of the component parts of the English Constitution, Paine discovers them compounded of two ancient tyrannies (the king and the House of Lords) "compounded with some new Republican materials" (the House of Commons, 7). To the objection that this system is a union of three powers mutually checking each other, Paine responds by setting up a false dilemma—"either the words have no meaning or they are flat contradictions." With this kind of heads-I-win-tails-you-don't logic Paine cannot lose. But how many of his American readers worried about bad logic in 1776? They also believed his down-to-earth explanations, especially when attached to a Biblical saying, as in the following instance:

Some writers have explained the English Constitution thus: the king they say is one, the People another; the Peers are a house in behalf of the King, the Commons in behalf of the People; But this hath all the distinctions of a house divided against itself. (8)

And he then goes on to add his common-sense comment:

. . . and tho' the expressions be pleasantly arranged, yet when examined they appear idle and ambiguous. [Such words, he says, are] words of sound only, and tho' they may amuse the ear, they cannot inform the mind. . . . (8)

Next, he asks, "*How came the king by a power which the people are afraid to trust, and always obliged to check?* Such a power could not be the gift of a wise People, neither can any Power, *which needs checking*, be from God.*" Paine finds the answer to this question two paragraphs later; it is self-evident that the source of the king's power comes from his being "the giver of places and pensions" (8). Paine concludes that "*it is wholly* [due] *to the constitution of the People, and not to the Constitution of the Government* that the Crown is not as oppressive in England as in Turkey" (9). He then proposes an inquiry into the "*constitutional errors* in the English form of government" (9).

This inquiry, he accomplishes in part two—"Of Monarchy and Hereditary Succession." Addressing himself to the question of the origin of kings, Paine writes: "Male and female are the distinctions of nature, good and bad the distinctions of Heaven; but how a race of Men came into the World so exalted above the rest, and distinguished like some new species, is worth inquiring into, and whether they are the means of happiness or of misery to mankind" (9). His verdict is for the latter: "In the early ages of the World, according to Scripture chronology there were no Kings; the consequence of which was there were no wars; it is the pride of Kings which throws mankind into confusion . . ." (9). In short, kings are unnatural and they are the prime cause of wars. Then, relying on the religious predispositions of his American readers,

Paine says, "Government by Kings was first introduced into the World by the Heathens [sic], from whom the children of Israel copied the custom. It was the most prosperous invention the Devil ever set on foot for the promotion of idolatry" (10). Having thus far argued mainly against kings as *unnatural*, he now ventures to discredit them with an elongated appeal to the Bible. Paine now turns to the second half of his title for this part—Hereditary Succession—presenting three vigorous arguments against it and stressing the dishonorable origin of kings. This section contains some of his most effective rhetoric:

One of the strongest natural proofs of the folly of hereditary right in kings, is that nature disapproves it, otherwise she would not so frequently turn it into ridicule, by giving mankind an *ass for a lion*.

....

Secondly, as no man at first could possess any other public honors than were bestowed upon him, so the givers of those honors could have no power to give away the right of posterity. . . . Because such an unwise, unjust, unnatural compact might (perhaps) in the next succession put them under the government of a rogue or a fool. (13)

....

Most wise men in their private sentiments have ever treated hereditary right with contempt; yet it is one of those evils which when once established is not easily removed: many submit from fear, others from superstition, and the more powerful part shares with the king the plunder of the rest.

....

. . . it is more than probable, that, could we take off the dark covering of antiquity and trace them to their first rise, we should find the first of them nothing better than the principal ruffian of some restless gang; whose savage manners or preeminence in subtility obtained him the title of chief among plunderers. . . .

Considering three possible origins of kings—lot, election, and usurpation—Paine states that William the Conqueror, from whom many English kings traced descent, was a usurper. Paine then concludes this second part with a list of evils attendant on hereditary succession:

Men who look upon themselves [as] born to reign, and others to obey, soon grow insolent. . . .

....

Another evil . . . is that the throne is subject to be possessed by a minor at any age. . . . The same national misfortune happens when a king worn out with age and infirmity enters the last stage of human weakness.

....

The most plausible plea which hath ever been offered in favor of hereditary succession is, that it preserves a Nation from civil wars; and were this true, it would be weighty; whereas it is the most barefaced falsity ever imposed upon mankind. The whole history of England disowns the fact (15).

Paine argues that, actually, hereditary succession is the *cause* rather than the preventative of civil wars—"monarchy and succession have laid . . . the world in blood and ashes" (16). In answer to his own query about the function or "business" of a king, he replies that

in England a king hath little more to do than to make war and give away places; which in plain terms is to empoverish [*sic*] the nation and set it together by the ears. A Pretty business indeed for a man to be allowed eight hundred thousand sterling a year for, and worshipped into the bargain! Of more worth is one honest man to society, and in the sight of God, than all the crowned ruffians that ever lived. (16)

Thus he concludes part two.

In the third part—"Thoughts on the Present State of Affairs"—the structure becomes a bit more complicated, but still may be quite easily outlined. There are five divisions in this part: 1. Paine first takes up four or five arguments of those urging reconciliation with Great Britain and systematically refutes each. 2. He next points out four disadvantages of continued connection with Great Britain. 3. Then he discusses the kinds of men who were espousing the doctrine of reconciliation—weak men, interested men, prejudiced men, and moderate men who think too highly of the European world—none of whom is to be trusted. In this section, too, he first argues for war—"since nothing but blows will do, for God's sake let us come to a final separation, and not leave the next generation to be cutting throats under the violated unmeaning names of parent and child" (23). 4. He imagines reconciliation and argues against it, equating it with ruin for the colonies. 5. He offers his own plan for an independent government with annual assemblies, congressional districts, a Continental Congress, etc.

In the fourth part—"Of the Present Ability of America; With Some Miscellaneous Reflections"—Paine presents an inventory of American resources to meet the demands of the forthcoming war: the number and *unity* of the men, the proportion of men to the need, the colonies' absence of debts, his plan for a navy, and a detailed list of natural resources. Wonderfully, in this list he includes not only cannon, saltpeter, and gunpowder but also the colonists' inherent "Resolution" and "courage" (35). The "Miscellaneous Reflections" include Paine's belief that it is the "the indispensable duty of government to protect all conscientious professors" of whatever religion as well as his belief that a large and equal electorate was absolutely necessary for such a government (37). He adds, "When we are planning for posterity, we ought to remember that virtue is not hereditary" (38).

In his conclusion, he advocates "an open and determined DECLARATION FOR INDEPENDANCE," urging that "until an Independance is declared, the [American] Continent will feel itself like a man who continues putting off some unpleasant business from day to day, yet knows it must be done, hates to set about it, wishes it over, and is continually haunted with the thoughts of its necessity" (39).

When the war began, the colonists soon found themselves with their backs against the wall. Hornberger writes that by December 19, 1776, "New Jersey was . . . well-nigh lost and Philadelphia panic-stricken. Washington had even written to his brother that 'if every nerve is not strained to recruit the new army with all possible expedition, I think the game is pretty nearly up.' " [41]

It was at this precarious juncture of events that Paine stepped into the light by printing, in the *Pennsylvania Journal*, over his by now well-known pen name of Common Sense the first of his sixteen papers entitled "The American Crisis." It was written, according to Foner, "on a drum-head by campfire while Paine was accompanying Washington's forces during the heartbreaking days of the retreat across New Jersey. The Revolution seemed to be lost; the enemy appeared to be invincible, and the morale of soldiers and civilians alike was at its lowest ebb." [42] *Crisis, no. I* was "almost immediately issued as a pamphlet." [43] It is a masterpiece of rhetoric. The technique of persuasion which Paine employs in piecing together again the shattered morale of the patriots deserves careful study.

Paine begins with a frank facing-up to the facts of the situation:

These are the times that try men's souls: The summer soldier and sunshine patriot will, in this crisis, shrink from the service of his country; but he that stands it NOW, deserves the love and thanks of man and woman. Tyranny, like hell, is not easily conquered; yet we have this consolation with us, that the harder the conflict, the more glorious the triumph. (50)

The key word in this opening is *consolation*, for in the first three paragraphs of this paper Paine is mainly consoling the colonists for their desperate situation. How does he account for their trouble? Independence should have been declared sooner! "We did not make a proper use of last winter, neither could we, while we were in a dependent state," he says. "But no great deal is lost yet; all that Howe has been doing for this month past, is rather a *ravage* than a *conquest*. . ." (50, my ital.) Paine defines neither of these words, and one wonders if his readers knew the difference. To be in a state of *ravage* would hardly seem very consoling, except that it reflects invidiously on Howe's humanity, except, too, that Paine says that "time and a little resolution would soon recover" their losses (50). Knowing the religious nature of his readers, he plays on it—this time with a real consolation:

God Almighty will not give up a people to military destruction or leave them unsupportedly to perish, who have so earnestly and so repeatedly sought to avoid the calamities of war, by every decent method which wisdom could invent. Neither have I so much of the infidel in me, as to suppose that he has relinquished the government of the world, and given it up to the care of devils; and as I do not, I cannot see on what grounds the king of Britain can look up to Heaven for help against us: a common murderer, a highwayman, or a housebreaker, has as good a pretence as he. (50–51)

Following his consolatory remarks, Paine next provides a long paragraph on *panics*. "All nations have been subject to them," he writes, particularly the English. Panics had their *uses*. They were "touchstones of sincerity and hypocrisy," serving to flush out Tories. "Many a disguised tory has lately shown his head, that shall penitentially solemnize with curses the day on which Howe arrived upon the Delaware," he says (51).

Then, after this short essay on panics and their uses, he brings out his own eye-witness acount of the events in question, the pell-mell, panicky retreat across New Jersey. "As I was with the troops at Fort Lee, and marched with them to the edge of Pennsylvania, I am well acquainted with many circumstances, which those who live at a distance, know little or nothing of," he writes (51). He persuades the reader that there were good reasons for leaving Fort Lee, near New York. (According to Hornberger's note, this fort was "hastily evacuated on November 20, the Americans even leaving their dinners cooking.") [44] "Our situation there was exceedingly cramped," he says: "our force was inconsiderable," ammunition and light artillery had been removed, the fort was only temporary, etc. (51–52). His description of the flight across Jersey makes it sound more like a deliberate and calculated withdrawal than a panic, albeit he does admit (probably in order not to tax credibility too much) that the troops bore the "long retreat" "with a manly and martial spirit" (52–53). And he observes, too, that Washington was the kind of leader whose "natural firmness" made him perform all the better when the going became difficult (53).

Although at this point in the essay Paine would appear only to have begun, he now announces that he will "conclude this paper with some miscellaneous remarks on the state of our affairs; and shall begin with asking the following question, Why is it that the enemy have left the New-England provinces, and made these middle ones the seat of war?" "The answer," he says, "is easy: New England is not infested with tories, and we are." Thus he makes Howe's victory look like an attempt at a British retreat to Philadelphia, a known center of Tories! From this point on he launches an emotionalized attack on Tories, beginning with a definition of the species:

And what is a tory? Good God! what is he? I should not be afraid to go with a hundred Whigs against a thousand tories, were they to attempt to get into arms. Every tory is a coward; for servile, slavish self-interested fear is the foundation of Toryism; and a man under such influence, though he may be cruel, never can be brave. (53)

He tries to persuade the reader that Howe, who really had the upper hand in the fighting, stood in need of troops. It was soldiers, not Tories, since these were cowards, that Howe needed. He then persuades his Tory readers (of whom there certainly were some), particularly those Tories who were pacifistically inclined, that Howe was their real enemy, since he was bringing the war into their own country, near Philadelphia. For the further discomfort of the Tories, Paine next predicts that a single successful battle will in the coming year settle the whole war in favor of the patriots.

Quitting his discussion of Tories, Paine turns now "with the warm ardor of a friend" to praise of the patriots and to encouraging them to greater efforts. Here we find some of his most wonderful rhetoric:

I love the man that can smile in trouble, that can gather strength from distress, and grow brave by reflection. 'Tis the business of little minds to shrink; but he whose heart is firm, and whose conscience approves his conduct, will pursue his principles unto death. (55)

Toward the close of this paper Paine refutes the objection of some Tories that Howe in victory would prove merciful to the Americans. "It is the madness of folly, to expect mercy from those who have refused to do justice," answers Paine.

Howe is mercifully inviting you to barbarous destruction [he advises the Tories], and men must be either rogues or fools that will not see it. I dwell not upon the vapors of imagination; I bring reason to your ears, and, in language as plain as A, B, C, hold up truth to your eyes. (56)

Repeating his argument that the retreat was orderly and controlled, Paine concludes with a personal testimony of courage and hope based on the past: "I thank *God* that I fear not," he writes.[45] "I see no real cause for fear. I know our situation well and can see the way out of it" (56). A new army is being collected, a new campaign planned, he tells his reader; and he concludes with a savage attack on cowardice.[46]

IX *Hugh Henry Brackenridge*

In his *Six Political Discourses, Founded on the Scripture* (Lancaster, [1778]), Hugh Henry Brackenridge seconded the motion as it were, of Tom Paine's *Common Sense* and early *Crisis* papers.[47] The sharpness of Brackenridge's attack on General Burgoyne, whom he calls a poet rather than a general, lacks the power of Paine's emotionalized onslaught on the British king, but it begins to approach it. (The first half of the fifth *Discourse* ridicules Burgoyne; the second half accuses him of "blasphemies," 62–70.)

Brackenridge makes several interesting rhetorical equations. Toryism is "the way of Cain," i.e., *murder*; Washington is Moses; and King George III, Satan.[48] (Brackenridge quotes Rev. 12:12—"The reign of the tyrant is the reign of Satan," and argues that the British king is *mad*, 79–80.) God himself is referred to as the "Admiral" of the American navy—in its victories over the British (55). Because of his proclamations, Burgoyne (in *Discourse* No. 5) becomes "Goliath" (64–65). Also, Brackenridge makes numerous allusions, or comparisons, having the effect of similar equations, to characters and incidents in the *Iliad*, *Don Quixote*, and Polybius (65–67). It is interesting to note, too, that in his prophecy of an American victory, he borrows one of Paine's arguments in *Common Sense*—the *unnaturalness* of a large territory's being subject to an island[49] (42).

For both Brackenridge and Paine the key terms in the *Discourses* and the *Crisis* were frequently *Tyranny* and *Toryism*. Both of these works were in the nature of propaganda. In fact, as Mason Lowance has pointed out, Paine was one of the first "media persuaders." His enormously expanded use of the public press (in newspaper, magazine, and pamphlet) made journalistic history. *Common Sense*, according to Hornberger, sold 125,000 copies during the first three months and underwent "fifteen or more editions" during the first year.[50] The *Crisis* papers also achieved wide circulation, appearing first in papers like the *Pennsylvania Journal* and in later editions in the form of pamphlets. (The first two *Crisis* papers, for example, were bound together and delivered abroad to Franklin in Paris.) [51] They were disseminated among Washington's troops at Valley Forge and elsewhere. "Each of the sixteen numbers," writes Hornerger, "circulated in the tens of thousands." [52] Moreover, they were written in a language beamed, or directed, at an audience of readers who need not have attended Harvard, Yale, or Princeton to understand what their author was saying with great clarity and simplicity albeit with extraordinary common sense. To be sure, Paine occasionally fell into a logical fallacy, but the grandeur of his spirited rhetoric—his ardent appeal to the fighting emotions, his scorn of Tories as cowards—transcended any niceties of academic nit-picking in book learning or logic. Thus his advent on the rhetorical scene, which Franklin and other leather apron printers had done much to prepare for in America, marked a very significant development. And he managed by dint of his superior power to arouse emotion as well as by the cogency of his well-organized *ad hoc* arguments to easily eclipse writers like Brackenridge who had received careful training in the academies of the day.

In this way the ideological ferment of the Revolutionary War came to a close. But as we shall see in the next chapter, the lull was only temporary. For when the actual shooting had quieted, the colonists were faced with creating a new government of their own on constitutional principles. In the postwar period and, indeed, until the end of the century, the war of ideas continued.

CHAPTER 6

The Adoption of the Constitution

I   *Shays' Rebellion—Minot* et al.

AFTER the Revolutionary War, the colonists found themselves in a severe economic depression. Loaded with debts, as a consequence of the costs of the war and their own extravagant buying from foreign ships that crowded the seaports immediately after the war, the colonists attempted to pay off these debts by raising taxes. The policies of unrelieved taxation, by both the Confederation and most of the states, began to tell on the poor farmers, to whom such policies seemed like robbery and tyranny— the very things they had sought to rid themselves of by means of the war. In western Massachusetts, especially, the farmers began to sense that their real enemies were the wealthy merchants in Boston and other towns, whom they blamed for their increasingly heavy load of debts, for the foreclosed mortgages on their farms, and, in some cases, for their imprisonment for debt.

Since many of these farmers were at the same time Revolutionary veterans, who knew the use of weapons, they resorted to desperate measures. Daniel Shays, who had been a captain in the Continental Army, organized his friends into a small rural army to back up a five-point program of demands: paper money, tax relief, a moratorium on debts, removal of the state capital from Boston to the center of Massachusetts, and abolition of imprisonment for debt. In the summer of 1786, Shays and his men "went in armed bands from place to place to break up court sittings and sheriff's sales." [1] That winter, about 1,200 strong, they advanced on Springfield, the site of an arsenal, to procure guns. There in January 1787 in a blinding snowstorm they encountered a state militia, organized and supported by loans from wealthy Boston merchants. Shays' men were defeated—several were killed, many captured, and the remainder scattered. Although Shays and his lieutenants were at first

165

sentenced to death, they were later pardoned and actually won a few concessions "in the way of tax relief and postponement of debt payments." [2]

Among the most important writings connected with this rebellion was that of George Richards Minot, whose *History of the Insurrection in Massachusetts in the Year 1786* (Worcester, Mass., 1788) represented a hostile view toward Shays. Nor was Minot alone in this attitude. Samuel Adams had also denounced Shays and his brave band as rebels and traitors. Abigail Adams, the wife of John Adams, writing to Thomas Jefferson in Paris, called Shays and his followers "ignorant, restless desperadoes, without conscience or principles." She hoped for the "most vigorous measures to quell and suppress" "these mobish insurgents." [3] Jefferson, however, took quite a different view of the episode. In his letter to James Madison (Januarary 30, 1787), he writes:

I hold . . . that a little rebellion now and then is a good thing, and as necessary in the political world as storms in the physical. Unsuccessful rebellions indeed generally establish the incroachments on the rights of the people which have produced them. An observation of this truth should render honest republican governors so mild in their punishment of rebellions, as not to discourage them too much. It is a medicine necessary for the sound health of government. [4]

But whatever one's feeling about the necessity or efficacy of rebellions, Shays' insurrection amounted to a significant "happening" in American history. As Current *et al.* say, it "affected the country as a whole by giving added urgency to the movement for a new Constitution." [5]

II   *The Defense of the Constitution: John Adams*

Once the new Constitution was written, the problem became how it was to be defended to those who were reluctant to adopt it.

John Adams was one of the first writers to anticipate an answer to this question. [6] In his gigantic, three-volume work entitled *A Defence of the Constitutions of the Government of the United States of America* (London, 1787–88), he argued for three *independent* branches (legislative, executive, and judicial), a strong executive, and a system of checks and balances. If there is any single point which receives greater emphasis than another in this vast compendium of governmental theory, it is the necessity for a checking and balancing power operating among the three branches of government. Adams differs radically from Tom Paine in finding even monarchy acceptable—*if*—and it's a big *if*—the nobles check the king, the ministers check the nobles, the armies check the nobles, etc. (I, ix). Basing his argument for a three-branched government on the authority of Cicero, whom he quotes (*Frag. de Repub.*), Adams states categorically that the laws can be "sure of protection, for any course of time, in no other form of government" (I, xxi). He draws an analogy with the music of Handel:

As the treble, the tenor, and the bass exist in nature, they will be heard in the concert; if they are arranged by Handel, in a skillful composition, they produce rapture the most exquisite that harmony can excite; but if they are confused together without order, they will
"Rend with tremendous sound your ears asunder." (I, xx)

Adams's *Defence* is 1,350 pages long, and is, in the strictest sense of the word, a true *compendium*, since it gathers together all known constitutions of the Western world. He considers in considerable detail every known European system of government! Is it any wonder that such vast erudition astonished his contemporaries?

I can give here only a rough idea of the structure of this enormous work. Briefly, he undertook to answer and correct earlier writings and criticism by Turgot (who espoused a unicameral government), De Mably, and Dr. Richard Price on various aspects of American political life. Beginning with the republic of San Marino in Italy (which had lasted for more than thirteen centuries), Adams points out similarities between it and Sparta and Rome and also between it and the state governments of Massachusetts, New York, and Maryland. Then he contrasts the Roman government with that of the United States of America. (I, 14, 15). Adams's method, in general, consists in showing exactly how the new Constitution of the United States he was arguing for marked an improvement over the foreign constitutions under discussion. He apparently follows an order of oldest to youngest in the arrangement of his material. Some of the discussions are object lessons in what to avoid—the constitution of Biscay, for example, where he points out that the people there have "established by law a contracted aristocracy under the appearance of a liberal democracy," and then adds, "Americans beware!" (I, 20).

Volume one of the *Defence* contains fifty-five letters. In the first group of ten letters, entitled "Democratical Republics," he includes besides the constitutions already mentioned those of the older Swiss cantons and the Low countries. The second group (letters 11–19 inclusive), entitled "Aristocratical Republics," embraces the government of various Swiss cities (Berne and Geneva, for example), the United Provinces of the Lowlands, and the Italian states of Lucca, Genoa, and Venice, giving the latter as a conspicuous example of the failure to employ the checking and balancing system he argues for. The third group (letters 20–23 inclusive), "Monarchical Republics," includes only England and Poland. Letter twenty-three is a recapitulation for this third group.

Beginning with letter twenty-four, Adams presents in three letters three successive views of ancient republics—respectively those of Swift, Franklin, and Price. He discusses Swift's *Contests and Dissensions between the Nobles and Commons of Athens and Rome*, criticizes Franklin and Turgot's unicameral legislature plan (he feared it would turn into an unchecked aristocracy), and introduces his own doctrine of "natural aristocracy" (of fortune, birth, and ability). Adams admits, though, that such an aristocracy in government can be *dangerous if unchecked*. He proposes that such gifted individuals be placed in an assembly (or Senate) and then checked by the power of a strong executive (I, 116–17). In the twenty-fifth letter Adams criticizes Price and defends minority rights. Next come "Mixed Governments" (letters 27, 28). Here he argues that neither monarchy, aristocracy, nor democracy (nor their degenerate forms—tyranny, oligarchy, or licentious anarchy) is effective; only a *mixed* form of all three (in which prince, lords, and commons check one another) will do (I, 145, 148). Here, too, like Madison (see *infra*), he supports a republican or representative government as more efficient than a simple democracy for states with large populations (I, 157). Letters 29 to 34 inclusive treat "Ancient Republics," as supported by the arguments of the philosophers. Letter 35 deals with Carthage as an example of "Ancient Democratical Republics"; letter 36, Rome as an example of an "Ancient Aristocratical Republic." Other headings for letters that follow are: "Ancient Monarchical Republics," mentioned in Tacitus and Homer (examples: Phaeacia and Ithaca)—letters 37, 38, 39; "Ancient Aristocratical Republic"—letter 40 (example: Sparta); "Ancient Democratical Republics"—letters 41–48 inclusive (examples: Athens, Corinth, Crete, Thebes, etc.); "Ancient Aristocratical

Republics"—letter 49 (example: Crotona, where Pythagoras lived);
"Ancient Democratical Republics"—letters 50–52 inclusive (examples: Sybaris, Locris, Rome); "Conclusion"—letter 53, dealing with
the American Congress; letter 54, criticizing Locke, Milton, and
Hume;[7] and letter 55, conclusion again . . . to all of which he adds
a "Postscript"! (In the "Postscript" he defends himself against the
accusation of his having asked Abbé De Mably for advice on the
framing of a constitution, admitting the charge, but saying it was "a
mere civility," I, 384.)

Volume II (445 pp.) expands Adams's principal argument, this
time in the form of five letters concerning various "Italian Republics
of the Middle Age." The second letter describes "Machiavelli's Plan
of a Perfect Commonwealth" (II, 241–50). The last one digresses
momentarily to describe the history of the government of
Neuchatel, indicating its similarities to those of America and
England and calling it a "happy mixture" of the three branches.
Adams's discussion of medieval Italian republics continues well into
volume three (pp. 1–209). Following this section (which also takes
the form of five letters), Adams treats "The Right Constitution of a
Commonwealth, Examined" (III, 209–506). Finally, he includes a
copy of the United States Constitution itself, a letter of George
Washington submitting it for ratification, and an elaborate index.

"On procuring Mr. Adams's book," writes William Livingston,
the first governor of New Jersey, "I set down with the utmost
eagerness and impatience to the perusal of it. From its title I had
formed high expectations . . . Judge then of my extreme mortifi-
cation, when after having followed the Doctor thro' all the rubbage
which with *profound erudition* and infinite pains he has collected
from the storehouses and magazines of antiquity, I came to the
conclusion, without encountering one single passage or argument
which could be stiled 'A Defence of the Constitutions of Government of the United States of America.' " With this bold attack
Livingston launches the beginning of his anonymous *Observations
on Government . . . by a Farmer of New Jersey* (New York,
1787).[8]

Notwithstanding Adams's great abilities, for which he gives him
credit, Livingston is constrained to call him

. . . nothing more than a state empiric [a quack], who prescribes one
single remedy for all disorders: Let what will be the situation of the patient,

let the disorder proceed from what cause it may, you have only to administer a dose of "Orders" and "Balances," and the body politic will be immediately restored to health and vigour. But what winds up the ridicule of this business to the highest pitch, is, that not a single scruple of this universal and so much boasted political nostrum, is to be found in any one of the [state] governments of the United States. (3–4)

Then, after quoting a number of short passages (most of them out of context), he concludes that Adams's way "is certainly a most singular mode of defending a cause" (6). Livingston has little trouble making his point that insufficient evidence exists to support a conclusion "in favor of any one form of government in exclusion of every other possible form" (8). He argues, against Adams, the *difficulty* of balancing the different branches of government: "Reason and experience both teach us how extremely difficult it must be to adjust the balance so as to preserve an equilibrium" (25). Too, he does not like Adams's proposal for an aristocracy. He writes:

. . . [H]owever eligible this scheme may be where an aristocracy is already established, yet as we are clearly not yet in this predicament,—as there is not the last trace or vestige of an aristocracy to be discovered yet in one of these States, it surely would be prudent in us to be thoroughly convinced of the absolute and unavoidable necessity of the case, before we submitted ourselves to a system of government so manifestly defective. (28)

And he charges Adams with trying to set up an interest "distinct and separate from that of the community at large" (28).

Livingston has other differences with Adams, too. For example, he does not see the virtue of the English constitution as subsisting in its executive (king) and nobles, as Adams had, but in its "legislation by *representation*, and trial by *jury* . . ." (33). He takes exception to Adams's dim view of human nature—that man is incapable of governing himself—exclaiming, "No, my fellow countrymen! let us make one more generous effort in favour of human nature" (6). As for Adams's aristocracy, Livingston says, "It can never be brought about in any way, unless by an accumulation of wealth in the hands of a few people . . ." (46). (He gives seven reasons why he regards this eventuality improbable.) [9] He also attacks Adams and De Lolme's proposition that extremely democratic governments cannot last long "without Orders and Balances" (50). "Is an hereditary monarch and nobility, the only possible expedient by means of which power can be limited and restrained? I thank God that the people of these States are not yet reduced to this dreadful alternative" (50–51).

In closing, Livingston argues for the new Federal Government. He suggests some amendments to the new Constitution, the main purpose of which was to curb the power of the presidency (54). For example, he thought the Chief Justice of the Supreme Court, rather than the president, should have the power of appointing other judges to the Court.

William Livingston and his brother Philip were both excellent writers. In the year 1787 William Pierce wrote of William Livingston, "His writings teem with satyr and a neatness of style," a judgment that might equally apply to Philip Livingston.[10] Pierce might have added that in the case of both these gifted brothers their writings also abounded with solid and far-sighted arguments.

III   The Federalist *Writers: Alexander Hamilton, James Madison, and John Jay*

The Federalist papers have been called "the most important work in political science that has ever been written, or is likely ever to be written, in the United States." [11] This series of eighty-five papers that appeared in New York City newspapers (October 27, 1787 to August 1788) over the pseudonym of "Publius" was written by Alexander Hamilton, James Madison, and John Jay. Hamilton supposedly wrote fifty-one of the papers; Madison, twenty-six; and Jay, five.[12] Jay was ill during the fall of 1787, Rossiter tells us, and this may account for the "skimpiness" of his contribution. Madison, a delegate to the Congress then meeting in New York, left for his home in Virginia in March 1788. (He made up in quality and profundity of thought any seeming lack in quantity.) Hamilton's authorship of the largest number of the papers is explained by the "intensity of his commitment." [13]

The object or purpose of this series of papers was to convince the citizens of New York to ratify the new Constitution. Without adoption by New York (one of the largest and most populous states) the success of the Constitution probably would have been seriously impaired. The audience for whom the papers were intended was "a select audience of reasonable, responsible, and established men. . . ."

On the ground of their interest for the modern reader I have selected the three following essays, which Clinton Rossiter lists as "by common consent of learned opinion" among "the cream of the eighty-five papers" [14]: No. 2, which introduces the subject of dangers from foreign force and influence, the discussion of which extends through the next three papers; No. 10, which deals with the perennial dangers of faction; and No. 23, which treats the thorny problem of the limit to be placed on national defense. Each of these papers represents an important aspect of the thought of the three writers.

Federalist No. 2 appeared in the *New York Independent Journal* (October 31, 1787). It was written by John Jay, wealthy New York lawyer and son-in-law of William Livingston. Jay states the question as follows: "Whether it would conduce more to the interest of the people of America that they should, to all general purposes, be one nation, under one federal government, than that they should divide themselves into separate confederacies and give to the head of each the same kind of powers which they are advised to place in one national government" (37). He precedes this statement of the question with two assumptions—that government is necessary and that "the people must cede to it some of their natural rights, in order to vest it with requisite powers" (37). Jay offers seven arguments: 1. the prosperity of the colonists depended on their continuing to be firmly united. 2. America constituted a natural geographical unity. [15] 3. America also possessed cultural unity. [16] 4. For all general purposes the American colonists had, during their immediately preceding history, acted as a united nation—"As a nation we have made peace and war; as a nation we have vanquished our common enemies; as a nation we have formed alliances, and made treaties, and entered into various compacts and conventions with foreign states" (39). 5. The Constitutional Convention in Philadelphia had been posited on the assumption that "ample security . . . could only be found in a national government . . ."—Jay takes time out to defend the constitution as the work of wise and virtuous patriots who had the confidence of the people and whose only motivation was love of their country (39). 6. The Continental Congress of 1774 had been a step towards union. Here again he defends the participants as "wise and experienced men" who were "individually interested in the public liberty and prosperity . . ." (40). 7. If the members of the Continental Congress were trustworthy men, how much more so were they in the Constitutional Convention, since many had taken part in both and since their patriotic principles and wisdom had been tried, tested, and improved by time and experience. As Jay puts it, they had "grown old in acquiring political information" and had, at the Convention, "carried into it their accumulated knowledge and experience" (41). Finally, in the long concluding paragraph, Jay stresses that the Congresses succeeding the first Continental one had always proceeded on the assumption that the preservation and perpetuation of the union was their object. He briefly attacks those who would "depreciate the importance of the Union" by "substituting a number of confederacies" in place of the plan of the Convention and closes in this manner:

I sincerely wish that it may be clearly foreseen by every good citizen that whenever the dissolution of the Union arrives, America will have reason to exclaim, in the words of the poet: "FAREWELL! A LONG FAREWELL TO ALL MY GREATNESS." (41)

In addition to extending the discussion in *Federalist Nos. 3, 4,* and *5,* Jay also wrote the sixty-fourth *Federalist* paper. This paper is important because it explains that the treaty-making power of the president with foreign governments is subject to a two-thirds vote of ratification by the United States Senate. At the end of this paper Jay draws attention to the fact that in the event of a proposed harmful treaty with a foreign nation drawn up by a large number of designing or unscrupulous participants (two-thirds of the Senate plus the president)—a situation he finds it difficult to imagine—the House of Representatives still had the power of impeachment to hold over the head of such a president. This, he thinks, would act as a deterrent to the making of such a treaty.

Madison's *Federalist No. 10* (November 23, 1787 in the *New York Packet*) is generally regarded as a classic statement of the problem of political factions, their potentially destructive nature, and their solution. He argues, of course, that the new Constitution offers "a proper cure" for "the dangerous vice" of faction (77).

In the first part of this paper (paragraphs one and two) Madison states the problem—the omnipresence of factions of one kind or another in the colonies during the postwar period—and defines a *faction* very carefully:

By a faction, I understand a number of citizens, whether amounting to a majority or minority of the whole, who are united and actuated by some common impulse of passion, or of interest, adverse to the rights of other citizens, or to the permanent and aggregate interests of the community. (78)

In the second part (paragraphs three to nine inclusive) he states
how factions may be cured—either by removing their causes or
controlling their effects. Considering first the removal of causes, he
sees, again, two ways of doing this—by "destroying the liberty"
which makes factions possible or "by giving to every citizen the
same opinions, the same passions, and the same interests" (78). The
first way (destruction of liberty) he characterizes as "worse than the
disease" itself; the second expedient (regimentation) is, considering
the basically individual nature of human beings, "impracticable."
The "diversity in the faculties of men" causes them to fall by nature
into various interest groups (or factions)—bankers, doctors, farmers,
merchants, manufacturers, etc. (78). For Madison "the latent causes
of faction are thus sown in the nature of man" (79). He illustrates his
theory with three general kinds of factions:

[1] A zeal for different opinions concerning religion, concerning government, and many other points, as well of speculation as of practice;
[2] an attachment to different leaders ambitiously contending for pre-
eminence and power;
[3] or to persons of other descriptions whose fortunes have been interesting
to the human passions. . . . (79)

The "propensity of mankind to fall into mutual animosities" (or
factions) is so strong, says Madison, "that where no substantial
occasion presents itself, the most frivolous and fanciful distinctions
have been sufficient to kindle their unfriendly passions and excite
their most violent conflicts." But the most common source of
factions lies in the "unequal distribution of property"—rich and
poor, have's and have not's, creditors and debtors. For this reason
nations often find themselves divided into various interest groups or
factions with "different sentiments [read passions] or views."
Because it is the function of government to regulate "these various
and interfering interests," "the spirit of party and faction" becomes
involved "in the necessary and ordinary operations of the government" (79). To illustrate, he shows how interest groups affect both
legislative and judicial systems in government. *Justice*, according to
Madison, ought "to hold the balance" between such interest groups
or factions (80).

In the last paragraph in this second part he takes up the objection
of his opponents that enlightened statesmen should be able to adjust
the clash between factions. The trouble with that view, writes

Madison, is that "enlightened statesmen will not always be at the helm" (80).

Having successfully proven that it is impossible to remove the causes of faction, Madison then moves logically, in part three, to his alternative proposal—controlling their effects. It will be remembered that factions can take the form of either *minority* or *majority*. It is easy enough to outvote (by superior force of numbers) a *minority* faction. But how is it possible to control a faction when it is in the *majority*? Here Madison considers first the so-called "pure" democracies (for example, the Greek city-states), finding them often scenes of great turbulence and generally ineffective at protecting the rights of minorities. Accordingly, he strikes on the device of a republic, by which he means a representative government, as the answer to the problem. By extending the size of the republic, he argues, you "take in a greater variety of parties and interests; you make it less probable that a majority of the whole will have a common motive to invade the rights of other citizens; or if such a common motive exists, it will be more difficult for all who feel it to discover their own strength and to act in unison with each other" (83). [17] Since the Constitution really amounted to an extension of the size of a republic (from one state to thirteen), the implication was clearly that it offered greatly improved chances of controlling these disturbing factions.

Federalist No. 23 by Alexander Hamilton (*New York Packet* for December 18, 1787) is a pure and simple argument for unlimited defense in order to preserve the new Union. Hamilton's thesis is clearly stated: the defense powers of the new government "ought to exist without limitation, *because it is impossible to foresee or define the extent and variety of national exigencies, or the correspondent extent and variety of the means which may be necessary to satisfy them*" (153). Arguing logically enough that "the *means* ought to be proportioned to the *end*," Hamilton presented an abstract argument that, given conditions at that time, probably seemed rational enough (153). But logic and abstract argument sometimes break down in the face of practical considerations. Surely this same argument of Hamilton's today is ridiculous (although it seems to be the basic premise of much jingoistic rhetoric by present-day militarists); for the lust for unending national security has led us down the perilous road to enormous stockpiling of atomic weapons and nuclear plants of various kinds—not to mention dangerous lasers and nerve gas—all of which, far from preserving our national security, rather threatens not only our own destruction but also that of the rest of the planet.

All this is not to deny the value of *Federalist No. 23* as an argument from the colonists' experience during the Revolutionary War. As Hamilton clearly explains, the attempt of Congress (acting under the Articles of Confederation) to impose levies of men and money on the various colonies for "common defense and general welfare" during the war had often not succeeded. Sometimes the colonies (or states) ignored these requests, or impositions, of Congress; sometimes they defied them. The result? Frequent bitter complaints from the states that did attempt to meet these demands of Congress against other states which for various reasons did not or could not. Hamilton's remedy—or rather that of the new Constitution—for the future prevention of such confusion necessitated a change in this old scheme, which he called "the vain project of legislating upon the States in their collective capacities." He writes: "We must extend the laws of the federal government to the individual citizens of America; we must discard the fallacious scheme of quotas and requisitions as equally impracticable and unjust" (154). By thus shifting the power of Congress from the *state* to the *individual*, the new Constitution, Hamilton argues, would bring about a far greater efficiency in the total defense posture of the national government. Thus the new government would be in a better position to survive.

Hamilton readily conceded that the administration of justice between citizens of the same state should properly fall under the "local" or state government, what later came to be called the doctrine of states' rights. But he did attack the "manifest inconsistency in devolving upon the federal government the care of general defense" while leaving within the hands of the state governments the *"effective"* power to ante up the men, money, and supplies (155-56).

In succeeding *Federalist* papers he takes up other facets of the problem. *No. 24*, for example, considers the objection which opponents of this new plan had raised against standing armies during peace time. *Nos. 25–29*, inclusive, continue with other specific aspects of this general problem, concluding with further arguments in favor of congressional regulation of the militia.

IV *George Mason and Objections to the Constitution*

One of the leading opponents of the new Constitution was George Mason, a wealthy Virginia landowner, who had earlier written against the Townshend Acts and drafted a document known as *The Declaration of Rights* (1776).[18] This latter work was vastly important, since it not only is supposed to have influenced Jefferson in his composition of *The Declaration of Independence* but also became the basis for the first ten amendments to the Constitution, known as the Bill of Rights.

Although Mason was a member of the Constitutional Convention, he refused to sign it, and he led the opposition to its ratification in the Virginia Convention. In a letter to George Washington, dated October 7, 1787, Mason writes:

I take the liberty to enclose to you my objections to the new Constitution of government, which a little moderation and temper at the end of the convention might have removed. . . . You will readily observe, that my objections are not numerous (the greater part of the enclosed paper containing reasonings upon the probable effects of the exceptionable parts), though in my mind some of them are capital ones. (1) [19]

Despite what he said in this letter, his objections were quite numerous, as we shall see by examining his broadside entitled *The Objections to the Proposed Federal Constitution* (1787). In the first place, he objected to the absence of a "declaration of rights" in the Constitution. Apparently, he was much concerned for state rights, because he argues that "the laws of the general government being paramount to the laws and constitution of the several states, the declaration of rights in the separate states, are no security" (324). He also objected to the fact that "enjoyment of the benefit of the common law" was not secured to the people (329). He objected, too, that the House of Representatives had "but the shadow only of representation" in contrast to the Senate, which had "power of altering all money bills, and originating appropriations of money" and the salaries of officers appointed, "in conjunction with the President of the United States—although they are not the representatives of the people, or amenable to them" (329). He feared that these, along with other great powers the Senate held, would destroy the balance of government "and enable them [the President and the Senate] to accomplish what usurpations they please, upon the rights and liberties of the people" (329). Furthermore, he thought that the judiciary under the new Constitution was "so constructed and extended, as to absorb and destroy the judiciaries of the several states; thereby rendering laws as tedious, intricate, and expensive, and justice as unattainable by a great part of the community, as in England; and enabling the rich to oppress the poor" (329–30). He also objected to the president's having no council, or cabinet, a situation which might lead to his becoming a "tool to the Senate" (330). Improper powers of appointment being thus lodged in the Senate, Mason worried that "an alarming dependence between that branch of the legislature and the supreme executive" might result. Moreover, he judged the office of vice-president as extraneous— Mason actually refers to the vice-president as "that unnecessary officer"—claiming that the fact that he presided over the Senate again "dangerously" blended "the executive and legislative powers." In addition, it tended to give one state "an unnecessary and unjust pre-eminence over the others" (330).[20]

Among the other matters which Mason objected to were these: the president's "unrestrained power of granting pardon for treason" (330); the House of Representatives' lack of control over the making of foreign treaties; the simple majority vote (instead of a two-third's vote) in the making of commercial and navigation laws, which gave the northern and eastern merchants and manufacturers an advantage over the primarily agricultural southern states (331); the state legislatures' lack of security for the people's rights against Congress's power to grant trade monopolies, "constitute new crimes, inflict unusual and severe punishments, and extend their power as far as they shall think proper" (331); the failure to specify liberty of the press, "trial by jury in civil cases," and "the danger of standing armies in time of peace" (330); state legislatures' being "restrained from laying export duties on their own produce" (331); the failure to prohibit "further importation of slaves for twenty-odd years, though such importations render the United States weaker, more vulnerable, and less capable of defence" (331); the prohibition upon the making of *ex post facto* laws (331–32).[21]

Mason then concluded his extensive list of objections with this gloomy prediction:

This government will commence in a moderate aristocracy; it is at present impossible to foresee whether it will, in its operation, produce a monarchy, or a corrupt oppressive aristocracy; it will most probably vibrate between the two, and then terminate in the one or the other. (6)

These objections of Mason were answered in cursory form by Madison in a letter to Washington (October 18, 1787). Iredell gave a more elaborate answer.[22] It goes without saying that most of Mason's objections were important. Although he objected to the Constitution in its first form, his own thinking eventually became so much a part of it—the most important part of it—that every American must be indebted to him for helping to insure some of our most fundamental rights.

V *Other Writers on the Constitution*

As one might expect, a whole host of other writers expressed themselves on the merits or disadvantages of the Constitution in the years 1787–88. Usually writers were either strongly *pro* or definitely *contra* in their positions with respect to the Constitution, and this led to the formation of themselves and their readers into the two earliest of our political parties—the Federalists (who supported the Constitution) and the Anti-Federalists (who resisted it).

Among the resisters perhaps the chief was Richard Henry Lee, whose *Letters from the Federal Farmer* (1787) accused the new government of being undemocratic, because it subordinated the majority to minority control. (As a United States Senator, Lee subsequently helped pass the Bill of Rights and himself introduced the tenth or "states rights" amendment.) Elbridge Gerry, who was later to become vice-president under Madison, objected strongly to eighteen specific points (which were later remedied by the Bill of Rights) in his *Observations on the New Constitution* ([Boston], 1788). Perhaps the strongest of these was his general feeling that it would lead to "an immediate tyranny," and end in "the most *uncontrolled despotism.*" George Clinton, first Governor of New York, wrote seven letters in the *New York Journal* under the pseudonym of Cato, objecting that the large states (like New York) would not have adequate representation. This view was answered by Hamilton's "Caesar" letters, which appeared in the *New York Daily Advertiser.*[23] Melancthon Smith was also an Anti-Federalist, although he later supported the Constitution. His *Address to the People of the State of New York By a Plebeian* (New York, 1788) assumed in its first sentence that the "advocates for the proposed new constitution" had already been "beaten off the field." He argued that some of the powers granted were dangerous, others not well defined, and the whole document much in need of amendment. Edmund Randolph wrote a *Letter on the Federal Constitution* (Richmond, 1787) in which he objected that it did not "shield against foreign hostility" or "domestic commotion." Nor would it promote trade and prosperity to his satisfaction (see Ford, p. 261).

The Federalist writers were naturally more numerous. We have

already alluded to James Iredell's *Answers to Mr. Mason's
Objections to the New Constitution by Marcus* (New Bern, N.C.,
1788). John Dickinson wrote a series of nine letters (*The Letters of
Fabius*) published "in the beginning of the Year 1788," according to
his own account, in separate newspapers.[24] Noah Webster wrote *An
Examination into the Leading Principles of the Constitution*
(Philadelphia, 1787). Pelatiah Webster also supported the plan for
the new government by refuting Anti-Federalist objections. See his
*Remarks on the Address of Sixteen Members of the Assembly of
Pennsylvania to their Constitutents dated September 29, 1787*
(1787) and *The Weakness of Brutus Exposed* (Philadelphia, 1787).[25]
Alexander Contee Hanson is supposedly the author of a work
entitled *Remarks on the Proposed Plan of a Federal Government,
Addressed to the Citizens of the United States of America, and
Particularly to the People of Maryland, by Aristides* (Annapolis,
[1788]), which favored adoption of the Constitution.[26]

David Ramsay, physician and historian and good friend of
Benjamin Rush, wrote at least two works defending the Constitution—*An Address to the Freemen of South-Carolina on the
. . . Constitution* (1788) and *A Dissertation on the Manner of the
Acquiring the Character and Privileges of a Citizen of the United
States* (1789).[27] This latter work is certainly of more importance than
it has been accorded. "The United States are a new nation,"
declares Ramsay, apparently after the ratification. He lists and
discusses five ways by which citizenship could be gained: 1. by
signature of the Declaration of Independence; 2. by an oath of
fidelity "agreeably to law"; 3. by tacit consent or acquiescence; 4. by
birth or inheritance (after 1763); 5. by adoption. Ramsay held a very
dignified notion of *citizenship*: "In the eye of reason and philosophy," he writes, "the political condition of citizenship is more
exalted than that of noblemen. Dukes and earls are the creatures of
kings, and can be made by them at pleasure; but citizens possess in
their own right original sovereignty" (1). In addition, Ramsay
refutes several Anti-Federalist objections to the Constitution and
advances several positive arguments for its adoption, one of which
was the advantage of a common currency for all thirteen states (5).

George Minot was also a Federalist. In his office of secretary for
the ratifying convention of Massachusetts, he played an important
part. He also wrote *Thoughts upon the Political Situation of the
United States of America* (1788), no mere pamphlet, but a book of
over 200 pages.[28]

Eventually, this great diversity of views about the Constitution resulted in the formation of two fairly clear political parties— Federalists (headed by Alexander Hamilton) and Republicans (whom Hamilton derogatorily called "Anti-Federalists," but who really were the followers of Jefferson, some of whom, like Madison, for example, had strongly supported the adoption of the Constitution.) The bitter clashes of these two conflicting parties, which (some think) almost destroyed the newly founded government, will be the subject of our final chapter.

CHAPTER 7

The Federalist Decade

I A Debate in the Senate

ALMOST from the beginning in the Senate, debates flared up which showed clearly the emergence of distinctly different points of view, which later developed into two political parties. Senator William Maclay, a representative of rural Pennsylvania, kept a vivid record of the debate in the early sessions. The entry in his *Journal* [1] for May 8, 1789 (apropos of a proper title for George Washington) reads as follows:

Mr. Elsworth moved for the report . . . on the subject of titles. . . . Mr. Lee led the business. He took his old ground—all the world, civilized and savage, called for titles; that there must be something in human nature that occasioned this general consent; that, therefore, he conceived it was right. Here he began to enumerate many nations who gave titles—such as Venice, Genoa, and others. The Greeks and Romans, it was said, had no titles, "but" (making a profound bow to the Chair [occupied by John Adams] "you were pleased to set us right in this with respect to the Conscript Fathers the other day." Here he repeated the Vice-President's speech of the 23d ultime [April], almost verbatim all over.

Mr. Ellsworth rose. He had a paper in his hat, which he looked constantly at. He repeated almost all that Mr. Lee had said, but got on the subject of kings—declared that the sentence in the primer *fear God and honor the king* was of great importance; that kings were of divine appointment; that Saul, the head and shoulders taller than the rest of the people, was elected by God and anointed by his appointment.

I sat, after he had done, for a considerable time, to see if anybody would rise. At last I got up and first answered Lee as well as I could with nearly the same arguments drawn from the Constitution, as I had used on the 23d ult. . . .

Izard got up. He dwelt almost entirely on the antiquity of kingly government. He could not, however, well get further back than Philip of Macedon. He seemed to have forgot both Homer and the Bible. He urged for something equivalent to nobility having been common among the

Romans, for they had three names that seemed to answer to honorable, or something like it, before and something behind. He did not say Esquire. Mr. Carrol rose and took my side of the question. . . . He spoke against kings. Mr. Lee and Mr. Izard were both up again. Ellsworth was up again. Langdon was up several times, but spoke short each time. Patterson was up, but there was no knowing which side he was of. . . . The Vice-President repeatedly helped the speakers for titles. Ellsworth was enumerating how common the appelation of President was. The Vice-President put him in mind that there were presidents of fire companies and of a cricket club. . . .

I collected myself for a last effort. I read the clause in the Constitution against titles of nobility; showed that the spirit of it was against not only granting titles by Congress, but against the permission of foreign potentates granting *any titles whatever*; that as to kingly government, it was equally out of the question . . . that they were both equally forbidden fruit of the Constitution.

. . . .

. . . "Excellency" was moved for as a title by Mr. Izard. It was withdrawn by Mr. Izard, and "highness" with some prefatory word, proposed by Mr. Lee. Now long harangues were made in favor of this title. "Elective" was placed before. It was insisted that such a dignified title would add greatly to the weight and authority of the Government both at home and abroad. I declared myself totally of a different opinion; that at present it was impossible to add to the respect entertained for General Washington. . . .

But I will minute no more. The debate lasted till half after three o'clock, and it ended in appointing a committee to consider of a title to be given to the President. This whole silly business is the work of Mr. Adams and Mr. Lee; Izard follows Lee, and the New England men, who always herd together, follow Mr. Adams. . . . for a court our House seems determined on, and to run into all the fooleries, fopperies, fineries, and pomp of royal etiquette; and all this for Mr. Adams. . . .

May 9th. . . . At length the committee came in and reported a title—*His Highness the President of the United States of America and Protector of the Rights of the Same.* Mr. Few had spoken a word or two with me, and signified his unwillingness to do anything hastily. He got up and spoke a great deal against hasty measures. . . .

I got up and expressed my opinion that what had fallen from the honorable gentleman from Georgia amounted to a motion for postponement, and asked leave to second him. . . . I could now see a visible anxiety in the Chair.

I had a fine, slack, and easy time of it to-day. . . .

Mr. Izard got up at last. He, too, was for a postponement. I could see the Vice-President kindled at him. . . . The members fixed themselves, and the question was called for.

Up now got the Vice-President, and for forty minutes did he harangue us from the chair. He began first on the subject of order, and found fault with everything almost, but down he came to particulars, and pointedly blamed a member for disorderly behavior. . . . The member he meant was Mr. Izard. All this was only prefatory. On he got to his favorite topic of titles, and ever the old ground of the immense advantage of, the absolute necessity of them. . . .

....

I rose. Mr. President, the Constitution of the United States has designated our Chief Magistrate by the appelation of the *President of the United States of America*. This is his title of office, nor can we alter, add to, or diminish it without infringing the Constitution. . . . As to grades of order or titles of nobility, nothing of the kind can be established by Congress.

Can, then, the President and Senate do that which is prohibited to the United States at large? Certainly not. Let us read the Constitution: *No title of nobility shall be granted by the United States*. The Constitution goes further. The servants of the public are prohibited from accepting them from any foreign state, king, or prince.

As we shall see, this extended debate over John Adams's endeavor to confer an appropriate title on the leader of the new government ultimately eventuated in what his political enemies referred to as his attempt to renew monarchy and royalty. (See, for example, Freneau's satiric poem "Stanzas to an Alien," published in 1799.) Earlier, much earlier, young Benjamin Franklin had remonstrated against the use of English titles. In the *New England Courant* for February 18, 1723, we read:

In old Time it was no disrespect for Men and Women to be call'd by their own Names: Adam was never called *Master* Adam; we never read of Noah *Esquire*, Lot *Knight* and *Baronet*, nor the *Right Honourable* Abraham, *Viscount* Mesopotamia, Baron of Carran; no, no, they were plain Men. . . . It was no Incivility then to mention their naked Names as they were expressed.[2]

Democratic sentiment against the use of titles in America thus had a long history. At issue in the Senate debate, however, as Maclay states, was the following sentence in the recently adopted *Constitution*: "No title of nobility shall be granted by the United States." In a sense, then, the debate was a highly important, early "test case" of the constitution between those who desired rigid enforcement of the principle of political equality and those who, for whatever reasons of gentility or decorum, were willing to take a more relaxed view.

II   *The French Revolution*

A. *John Adams*

John Adams's admiration for, and his attempt to imitate to some degree, English constitutional government provoked the above unflattering portrait of him by Senator Maclay. In a series of thirty-two letters to John Fenno's *Gazette of the United States* (1789–90) Adams contributed to his further unpopularity and that of his conservative Federalist party. These letters were published in a collected edition in 1791 under the title of *Discourses of Davila*. The letters, particularly the last in the series, so aroused Jefferson and his followers that they helped solidify the opposition to Adams (and Hamilton) under a new party name—the Republicans (a liberal group having no connection with the present-day Republican party, but rather a group which the present Democratic party claims as its ancestor).

Although Adams himself apparently thought of these *Discourses* as his fourth volume of the *Defence of the Constitutions of the United States*, they also show some of his reactions to the French Revolution, an event which for the entire last decade of the eighteenth century was to affect the course of party politics in America. (As one historian has pointed out, it was repulsion from Adams and Hamilton's admiration for the British Constitution, rather than any special attraction to France, which led Jefferson "to regard the French alliance as his polar star.") [3] The *Discourses of Davila* consist mainly of translations from Enrico Caterino Davila's *History of the Civil Wars of France*, which raged during the sixteenth century. [4] In addition, the *Discourses* present Adams's reflections on human nature, as related to politics, much of which (in the ninth paper) was drawn from Adam Smith's *Theory of the Moral Sentiments*. [5]

In most of the first four discourses Adams argues that man is driven by the desire for attention from his fellow beings and will do almost anything to satisfy this desire. "The poor man's conscience is clear; yet he is ashamed. His character is irreproachable; yet he is neglected and despised. . . . Mankind takes no notice of him" (183). But "riches attract the attention, consideration, and congratulations of mankind; it is not because the rich have really more of ease and pleasure than the poor. Riches force the opinion on a man that he is the object of the congratulations of others . . ." (182). Adams admits that "there is a voice within us which seems to intimate that real merit should govern the world, and that men ought to be respected only in proportion to their talents, virtues, and services. But the question always has been, how can this arrangement be accomplished? How shall the man of merit be discovered?" (185). "Real merit," he goes on to say, is often "remote from the knowledge of whole nations. . . ." "Nations, perceiving that the still small voice of merit was drowned in the insolent roar . . . of impudence and knavery in national elections without a possibility of remedy, have sought for something more permanent than the popular voice to designate honor" (186). This attempt led historically to the rise of a class of nobles (or aristocracy) during the feudal period. This leads Adams to restate one of his favorite principles of government—the need to control the aristocracy. According to Adams, such control could proceed effectively only by several groups—church, kings, and common people (188).

But if the common people are advised to aim at collecting the whole sovereignty in single national assemblies, as they are by the Duke de la Rochefoucauld and the Marquis of Condorcet, or at the abolition of the regal executive authority, or at a division of the executive power, as they are by a posthumous publication of the Abbé de Mably—they will fail of their desired liberty as certainly as emulation and rivalry are founded in human nature and inseparable from civil affairs. . . . And if a balance of passions and interests is not scientifically concerted, the present struggle in Europe [the French Revolution] will be little beneficial to mankind and produce nothing but another thousand years of feudal fanaticism under new and strange names. (188)

Adams urges, further, that the increase of knowledge among the intellectual classes makes more necessary than ever the system of checks and balances he favors. "Bad men increase in knowledge as fast as good men," he writes, "and science, arts, taste, sense, and letters are employed for the purposes of injustice and tyranny as well as those of law and liberty, for corruption as well as virtue" (190). Then, in a ringing rhetorical passage he directly addresses the French nation:

FRENCHMEN! Act and think like yourselves! confessing human nature, be magnanimous and wise . . . avow the feelings of men. The affectation of being exempted from passions is inhuman. . . . Consider that government is intended to set bounds to passions which nature has not limited; and to assist reason, conscience, justice, and truth in controlling interest which without it would be as unjust as uncontrollable. (190–91)

Turning at this point to his own nation, Adams writes, "AMER-ICANS! . . . In a well-balanced government, reason, conscience, truth and virtue must be respected by all parties for the public good" (191).

B. *Thomas Paine*

The reactions of professional revolutionist Tom Paine to the French Revolution were decidedly different from those of conservative John Adams. They took the form of Paine's longest written work, *The Rights of Man* (London, 1791), part one of which is dedicated to George Washington.[6] In this work Paine answered Burke's *Reflections on the French Revolution* (November 1, 1790), in which Burke had attacked Dr. Richard Price's sermon of the previous November 4, a sermon which made three points—*viz.*, that the English people had the right to choose their own governors, "to cashier them for misconduct," and to frame a government.[7] Burke had argued that two acts of Parliament during the reign of William and Mary bound the English people *forever* to obey the throne and that the same obedience applied in the case of the common people to the king of France. To this main argument of Burke, Paine retorted:

There never did, there never will, and there never can exist a Parliament, or any description of men, or any generation of men in any country, possessed of the right or the power of binding and controlling posterity to the "end of time," of commanding forever how the world shall be governed or who shall govern it; and therefore all such clauses . . . are in themselves null and void.

Every age and generation must be free to act for itself, *in all cases*, as the ages and generations which preceded it. The vanity and presumption of governing beyond the grave is the most ridiculous and insolent of all tyrannies. (I, 251)

Paine's ensuing arguments in part one are more detailed and rest on the natural rights theory. He also takes note of the new French constitution, which had abolished titles and, indeed, the whole class of the so-called aristocracy. "Titles," he remarks, "are like circles drawn by the magician's wand to contract the sphere of man's felicity. He lives immured within the Bastile of a word and surveys at a distance the envied life of man" (I, 287). Part one also contains the famous seventeen-point *Declaration of the Rights of Man*, passed by the French National Assembly, and Paine's "observations" on them (I, 313–17). Part two, dedicated to Lafayette, is less a reply to Burke than an exposition of Paine's own political principles. It contains an extensive comparison between the "English and French Constitutions." Part three, addressed to the English people, demands that they call a national assembly and form a republic. It resulted in Paine's being outlawed and his effigy being burned throughout England.

John Quincy Adams replied to Paine's *Rights of Man* with a series of eleven letters in *The Columbian Centinel* (June 8 to July 27, 1791).[8] These letters were written over the signature of "Publicola." John Quincy Adams, needless to say, was a Federalist.

At least two other important works of Tom Paine stem from the French Revolution, in which he took so active a part—*The Age of Reason* (part 1, 1794; part 2, 1796), the classic exposition on Deism and a defense of the French abolition of a national priesthood (and church), and his *Dissertation on the First Principles of Government* (Paris, 1795), which contains much of his most important political thought.[9] In the first part of this latter document Paine refutes hereditary systems of government; in the second, he defends representative government as right and proper. Many of his arguments in part two attack the aristocracy. The third, very brief part consists of "some observations on the means of *preserving liberty*" (II, 587). He justifies insurrections as means to overthrow despotism, asserts that the moral principle of revolutions is to instruct, not to destroy, and finally sees a constitution as necessary to "*prevent governing by party*" (II, 587–88).

Paine's last important work which falls in the period under discussion, *Agrarian Justice* (Paris, 1797), resulted from the conspiracy of Babeuf, a French Agrarian leader, whose movement for reform was crushed in May 1796.[10] In this work Paine presents a socialistic argument for "Improving the Condition of the Unpropertied." [11] Whatever one may think of the practical details of this socialistic plan to remedy economic injustice, there is much appeal in the fundamental premise on which it rests—that "the earth, in its natural uncultivated state," is the "COMMON PROPERTY OF THE HUMAN RACE." [12] As a consequence of this premise, according to *Agrarian Justice*, every human being born is heir to some property, either in land or other capital. The principal cause of poverty, according to Paine, is the dispossession among the numerous poor of this "natural inheritance" through a "landed monopoly" owned by the rich few. Thus he argues for property restitution to the poor as a *right*, rather than a *charity*. In his own words such restitution would amount not to "bounty but justice" (I, 617).

We might summarize our discussion of these works in terms of their aims, each being directed at a different form of tyranny. In the *Rights of Man* Paine aimed to free the English as well as the French—in fact, all men—from the tyranny of despotic government by a hereditary aristocracy. (This freedom he would achieve, as he explained in his *Dissertation on the First Principles of Government*, even by violence if necessary.) In *The Age of Reason*, which really was an educational work, he aimed at a different phase of freedom, freedom from the tyranny of a powerful wing of the government, the state church, which in America, England, and France had tended, in his view, to enslave the mind of man by means of the age-old devices of hearsay evidence (revelation), mystery, miracle, and prophecy. Here Paine's war on tyranny takes a somewhat paradoxical turn, invading the privacy of an individual's thinking and often emotionalized religious beliefs for the purpose of persuading that individual not to follow other "invaders," or enslavers, of his inner thoughts—specifically, the doctrines of the state church and the anti-Deistic dogmas found in the Bible. *Agrarian Justice* further extends the range of Paine's thinking, in that it represents an attempt to correct a third, totally different form of tyranny—that of economic injustice—of the few rich over the poor many. (Needless to say, this last marks a very significant development in government theory, one that has had such important consequences in the twentieth century as the efforts of governments, acting both individually and collectively, to battle poverty conditions throughout the world.) It is worth noting, finally, that in each case the natural-rights theory serves as a basis for the highly individualized turn of the argument. According to Paine's view of this theory, political liberty, once achieved, would be best preserved by constitutional means.

C. *Joel Barlow*

Concerning Joel Barlow, John Adams once wrote, "Tom Paine is not a more worthless fellow." [13] Parrington tells us, however, that Barlow's *Advice to the Privileged Orders* was eulogized by Fox in the House of Commons and suppressed by the Pitt ministry. [14] Like Paine, Barlow went into hiding in England when he was proscribed. Like Paine, he was made an honorary French citizen because of his active part in the French Revolution. Like Paine again, he wrote probably some of the best and most extensively read political rhetoric of the decade.[15]

Barlow's *Advice* is certainly a work of major political importance by any standards. His purpose, as stated in the introduction, is to examine "the nature and consequences of a similar revolution [to that of the French Revolution] in government, as it will affect the following objects, which make up the affairs of nations in the present state of Europe:

I.   The feudal System,
II.   The Church,
III. The Military,
IV.   The Administration of Justice. . . ." (3–4) [16]

These are the four "privileged orders" referred to in the title. Barlow assures the reader that "the interest of kings and hereditary succession will not be forgotten in this arrangement; they will be treated with the privileged orders under the several heads to which their different claims belong" (4). In a rather grim footnote to his outline, he adds, "It must be of vast importance to all the classes of society, as it now stands classed in Europe, to calculate before hand what they are to gain or to lose by the approaching change [revolution]; that, like prudent stock-jobbers, they may buy in or sell out, according as this great event shall affect them" (5). It is obvious from this statement that for him, at least, the American Revolution, and, indeed, the French Revolution, were only the opening shots of a more comprehensive, world-wide revolution, the revolution against monarchy in favor of republican government.[17]

How, asks Barlow, will the privileged orders (aristocracy, clergy, military, and judiciary) "be affected by the new order of things" (6)? Admitting that he has a Herculean task, he nevertheless hopes to persuade "those who now live by abuses" that the "new order" will be "less injurious" to them "than is commonly imagined" (7). Barlow plainly thinks of the French Revolution as basically *rational*, for he writes that "it is the work of argument and rational conviction . . . an operation designed for the benefit of the people; it originated in the people, and was conducted by the people" (3). He even argues that in point of "indiscriminate ferocity and private plunder" French mobs were less dangerous than English mobs.

A popular commotion in Paris was uniformly directed to a certain well-explained object; from which it never was known to deviate. Whether this object were to hang a man, to arrest the king, to intimidate the court, or to break the furniture of a hotel, all other persons and all other property, that fell in the way of the mob, were perfectly safe. (8)

Taking it for granted that a general revolution is at hand "whose progress is irresistible," he writes, "My object is to contemplate its probable effects, and to comfort those who are afflicted at the prospect" (120).

Barlow attacks the feudal system for swelling "the inequality of wealth," habituating the people "to believe in an unnatural inequality in the rights of men, and by this means prepar[ing] them for servility and oppression." The feudal system also prevented the "improvement of lands," impeded "the progress of industry and cultivation, which are best promoted on small estates, where proprietors cultivate for themselves," and discouraged the growth of population (then thought to be a good thing) "by inducing a life of celibacy" (among the clergy) (26). By destroying the feudalistic institutions of *primogeniture* and *entail* and by adding the freedom of the press, a people might ensure "the continuance of liberty in any country where it is once established" (42).

In his second chapter Barlow attacks the state church, which appears to him "like a giant, stalking over society, and wielding the sword of slaughter; but . . . likewise perform[ing] the office of silent disease and of unperceived decay." To him it seems "a canker corroding the vitals of the moral world, and debasing all that is noble in man" (57).

In his third chapter, dealing with the military, he attacks standing armies and offensive wars. He argues that from Roman times there has never been "what may properly be called a *popular* offensive war; I mean a war that would have been undertaken by the people, had they enjoyed a free government, so organized as to have enabled them to deliberate before they acted, and to suffer nothing to be carried into execution but the national will" (86). He also argues that the rise of "free" governments will lead to greater ease in settling territorial disputes, which he considers a frequent cause of wars (99).

In many ways, Barlow's fourth chapter, in which he takes the judiciary to task, is the most interesting. "It may be safely pronounced," he writes here, *"that a state has no right to punish a man, to whom it has given no previous instruction. . . ."* (108) What did Barlow mean by *instruction?*

Knowledge is a part of the stock of society; and an indispensable part to be allotted in the portion of the claimant, is *instruction* relative to the new arrangement of natural right [brought about by changes in society]. To withhold this instruction therefore would be, not merely the omission of a duty, but the commission of a crime; and society in this case would sin against the man, before the man could sin against society. (112)

He carries this point even further, arguing that

In some cases where a person is born of poor parents, or finds himself brought into the community of men without the means of subsistence, society is bound in duty to furnish him the means. She ought not only to instruct him in the artificial laws by which property is secured, but in the artificial industry by which it is obtained. She is bound, in justice as well as policy, to give him some art or trade. For the reason of his incapacity is, that *she* has usurped his birthright; and this is restoring it to him in another form, more convenient for both parties. The failure of society in this branch of her duty, is the occasion of much the greater part of the evils that call for criminal jurisprudence. The individual feels that he is robbed of his natural right; he cannot bring his process to reclaim it from the great community, by which he is overpowered; he therefore feels authorized in reprisal; in taking another's goods to replace his own. And it must be confessed, that in numberless instances the conduct of society justifies him in this proceeding; she has seized upon his property, and commenced the war against him. (112–13)

Having thus analyzed what he believes to be the basic causes of crime, Barlow then presents by way of illustration a typical law case, in which he sees only *fees* and *oppression* as the purpose of the law (143). He therefore urges legal reform (147).

D.   *Other Writers—Gouverneur Morris, Noah Webster,* et al.

There were, of course many other American writers of this period who commented on the French Revolution. The Federalists, as we have already seen in the case of John Adams, naturally took quite a different view from that of Paine and Barlow—Noah Webster, for example, in *The Revolution in France* (New York, 1794). Gouverneur Morris in his *Diary of the French Revolution* (not published until 1938) took at times a cynical attitude toward the new democracy.

Others, like Theodore Dwight (also a vehement Federalist) in his *Oration Spoken before the Connecticut Society of the Cincinnati* (July 4, 1792), saw—at least momentarily—the French Revolution as bringing freedom to 20 million Frenchmen and credited the French chapter of the Cincinnati with the success of this event (see pp. 11–12). To the two principal leaders of the Federalist party, however, the French Revolution was something to be feared.

III   *The Bank Question and the Challenge to the "Paper Aristocracy"*

A.   *Alexander Hamilton*

Although he and John Adams often saw eye-to-eye on the dangers of the French Revolution and on matters of money and politics, Alexander Hamilton did not agree with Adams's *Discourses of Davila*. Crediting Adams with the best of intentions, he nevertheless thought these *Discourses* had "a tendency to weaken the present government," a government, incidentally, of which Hamilton did not really approve. (In a conversation with Jefferson he opted for the British form, although he was for giving the new American form a fair trial and did admit that its success thus far had exceeded his expectations.) [18] To Jefferson the *Discourses of Davila* and the *Defence of the Constitutions* were significant as indicating Adams's dangerous tendency towards hereditary monarchy. Indeed, their political importance lay in the fact that they were generally interpreted in this way. [19] The paths of these three men now began to diverge rather sharply.

Fearing the French and believing that the American government therefore needed strengthening, Hamilton revived his plan for a national bank, which he had written about earlier in a letter during the year 1779. [20] As Secretary of the Treasury, Hamilton had also outlined in his *First Report on Public Credit*, dated January 9, 1790, the means he proposed for strengthening the government—as one writer puts it, "buttressing the government by enlisting the moneyed classes in its support." [21] More specifically, he wanted to consolidate the numerous state debts into one large public or national debt and to pay it off by means of taxes and a sinking fund. [22] Putting the government on a sounder fiscal policy, he writes, would serve various purposes: it would restore the value of landed property and furnish new resources to agriculture and commerce, but, above all, it would cement the union of the states more closely, thus offering greater security against the French and other possible foreign attacks. Among these different proposals for stiffening the central government, his idea of a national bank loomed largest.

Differences with Jefferson and Edmund Randolph in Washington's cabinet had led Hamilton to put his views on the bank in writing. In a work entitled *The Argument of the Secretary of the Treasury upon the Constitutionality of a National Bank*, dated Philadelphia, February 23, 1791, he explains his differences with the Secretary of State (Jefferson) and the Attorney General (Randolph) at "the order of the President." [23] First he states his basic premise—that "every power vested in a government, is in its Nature SOVEREIGN, and includes by *force* of the *term*, a right to employ all the means requisite, and fairly applicable, to the attainment of the ends of such power and which are not precluded by restrictions and exceptions specified in the constitution" (4). Then he states the question and clarifies his position on it: "Whether the United States have the power to *erect* a corporation; that is to say to give a legal or certified capacity to one or more persons, distinct from the natural? For it is unquestionably incident to sovereign power to erect corporations; and, consequently, to that of the United States, in relation to the objects intrusted to the management of the government" (5). He then argues that the power to erect corporations is "implied" in the Constitution (7). The question he next faces then becomes whether any of the so-called "implied" powers violated "acknowledged objects or lawful ends" of the government. Here he supplies an interesting example. Imagine, he asks the reader, Congress setting up a special police force to superintend Philadelphia. This would violate the constitution, he says. But, he adds, a police force "may be erected [by Congress] in relation to the collection of taxes, or to the trade with foreign countries, or to the trade between the States, or with the Indian tribes; because it is the province of the federal government to regulate these objects. . .because it is incident to a general *sovereign* or *legislative* power to regulate a thing, to employ all the means which relate to its regulation to the best and greatest advantage" (7). For Hamilton a corporation is not "some independent substantive thing, as a political engine, and of peculiar magnitude and moment . . ." but "a means to an end" (7). And he concludes that the end to which his bank proposal relates comes within the specified powers of the Constitution and is "not forbidden by any particular provision of the constitution" (13). From here on he attacks Jefferson's objections—that the bank as a corporation violated state laws, the law against monopoly, etc. (13–17). He also tries to refute Randolph's objections (17–24), arguing against Randolph that the congressional power to create corporations was even included under at least one of the *express* powers (that governing jurisdiction in a ten-mile radius of the capital) as well as under those *implied*. Finally, he outlines his plan for the bank in detail, again stressing that, *"politically* speaking," the bank is necessary to carrying out the *powers* of government, particularly the powers of collecting taxes, borrowing money, regulating trade between the states, and raising and maintaining fleets and armies (25).

On December 5, 1791, Hamilton issued his third and possibly most important statement on fiscal policy. Since this long document, *Report on Manufactures*, has been well analyzed by other writers,[24] I shall present only a few of its ideas.

In the *Report* Hamilton encourages manufactures, on the theory that their increase will contribute to the security and economic development of the country. "Not only the wealth," he writes, "but the independence and security of a country appear to be materially connected with the prosperity of manufactures." (He uses some of Adam Smith's ideas, especially that of division of labor.) Departing from the orthodox economic theory of Quesnay and the physiocrats that agriculture was the "most beneficial and productive object of human industry," i.e., the true source of a nation's wealth, he argues instead for a system of manufactures based on protective tariffs, rewards and fines, and encouragement of inventions. He would set up a board of commissioners to oversee and promote "arts, agriculture, manufactures, and commerce." As Prescott says, this report was extremely important in that it "contains the germ of our protective system, our Department of Commerce, and our economic commissions."[25] But it and the other two documents we have been considering are important in yet another way, as we shall see in reviewing John Taylor of Caroline's reactions to them.

B. *John Taylor of Caroline*

John Taylor of Caroline (a county in eastern Virginia) is best remembered today as the leading theorist on Jeffersonian democracy, agrarianism, and states' rights. He lived from 1753 to 1824. During the years 1792–1794 while serving as United States Senator he reacted violently against Hamilton's money policies, especially to taxes clogging the circulation of newspapers and to secret legislative sessions at which some of these policies were instituted. " 'Tis the right and the duty of a free people to watch attentively the movements of every department of public trust," he writes in *An Examination of the Late Proceedings in Congress, Respecting the Official Conduct of the Secretary of the Treasury* (March 8, 1793).[26] " 'Tis particularly their duty to watch attentively the conduct of the legislature" (3).

Taylor objected specifically to the enormous financial power Hamilton had gained from Congress to pay off the national debt by raising taxes, controlling the sinking fund, and administering the new federal bank. He writes: "It has depended on the Secretary to say when money could or could not be furnished for the sinking fund, out of the funds appropriated for the purpose, and even out of monies borrowed for and legally available for the purpose" (7). In Taylor's view Hamilton was like a great landlord and "man of revenue" presiding over innumerable tenants or ordinary citizens, especially *farmers*. To Taylor, Hamilton and his followers (in Congress and in the banks) represented a "ministerial" faction "leagued together upon principles to a certain degree hostile to the community" (8). " 'Tis the first principle of a free government that those who impose the tax should feel the effect," he writes, but in this case the Hamilton faction has "not only violated, but reversed" the rule (9).

He draws up a list of charges against Hamilton's mishandling of a loan from France and Holland. In his opinion Hamilton had violated both the law and the president's instructions by borrowing for the sinking fund $1 million more than authorized, had lost interest money due the United States, had borrowed from the national bank "when there was no occasion for such loans," had violated faith with France by not paying back the proper amounts at times stipulated, and had done all this without the knowledge of Congress and the president (20–22). In trying to discover a motive for this terrible misuse of funds, Taylor finds himself at a loss to understand Hamilton's action. The money in question would, if it had been paid back properly, have helped the French "to repel the invasion under the Duke of Brunswick" (23). (Hamilton was, of course, anti-French in his sympathies.) Taylor can only infer that the misapplied money was "intended solely to aid the bank here" and the political associates of Hamilton who were "speculators" (23–24). He therefore claims that the Hamilton faction is "undermining the great pillars of the government, in express violation of its powers, and [is] capable, as an engine of corruption, of sapping the foundation of public virtue, and polluting all its measures . . ." (27).

The hard core of this faction, according to Taylor, was twenty-one members (of the thirty-five-member House) who were at that time stockholders in the bank (36n). It was this group, along with the Secretary of Treasury, that constituted, for Taylor, "a powerful faction, in two departments of the government," a very great danger to the "rights and interests of the community" (27).

In *A Definition of Parties: Political Effects of the Paper System Considered* (1794) Taylor consequently portrays the American nation in a desperate condition, "the national good struggling for life, under the grasp of . . . [Hamilton's] interested junto."[27] At this time, he points out, the population of the United States was 5 million. These 5 million were dominated by Hamilton's faction, or junto, who in the aggregate, counting those outside Congress, amounted to an estimated total of 5,000. He then asks, "Did the constitution intend to produce a government, chiefly upon the will of numbers or upon the will of wealth?" "Obviously the former," he replies in answer to his own question. It was Taylor's deepest conviction that Hamilton's money system, which he calls a "paper system," was the most glaring outrage ever perpetrated upon the American people, in so far as it usurped not only the *rights of man* but also the *rights of property* as the latter term was understood at the time of the constitutional convention. "Is this a government of numbers?" he asks. "No—Of property in general?—No—It is a government of paper."

Paper is *in fact* the only representative, both of numbers and of property, bestowed by a faction upon itself, for the purpose of transferring to itself, the property of others. An effect which never would have been intended by the Constitution, consigning to that instrument, the guardianship either of the rights of men, or of property. . . . Will the great majority of the people . . . sell their birth-right for a mess of paper, into which they themselves have been cooked; but of which they can never taste? (6)

After listing the various bad effects of this government by a paper system, prominent among which was its dispensing "*unequal wealth*" instead of "*public welfare*," he argues that *land* rather than paper is "the most solid foundation for a government built on one species of property" (9).[28] Toward the end of this pamphlet he writes:

For the truth is, that a secretary of the treasury—an incorporated bank—and a funding system, constitute substantially a phalanx of privileged orders, if they can influence the legislature. The first will form the legislature, by the magic of private interest. The second is a successional body having exclusive rights and legislative weight, without election or representation—and the third is a mode of representation, equivalent to the rotten boroughs of England.

Accordingly, our privileged orders have openly sympathized with the privileged orders combined for the suppression of republicanism in France. . . . (16)

Taylor's conclusion? That the commonwealth cannot be safely entrusted to the hands of "such a faction" (16).

In *An Enquiry into the Principles and Tendencies of Certain Public Measures* (1794) Taylor "called upon agrarian America to mobilize against the menace of chartered banks, protective tariffs, and moneyed corporations." [29] These were the tools of the new "paper aristocracy" which were being used to exploit other classes. In later works he warns that unless corporations are checked they will "erect a new moneyed aristocracy" that will "sink America to the level of former aristocracies." [30]

The relevance of Taylor's work to our own times, an age characterized by national and international corporations and labor unions exerting enormous political and economic pressures on governments and individual citizens alike, seems obvious. In his own day Taylor was important in defining the agrarian ideal, a position that has often been identified with Jeffersonian democracy, in contrast to the Hamiltonian banking and manufacturing system supporting our entire industrial economy. The regional separation between these two traditions (South and North, respectively) persisted all through the nineteenth century, through the Civil War, and into the twentieth century, even to this day, and it gives a very special significance to these writings of Taylor and Hamilton.

IV *The Jay Treaty and the Whiskey Rebellion*

The Jay treaty with Great Britain in late 1794 evoked considerable response from proponents of the two parties under discussion.

In effect, it abrogated the treaty of alliance with France in 1778. Robert R. Livingston in his *Observations on Jay's Treaty* regarded it as tantamount to a war with France. Mathew Carey, a Philadelphia printer, friend of Benjamin Franklin, and strong Jeffersonian Republican, brought out in 1796 a collection of essays and speeches relating to this treaty—*The American Remembrancer* (Philadelphia, 1795–96). Carey also wrote other works on this event—see, for example, his *Address to the House of Representatives . . . on Lord Grenville's Treaty* (Philadelphia, 1796). Benjamin Bache, Franklin's grandson, leaked the treaty to the public, in his newspaper the *Aurora*. The outcry against Jay was immediate. And all was confusion. Jay himself observed that "he could have found his way across the country by the light of his burning effigies in which he was represented selling his country for British gold." [31]

Hamilton and Rufus King attempted to placate the aroused indignation of the country with a series of thirty-eight newspaper articles signed by "Camillus." [32] At approximately this same time Hamilton, despite his brilliance at financial measures, found himself in further serious trouble. His excise taxes on whiskey in western Pennsylvania had aroused so much resentment that they almost precipitated a civil war. Hugh Henry Brackenridge, a western Pennsylvanian himself and an ardent opponent of Hamilton, wrote a fairly unbiased account of this rebellion—*Incidents of the Insurrection in the Western Part of Pennsylvania, In the Year 1794* (Philadelphia, 1795). Earlier, Albert Gallatin, a strong Republican spokesman, had published a *Speech . . . in the House of Representatives . . . With Notes on the Western Insurrection* (Philadelphia, 1794).

The tumult of events triggered by the French Revolution, the failure of Genêt's mission, the division into two bitterly opposed political parties (brought on largely by Hamilton's money policies), the Whiskey Rebellion, and the Jay Treaty seemed to be leading the country down the perilous road to anarchy. No wonder, then, that when John Adams stepped into the presidential chair he felt the need to take a strong hand.

V   *The Alien and Sedition Acts*

By 1798 the events referred to above, along with the conflict between the two opposing parties, had reached such a degree of intensity that war with France was no longer merely talked about; it had begun. In the undeclared war of 1798 that followed the XYZ Affair (in which three agents of Talleyrand demanded a bribe as the price of a favorable treaty with France) more than eighty French armed ships were seized by American privateers and warships.[33] The harsh criticism of the American press, directed mainly at the conduct of the executive, at last became too much for John Adams and his Federalist party. As a consequence the Alien and Sedition Acts of 1798 were passed as a wartime necessity. According to these laws, all aliens were required to live fourteen years in the United States before becoming citizens, the president had the arbitrary power to remove from the country any alien considered dangerous to the nation, and false or malicious writings aimed at the president or his government were punishable by fine or imprisonment. The difficulty, of course, came in defining what was *false* or *malicious*. In reality, almost any criticism directed at these laws was considered punishable, and freedom of the press ceased to exist. These unjust laws further weakened the already seriously weakened Federalists, who had suffered a split between Hamilton and Adams. They also gave rise to a number of pamphlets and other writings, among which were the Kentucky and Virginia Resolutions, drafted respectively by Jefferson and Madison, two of Adams's strongest opponents.

Even before the passage of the Alien and Sedition laws John Dickinson had warned his countrymen of the increasing military power of France. In his second series of Fabius *Letters* (1797) (see *supra*) he equated France and Rome as military republics.[34] Still, Dickinson felt that there was less to fear from the new French republic than from its old hereditary rulers (106). In general, he defends the French in these letters, particularly in the twelfth letter, where he reminds his American readers that "FRENCH-MEN fought, bled, and died for us" (143). In an impassioned peroration in the fifteenth letter he writes that we owe our *"peace, liberty*, and *safety"* to France. "HEAVEN FORBID! that *American gratitude* should become a by-word among civilized nations to the latest ages, emphatically to describe that supremacy of depravity, which no other terms can fully define" (192).

Albert Gallatin, a Swiss-born immigrant and fellow Pennsylvanian of Dickinson, had also criticized the Federalists in a series of seventeen letters, under the title of *An Examination of the Conduct of the Executive of the United States, towards the French Republic* (Philadelphia, 1797). The purpose of these letters was to provide "an antidote to the circulating poison" of the "Administration," which had attempted to justify its conduct, "to criminate the French Republic, and to alienate the American affections from their friends and allies" (iii). Gallatin attacks Adams in the very first letter, but he also charges Washington with acting like a Roman pontiff by forming treaties independently of Congress, an action which Gallatin termed "usurpation" (39, 40). Moreover, Washington had, Gallatin claims, created a small Executive Council—consisting of the Secretaries of Treasury, State, and War and the Attorney General—to supplant the Senate's advisory power (42). The entire executive department was becoming more and more like a "Puppet Show" with the President playing the part of Punch and his department heads that of "Jugglers" (43). He calls Hamilton "the virtual President of the United States" and criticizes his monarchical tendencies visible in the Pacificus letters, which he rightly thought Hamilton had written.[35] He accuses the Federalists of breaking faith with Spain and the Indians. After drawing up a long list of particular abuses, he concludes, "I could swell the black catalogue of infractions to a size, which would perhaps appal the Executive himself . . ." (62).

Gallatin was a hard-hitting writer and an ardent Republican spokesman. At least one authority thinks that the Alien and Sedition Acts were partly aimed at him.[36] But they were certainly aimed at many others—including Benjamin Franklin Bache, whom the Federalists called "Lightning Rod Junior" in reference to his illustrious grandfather and to Bache's strong pro-French and Anti-Federalist writings in his Philadelphia newspaper *Aurora*. Mathew Carey and Philip Freneau were two of many other Republican editors on the Federalists' enemy list.[37]

Toward the close of the century Mathew Carey, also of Philadelphia, carried on a paper war with an English immigrant, one William Cobbett, who wrote under the pseudonym of Peter Porcupine. Cobbett's savage, sarcastic humor in *A Bone to Gnaw for the Democrats* was leveled at Bache. It attracted the attention of Hamilton, and Porcupine forthwith became the leading Federalist writer with his *Porcupine Gazette*, which urged alliance with England. Mathew Carey wrote in an ironic vein a forty-eight-page pamphlet, *A Plumb Pudding for the humane, chaste, valiant, enlightened Peter Porcupine* (Philadelphia, 1799).

James T. Callender, another anti-Adams writer, also returned some of Cobbett's sharp quills. In his *The Prospect Before Us*

(Richmond, 1800),[38] he writes, "His whole conduct, since he became president, exposes him to great and severe censure; and every day adds an item to the catalogue of his errors" (II, 87). Writing from jail, where he himself was feeling the razor edge of the Alien and Sedition laws, Callender bitterly comments, "Away with your pretended *freedom of the press!* The phrase is nothing but a trap door" (II, 100).

In New England, too, the paper war between the Federalists and the Anti-Federalist Republicans was in process. Timothy Dwight worried about uniformity in religion, since Paine and other Republicans had been accused of atheism. (See Dwight's sermon *The Duty of Americans, at the Present Crisis* ([New Haven, 1798]). Joseph Dennie in his *Lay Preacher* and *The Spirit of the Farmer's Museum and Lay Preacher's Gazette* represented a strongly Federalist position. In the sermon "Favor Is Deceitful" (from *The Lay Preacher*) he attacked Paine's *The Rights of Man* and *The Age of Reason.* In contrast, William Manning, an unlettered farmer, wrote a series of essays entitled *The Key of Libberty* for the *Boston Independent Chronicle* (1798), an Anti-Federalist newspaper, in which he argued that "the gratest dainger the Many are under in . . . money matters are from the Juditial & Executive Officers. . . ." [39] But it was Freneau's *Letters on Various Interesting and Important Subjects . . . By Robert Slender, O. S. M.* [one of the Swinish multitude], contributed originally to the *Aurora* and later published by D. Hogan (Philadelphia, 1799), which probably helped more than anything to turn the tide against the Federalists.

In the first letter of this series Freneau assumes the ironical mask of a "Monarchist" and writes to correct the idea some of the editor's correspondents had that "princes or presidents ought always to act fairly, openly and ingenuously: that they ought not only to see that the law should be obeyed, but should in their actions, strictly act in conformity to both the letter and the spirit of the law themselves" (9). "I am bold to affirm," writes the Monarchist, "that I can prove the contrary" of this proposition (10). And he proceeds to a long disquisition from antiquity (in which he apes Adams's *Defence of the Constitutions*) to prove his point that the nature of "governors or princes" places them "in certain cases supreme above all law." From which he deduces the following particulars:

1st. An irrefragable argument for the justice of the Alien Bill. Those people who are most affected by it, and against whom it was made, are inimical to all good government. Witness the troubles they raised in Ireland, where . . . for many hundred years past, the government hath been *temperate, humane,* and just.

2nd. It was necessary, by the Sedition Law, to clip the wings of some men, and to shew the *heinous* nature of speaking against persons high in trust. (13)

The conclusion to this letter reads as follows:

> Let us never judge governors by those rules by which we ourselves are to abide and be governed; but rest satisfied under whatever laws, decrees, or ordinances the rulers frame, still remembering this grand advice (which is my last authority) [that] whosoever resisteth the power, resisteth the ordinance of God, and that they who resist shall receive to themselves DAMNATION.
>
> A MONARCHIST (14)

With the defeat of Adams and the election of Jefferson in 1800 a new century began. Temporarily, government by what Adams had called "the rich, the well-born, and the able" was repudiated. Temporarily, at least, liberal principles triumphed and the party of farmers, tradesmen, mechanics, and small shopkeepers was to have its day.

The struggle whereby—on the surface, at least—the common man emerged victorious at the end of the Federalist decade was a complex one. Let us look back over these ten years by way of reminding ourselves what the main issues were.

The debate in the Senate concerning titles set the tone for the entire decade. Was there to be a king in the new American government, despite Paine's brilliant rhetoric against the institution of monarchy in *Common Sense?* Was there to be a class of nobles, aristocrats, despite the provision in the Constitution against them? In his *Discourses of Davila* Adams himself saw the need to control the aristocracy. But his belief in monarchy as one of the limiting factors on the aristocracy made him suspect. (Here Jefferson saw his opportunity for opposition.) Adams's distrust of the passionate actions of the French people during their Revolution led to his appeal (to both the French and the Americans) for "reason, conscience, truth, and virtue" as necessary for the public good.

It was the French Revolution, then, that intensified the polarization between parties in the 1790s. The democratic sympathies of Jefferson, Paine, Barlow, Freneau, and Gallatin for the

French crystalized sentiment against security-conscious Adams and
Hamilton and the Federalists, who were fearful of possible attacks
by foreign foes. Increasingly throughout the decade this became the
pattern of conflict, culminating in the Jeffersonian Republicans'
opposition to the Alien and Sedition laws of the "monarchical"
Adams administration. The debate between Hamilton and John
Taylor of Caroline in which the manufacturing and banking interests
squared off against southern Agrarians further intensified this
conflict of the two principal parties by carrying it into the economic
area, as did Paine's *Agrarian Justice*. Both parties, of course, made
appeals to *reason*. Paine's classic work on Deism, *The Age of
Reason*, was not, however, the kind of *reason* that the New England
Federalists respected; for, if Timothy Dwight may be considered an
example, they identified it with the dangerous infidelism they
associated with the Reign of Terror.

In closing, what can we say about the main issues and themes in
American political writing during the period 1588-1800? A few
generalizations may be in order.

First, there was the issue of how to set up a commonwealth on
biblical principles, a problem faced by a small group that thought of
itself as candidates for eternal salvation (the Elect). Differences of
opinion in the struggle for religious freedom, the hand of the clergy
in framing civil law, the separation of the powers of church and
state, the limitation of the power of the magistrates—all these might
be regarded as themes associated with this attempt to set up a city
on a hill, a kind of utopian government in this world that would
herald the divine reward to be experienced by the very small band
of the Elect in the hereafter.

Second, there was the question of how to decide which forms of
church government and doctrine were to be tolerated. Here the
Half-Way Covenant became the focus of many debates, as did the
Stoddard-Taylor controversy over church membership, the results
of which were important for the later history of revivalism,
including the Great Awakening. Emerging themes were the greater
toleration of diversity in the local churches, the transformation of
New England from a narrow "sectarian community" to a secular
society, the widening separation between church and state, and the
decline of theocracy generally but withal a curious persistence in
the effects of religious changes on matters political. John Wise's
statement of the natural rights theory in his defense of New England

church government might be cited here as representing an important change in focus from church government to civil government.

Third, there was the question of the rights of the individual, *vis-à-vis* the government and the economic system, that found expression in the antislavery literature. This crusade, as we have seen, followed a very complicated path—pioneered at first by a few brave Quaker souls but finally coming to a climax in the large-scale political action represented by early proposals for gradual emancipation and the near prospect of an end to importation of slaves.

All the while, of course, economic issues were becoming more and more important and were assuming an explicit role in political rhetoric. Consequently, during the pre-Revolutionary period of the stamp tax and other taxes as well as during the Revolution itself the rights of individual colonists to resist slavery, as they encountered it, or *felt* they encountered it, in the British economic and political system, bore a kind of parallel to the demand for individual rights given expression during the antislavery crusade. Tom Paine, our first large media persuader, or propagandist, unified public opinion in the colonies to the point where his calls for separation from Britain and for war no longer fell on deaf ears. Jefferson then announced the birth of a new nation on a formal rationale of natural rights.

Finally, during the 1780s and 1790s the issue became how the new government, the post-Revolutionary government, should relate to various economic interests or classes in American society. Exacerbating the polarization of economic interests and parties in this period were the mutual accusations hurled at each other by the Republicans and Federalists as they respectively espoused their sympathies for France and Britain. This hardening of conflict came to a head in the controversy over Adams's "monarchical" administration and in the "paper war" between Hamilton and John Taylor of Caroline concerning the bank question and the rise of a new money aristocracy dominating Congress.

In general, it might be said that the movement during these two centuries proceeded from the religious and governmental to the economic and governmental. By the time of the American Revolution, as Larzer Ziff has brilliantly illustrated in a recent article,[40] Thomas Paine, deist and propagandist, would employ (without regard for consistency) religious doctrines such as original sin, which underlay Covenant theology, in his purely political rhetoric for fracturing the British empire with *Common Sense*; and John Adams (in his rhetoric against the Stamp Act) could take a "secular" view of Puritan history.[41] Ultimately the spiritual hopes of the small body of the Elect for otherworldly happiness were transmuted into the more secular concern for the economic rights of all persons alive *in this world*, as we have seen in Paine's *Agrarian Justice*.

These few generalizations cannot possibly express the total texture of American political writing in the period 1588–1800. They do suggest, however, a structure of major political preoccupations which can help us keep our bearings as we review the centuries which culminated in the establishment of the United States of America.

Notes and References

Chapter One

1. Edmund S. Morgan, *The Puritan Dilemma, The Story of John Winthrop* (Boston, 1958), p. 180.

2. Thomas Harriot, *A Briefe and True Report of the New Found Land of Virginia*, The Complete 1590 Theodor De Bry Edition, with an intro. by Paul Hulton (New York, 1972), p. 22. This text of this Dover facsimile reprint is identical with the original 1588 edition, which lacked the illustrations of the De Bry ed.

3. *Ibid.*, pp. 25, 26.

4. See *Of Plymouth Plantation*, chap. 1, and *passim*.

5. Perry Miller and Thomas Johnson, *The Puritans* (Boston, 1938), p. 10.

6. *Ibid.*, p. 58.

7. Morgan, p. 93. See Miller and Johnson, pp. 189–91, for a detailed explanation of Winthrop's understanding of how "political doctrine became part and parcel of the theological." Samuel Eliot Morison and Henry Steele Commager, *The Growth of the American Republic* (New York, 1942), I, 53, note that "Church and State in New England were dominated by the covenant idea" and that each Congregational church and settlement thought of its particular covenant with God as something *new* and *individualized*. They cite a passage from Winthrop's *A Model of Christian Charity*—"We are entered into a covenant with God, . . . the Lord hath given us leave to draw our own Articles," and "He will expect a strict performance."

8. Sidney E. Ahlstrom, *A Religious History of the American People* (New Haven, 1975), p. 131.

9. *Ibid.*, p. 87, for Ahlstrom's belief that the groundwork for Covenant Theology was laid as early as 1553. For further information, see Phyllis M. and Nicholas R. Jones, eds., *Salvation in New England: Selections from the Sermons of the First Preachers* (Austin, 1977), p. 28, where they assert that "no work explicates federal [or covenant] theology . . . as fully as the . . . *Gospel-Covenant*" sermon of Peter Bulkeley of Concord, Mass. Pp. 30–41 reproduce this sermon. Part of the "breadth and excitement" of this sermon, in their opinion, is "its continual expansion from the individual

in covenant with God to the church and state in league with him." The
doctrine of the covenant explained "God's special relationship with his
chosen followers, be they organized in a church community or a public
state," p. 28.

10. Apparently banishment from God's chosen people was then regarded
as a "capital punishment." The "or" on the title page of the *Abstract* is
undoubtedly a misprint, since "of " replaces it in the listing of the title on
page one.

11. Pp. 10–11 of the original edition in the Houghton Memorial library.
This work has been ascribed to John Cotton. See Samuel Eliot Morison,
Builders of the Bay Colony, 2nd rev. ed. (Boston, 1958), pp. 227–28.
Nathaniel Ward is supposed to have drawn on this *Abstract* in composing
his *Body of Liberties* (Nov. 1641). Morison, p. 229, also says that John
Davenport used it in constructing his fundamental law of Conn.

12. Pp. 95–96.

13. Reproduced in Roy Harvey Pearce, *Colonial American Writing*
(New York, 1969), pp. 116–17, my source for this and the short quotations
in the paragraph following.

14. See Morgan, p. 89, who adds that they did not even retain the
powers given them by the charter.

15. Usually the *text* was a biblical quotation. Winthrop's sermon, as here
printed by the Mass. Hist. Soc., gives the text in his own words—which was
unusual. But he does clarify the Biblical source of his text in his third proof,
where he refers to its source in Ezek. 16:17 and Proverbs 3:9.

16. Cf. the already noted distinction between the *covenant of works* and
the *covenant of grace*.

17. This speech has been extensively published in anthologies of
American literature. See, for example, Willard Thorp *et al.*, eds., *American
Issues, I, The Social Record* (New York, 1944), pp. 56–57.

18. Morgan, p. 134. Morgan's account of this controversy (in his tenth
chapter, of *Puritan Dilemma*) is excellent. See p. 212 for other accounts;
also, Emery Battis, *Saints and Sinners, Anne Hutchinson and the
Antinomian Controversy in the Massachusetts Bay Colony* (Chapel Hill,
1962), and David D. Hall, *The Antinomian Controversy, 1636–38, A
Documentary History* (Middletown, Conn., 1968).

19. Hall, p. 9. See also Morgan, p. 146, for information about these
immigrants from Grindleton Chapel in England, who held beliefs similar to
those of Anne Hutchinson.

20. *The Puritans*, p. 771. Quotations in this and from the paragraphs
following are from pp. 199–202, *passim*.

21. *Ibid.* An allusion to Roger Williams, according to Miller: "With
characteristic generosity, Winthrop is insinuating that in spite of his error
Williams might still be a genuine Christian (cf. Bradford's similar judgment,
p. 111) though Winthrop is clear that Williams' errors merited banishment,
however holy Williams himself might be."

22. Miller and Johnson, p. 202. My bracketed emendation.

23. Parenthetical page citations in this and the two following paragraphs are to the American Antiquarian Soc. (hereafter AAS) copy of *A Journal of the Transactions and Occurrences and Settlements of Massachusetts and other New England Colonies, from 1630 to 1644* (Hartford, 1790), Evans no. 23086, p. 144. Miller and Johnson, p. 767, n. 19, claim that this contention by the Mass. Court was "unjustified" but a matter of practice until the revocation of the charter in 1684.

24. Winthrop's *Journal* was published under the title of *The History of New England from 1630 to 1649* by James Savage (Boston, 1853), 2 vols. The quotation I have used here is reproduced in Edmund S. Morgan, *Puritan Political Ideas, 1558–1794* (Indianapolis, 1965), p. 137.

25. Morgan, *Puritan Political Ideas*, pp. 138–39. Morgan's translation of the Latin quotation.

26. *Ibid.*, p. 20.

27. Perry Miller, *Roger Williams, His Contribution to the American Tradition* (New York, 1965), pp. 236–40.

28. Miller's *Roger Williams* is an excellent abridgment of the total thought of this writer. See also, among others, Henry Chupack, *Roger Williams* (New York, 1969), pp. 62–144; Edmund S. Morgan, *Roger Williams, The Church and the State* (New York, 1967), pp. 86–142; and Everett H. Emerson *John Cotton* (New York, 1965), pp. 133–40. See also, Larzer Ziff, *The Career of John Cotton* (Princeton, 1962) and numerous anthologies of American literature.

29. Miller, *RW*, pp. 18, 25. See also Miller and Johnson, *The Puritans*, p. 215.

30. Quoted in Emerson, pp. 143, 165. The original source is Thomas Hutchinson, *Hist. of Mass. Bay*, I (1764), p. 412.

31. Miller and Johnson, *The Puritans*, p. 209.

32. *Ibid.*, p. 208.

33. See Emerson, pp. 149–51, for discussion of this work.

34. *Ibid.*, p. 149.

35. *Ibid.*, p. 150.

36. See Miller, *RW*, pp. 108–44, for the specific arguments of Part I, in which Williams replied to Cotton's work entitled *The Answer of Mr. John Cotton of Boston in New-England, to the Aforesaid Arguments Against Persecution For Cause of Conscience Professedly Maintaining Persecution For Cause of Conscience*. Cotton's *Answer*, a manuscript that had fallen into Williams's hands in 1636, was directed at an Anabaptist work against persecution which had been published in England in 1620. See Miller, p. 74. In Part II Williams was answering the nonseparatist ideas expressed in the *Model* of the Massachusetts Bay ministers association. See pp. 144–56 of Miller.

37. *Ibid.*, p. 166.

38. *Ibid.*, pp. 194–95.

39. *Ibid.*, p. 235. Miller states that the pastorate of John Cotton, Jr., was not happy in that Separatist colony.

40. *Ibid.*, p. 238.

41. *Ibid.*, p. 241. Towards the end of the century Francis Pastorius defended the religious freedom of the Quakers in *Four Boasting Disputers of this World Briefly Rebuked* (New York, 1697). This work answered a pamphlet entitled *Advice for All Professors and Writers*, which apparently had been written by the followers of George Keith, the apostate Quaker, and which had misrepresented some of the Quakers' religious principles as well as slandered William Penn and others of this sect. Although William Penn spent only four years in America, he has been so completely identified with the cause of religious toleration, specifically by means of his constitution of Pennsylvania (written with Algernon Sidney) and other writings on politics and religion, such as *No Cross, No Crown* (1669), that he deserves a reassessment in more detail than I can possibly provide here.

42. Miller, *RW*, p. 254.

43. *Ibid.*, pp. v–vi.

44. Morgan, *Puritan Political Ideas*, pp. 222–223.

45. Perry Miller, "Thomas Hooker and the Democracy of Early Conn.," *NEQ*, IV (1931), 663, 690, writes that Hooker was not as democratic as Parrington and James Truslow Adams would have us believe. See also p. 698.

46. See *ibid.*, pp. 694–95, for other differences from Mass.

47. *Ibid.*, p. 712.

48. *Ibid.*, p. 709, for this and the preceding quotation.

49. Miller and Johnson, *The Puritans*, pp. 160, 143, 768.

50. Vernon Louis Parrington, *The Colonial Mind, 1620–1800* (New York, 1927), pp. 76–77.

51. *Puritan Political Ideas*, p. 178.

52. *Ibid.*

53. Morgan, *Puritan Political Ideas*, p. 175. Winthrop, of course, in his *Discourse on Arbitrary Government* (see pp. 149–60, of Morgan, *idem*) had argued for greater discretionary power for the magistrates in applying the law. His opponents had charged that giving magistrates discretionary power to fix penalties would constitute arbitrary government. Winthrop had answered that since both citizens (he calls them *Freemen*) and magistrates were limited "by certaine Rules," the government might be regarded as a mixed aristocracy in "no waye Arbitrary." (*Freemen* were originally stockholders of the Mass. Bay Co., but later the term came to refer to citizens.)

54. *John Cotton*, pp. 157, 158.

Chapter Two

1. The title page of this Harvard College Library original edition describes this work (in the subtitle) as "A short view of New-England's

present Government, both Ecclesiasticall and Civil, compared with the anciently-received and established Government of England, in some materiall points; fit for the gravest consideration in these times." Page references are to this edition in the Houghton Library.

2. Lechford, *Plain Dealing*, p. 40. The preface is dated January 17, 1641. Lechford was apparently back in England at this time. See Miller, *The Puritans*, p. 401, for further details on Lechford's own non-church membership and his debarment from the law for attempting to influence a jury in Massachusetts.

3. Printed in 1649 as *A Platform of Church-Discipline*. Like the Half-Way Covenant, it was drafted by Richard Mather, amended, and adopted by a church synod.

4. See Perry Miller, *Orthodoxy in Massachusetts, 1630–1650* (Boston, 1959), pp. 200–11, for discussion of this controversy. Miller, incidentally, dates the beginning of this controversy as early as 1637. See p. 203.

5. *Plain Dealing*, p. 58. Lechford did admit, however, that the Puritan principle of separation between churches and state had begun to be observed, p. 14.

Another important criticism, related to controversies over baptism and church membership as affecting citizenship in this world and salvation in the next, was that of the conversion of the Indians. Lechford denied that the Puritan churches had a valid right to convert the Indians, since in this act they were operating outside their patent from the king and the rules of the Anglican Church.

6. Thomas Jefferson Wertenbaker, *The Puritan Oligarchy* (New York, 1947), p. 67. Quoted by permission from Charles Scribner's Sons.

7. Norman Grabo, *Edward Taylor* (New York, 1962), pp. 13–14. The duel began in 1679 in western Massachusetts and continued practically until Taylor's death in 1729, at which time Stoddard's more liberal views on easier admission to church membership triumphed.

8. Robert G. Pope, *The Half-Way Covenant, Church Membership in Puritan New England* (Princeton, 1969), p. 14.

9. *Ibid.*, pp. 6–7. Most of the contemporary writings on the Half-Way Covenant (except I. Mather's *First Principles of New England*) appeared between 1662 and 1664. See Pope, pp. 55n–56n for a list of these.

10. *Ibid.*, pp. 134–35.

11. *Ibid.*, p. 30.

12. *Ibid.*, p. 41.

13. *Ibid.*

14. *Ibid.*, pp. 15, 17. Pp. 51, 52, give possible reasons why Increase Mather opposed his father's views until after the latter's death.

15. *Ibid.*, pp. 95, 127. Toward the end of the century (1689–96) in Stonington, Conn., practically everyone in town was a church member, p. 119.

16. *Ibid.*, p. 153.

17. *Ibid.*, p. 152.

18. *Ibid.*, pp. 167–79. Massachusetts law prohibited gathering a church without the approval of both *elders* and *magistrates*, p. 174.

19. *Ibid.*, p. 179.

20. *Ibid.*, p. 183.

21. *Ibid.*, p. 186.

22. *Ibid.*, pp. 68, 241, 243.

23. *Ibid.*, pp. 165–66.

24. *Ibid.*, pp. 130, 131, 73.

25. *Ibid.*, pp. 54, 180, 8, 275–76 respectively for the remaining material in this paragraph.

26. *Ibid.*, p. 276.

27. Miller, *The Puritans*, p. 237.

28. *Ibid.*

29. *Ibid.*, p. 238.

30. *Ibid.*

31. Kenneth B. Murdock, *Selections from Cotton Mather* (New York, 1926), p. xii.

32. Kenneth B. Murdock, *Increase Mather, The Foremost American Puritan* (New York, 1966), p. 156, for this date. See S. E. Morison and H. S. Commager, *The Growth of the American Republic* (New York, 1948), p. 82, for reasons for the revocation of the charter.

33. *Ibid.*, Morison and Commager, p. 84. See also Richard N. Current *et al.*, *American History, A Survey* (New York, 1965), pp. 54–56, for a succinct account of this historical episode.

34. It should be noted that, during this period at least, Increase Mather himself never actually opposed religious toleration or so-called liberty of conscience. Murdock, *Increase Mather*, repeatedly makes this point. See pp. 162–63, 182–83, 206–207, 238. But at the same time Mather also held out for restoration of the old charter. The new charter, eventually granted by William III, did, however, extend the power of the franchise to non-church members and certain property holders, thus curtailing the power of Mather and others of the clergy.

35. A note on the verso (opposite the title page) of the Houghton Library copy I used reads: "This pamphlet was written and printed in December, 1688. The date on binding is an error. M.B.J." But Murdock, *Increase Mather*, pp. 213 and 213n, argues for sometime after January 2, 1689, since the events of this day are referred to in the text. My parenthetical page references are to the Houghton copy. Murdock used the copy in the *Andros Tracts*, II, 3ff.

36. Murdock, *Increase Mather*, pp. 212–13, interprets Increase Mather's diary for Dec. 5, 1688, to mean that Mather had finished this pamphlet on that day. But it was not printed before Jan. 2, 1689. (James's final escape from England occurred in December. William III was ensconced in Whitehall on December 23, p. 209.) The copy which Murdock used in the *Andros Tracts* includes at the end of the eight-page pamphlet

The humble Application of Henry Lord Bishop of London and also *The Address of the Nonconformist Ministers* to William of Orange. The *Address* was delivered on January 2, 1689.

37. Murdock, *Increase Mather*, p. 213n.

38. *Ibid.*, p. 220. Murdock summarizes the arguments on pp. 221–23. A pamphlet in *Andros Tracts*, II, 137–47, answers (in its general argument against restoration of the charters) many of the arguments of *New England Vindicated* and may be a later edition of the original pamphlet which *New England Vindicated*, in reply to certain "Considerations," answered. Since the original pamphlet carried the word "Considerations" in its title (see Murdock, *Increase Mather*, p. 220), Mather calls the anonymous authors of this pamphlet "Considerators." *Andros Tracts*, II, 111–24 (Boston, 1869) is a transcript of a copy of *New England Vindicated* in the British Museum. It is this transcript to which my parenthetical page numbers refer. The surmised date is 1688, soon after Increase Mather's arrival in London and "antecedent to the overthrow of Andros," p. 113n.

39. The fact that Andros was first appointed in June 1686 and that "Mather arrived in London in May 1688" has raised the possibility that he may have only inspired rather than written this document. See p. 121n. But this seems unlikely. Mather's statement could just as well be construed as meaning less than three years.

40. Murdock, *Increase Mather*, opposite p. 222, reproduces the title and the first page of this second vindication, which he attributes to Increase Mather on grounds of form and style. See pp. 223–24 for further information upon this incomplete but apparently *unique* copy.

41. Murdock, *Increase Mather*, pp. 224–25, summarizes the main arguments of this work.

42. *Ibid.*, pp. 227–28.

43. *Ibid.*, p. 228.

44. *Ibid.*

45. *Ibid.*, p. 231.

46. *Ibid.*, p. 233.

47. *Andros Tracts*, II, 225–30.

48. *Increase Mather*, p. 236.

49. *Ibid.*, p. 275, for the quotation and for further information about this tract, including its publication in England rather than in America.

50. See *Andros Tracts*, I, 63 ff. "S. S." might refer to Samuel Sewall. A better possibility would seem to be Samuel Shrimpton, apparently one of Andros's council, whose name is listed along with those of William Stoughton, Thomas Hinckley, Wait Winthrop, and Barthol Gedney at the end of the pamphlet bound with this one. See pp. 51–59. Murdock, *Increase Mather*, p. 235n, expresses the opinion that Mather did not write *The Revolution in New-England Justified*. *The Revolution* is a fifty-page pamphlet; the other pamphlet *A Narrative* (pp. 51–59) is dated Boston, January 27, 1690, on p. 59.

51. This *Narrative* dissociated those listed in the preceding note from the crimes of the Andros administration.

52. See Murdock, *Increase Mather*, pp. 167–77, for discussion of this book.

53. *Ibid.*, p. 317.

54. David Levin, *What Happened in Salem?* (New York, 1960), 2nd ed., pp. xiv–xv. See also, Harvey Wish, ed., *The Diary of Samuel Sewall* (abridged; New York, 1967), pp. 184–85; Chadwick Hansen, *Witchcraft at Salem* (New York, 1970), pp. 160–67, which I have used in some of the information which follows.

55. Levin, p. xvi. According to the theory of "spectral evidence," if a person testified that the shape of another person appeared to him, that shape was immediately suspect, and accordingly the person it represented was considered a witch, since innocent persons were not believed to have such power. The devil or his agents could not take the shape of an *innocent* person. Such evidence, of course, rested only on hearsay, rather than on any real evidence.

56. *Increase Mather*, pp. 304–305.

57. *Ibid.*, p. 300. See pp. 300–301 for further arguments—*viz.*, that "ducking" and other methods employed during the trial were unsound, whereas a free and voluntary confession by a witch or sworn testimony by at least two credible witnesses (who were not witches) might be sound.

58. Levin, pp. 96 ff.

59. Frederick C. Drake, "Witchcraft in the American Colonies, 1647–1662," *Am. Quart.* XX (Winter 1968), 694–725, calls attention to "over 95 incidents involving colonial people with witchcraft before 1692," p. 697.

60. Kenneth Murdock, *Selections from Cotton Mather* (New York, 1926), Hafner Library of Classics reprint, p. xxxv. Hereafter *Cotton Mather*.

61. Levin, p. 112. Pp. 112–16 reproduce the Burroughs trial.

62. Theodore Hornberger *et al.*, *The Literature of the U.S.*, 3rd ed. (Chicago, 1966), I, 138. Hornberger's assessment seems fair; he informs us that most educated men of that day believed in evil spirits as well as good ones. Not to have done so would have been to sell out to materialism, as they saw it.

63. Levin, pp. 107 and 109, respectively, for these two quotations.

64. *Ibid.*, p. 111. Levin notes that this letter was reprinted in the London (1862) edition of *The Wonders of the Invisible World.* On grounds of language similar to that of the letter to Judge Richards, he thinks C. Mather wrote it.

65. Russel Nye and Norman S. Grabo, *American Thought and Writing, The Colonial Period* (Boston, 1965), I, 233, explain the late appearance of Calef's book by saying that "he waited until 1697 when both judges and jurors expressed remorse and contrition for the parts they played in the trials, and then sent his assembled material to London for publication." But

the excerpt which they present from this book is dated January 12, 1696. On January 14, 1697, Samuel Sewall did public penance in church for his part in the trials, in which he had figured as a judge. For Increase Mather's "Reply to Calef " (1701), see *Andros Tracts*, II, 313–23.

66. This is Murdock's considered conclusion. See *Increase Mather*, p. 316.

67. *Ibid.*, p. 315. Pp. 314–16 discuss this matter at length.

68. *Ibid.*, p. 332.

69. *Ibid.*, p. 333n.

70. *Cotton Mather*, pp. xlv–xlvi.

71. *Ibid.*, pp. 364–65.

72. *Ibid.*, pp. 365–66, for all quotations in this paragraph.

73. *Ibid.*, pp. 368–70; p. 367 for the short quotation preceding this one.

74. *Ibid.*, pp. 370–71, reproduce the text of this brief fable. Quotations in this paragraph are from these pages.

75. *Ibid.*, pp. liv–lv.

76. *Ibid.*, p. lv.

77. *Ibid.*, p. 149, where the reproduced verse of the title page gives the date April 27, 1697.

78. *Ibid.*, p. xlvii, for this and the preceding quotation.

79. See Cotton Mather, *Manuductio ad Ministerium* (Boston, 1726), pp. 44–46.

80. See Murdock, *Cotton Mather*, p. xxxi. Further politically significant writings by Cotton Mather include: several sermons dealing with the Andros affair (and related matters) and the new charter—*The Serviceable Man* (c. 1689), *The Way to Prosperity* (c. 1689), *The Wonderful Works of God* (December 19, 1689), and *The Present State of New-England. Considered in a Discourse on the Necessities and Advantages of a Public Spirit . . . Upon the News of an Invasion by bloody Indians and French-Men, begun upon Us* (March 20, 1690); his artillery election-day sermons—such as *Soldiers Counseled and Comforted, Military Duties*, and *Expectanda, or Things to be Look'd for*—which encouraged soldiers in their various battles with the French and the Indians; his other sermons, such as the Jeremiah-like *Things for a Distressed People to Think Upon* (1696), dealing with a variety of troubles, his dissatisfactions with Governor Stoughton, the attempt of the king and the royal governor to exercise increasing political power over Harvard, the unsuccessful attempt at assassinating the king, etc.; *The Deplorable State of New England By Reason of a Covetous and Treacherous Governor* [Jos. Dudley, who became governor in 1702] (Boston, reprinted 1720), which should be compared with Increase Mather's *The Public Spirited Man* (Boston, 1702) on the same subject; *A Faithful Monitor* (1704), which was a latter-day abstract of the laws of New England; his *Parentator* (1724) or biography of his father on the occasion of his death in 1723; and his *Christian Loyalty* (1727), dealing with the accession of George II to the English throne.

81. Pope, p. 253. The quotation is by Pope, who adds that the

autonomy of the individual congregation, in the rapidly changing society of Massachusetts, "proved to be the undoing of religious uniformity," p. 260.

82. *Ibid.*, p. 254n. The title of the sermon was *A Discourse Concerning the Danger of Apostasy.* See Mason I. Lowance and Everett H. Emerson, eds., "Increase Mather's Confutation of Solomon Stoddard's 'Observations Concerning the Lord's Supper' 1680," *Proc. AAS,* LXXXIII, I (Oct. 1973), 31.

83. James P. Walsh, "Solomon Stoddard's Open Communion: A Reexamination," *NEQ,* XLIII (March 1970), 108.

84. Lowance and Emerson, pp. 29–66.

85. James D. Hart, *The Oxford Companion to American Literature* (New York, 1941), p. 728.

86. Thomas A. Schafer, "Solomon Stoddard and the Theology of the Revival," in *A Miscellany of American Christianity,* ed. by Stuart C. Henry (Durham, 1963), p. 331.

87. Lowance and Emerson, p. 32.

88. *Ibid.*, p. 33.

89. Schafer, p. 332; Walsh, pp. 108–109.

90. Mason I. Lowance, Jr., *Increase Mather* (New York, 1974), p. 6.

91. Kenneth Murdock, *Increase Mather* (New York, 1966), pp. 359–63. See Evans microcard 938, which I have used as text.

92. *The Order of the Gospel,* p. 1 of *"Epistle Dedicatory"* for the first quotation; p. 5 for the second.

93. *Ibid.*, p. 5.

94. Evans 966 gives "[New York] 1700 [Wm. Bradford]" as conjectured place and publisher. Cf. Murdock, *Increase Mather,* p. 365.

95. Murdock, *Increase Mather,* appendix D, does not list this work, but it was obviously written by one of his sympathizers.

96. *Ibid.*, p. 364.

97. *Ibid.*, pp. 369, 370.

98. Evans 1372. Boston, 1708.

99. Lowance, *Increase Mather,* p. 18.

100. Evans 1366. Boston, 1708.

101. Miller and Johnson, *The Puritans,* pp. 85–86. For Edward Taylor, another of Stoddard's opponents, the "proper administration of the sacraments" was the "crucial question of the entire Reformation." See Norman S. Grabo, "The Poet to the Pope," *American Lit.,* XXXII (May 1960), 198.

102. Grabo, *Edward Taylor* (New York, 1961), pp. 13, 14. For Taylor's twelve objections in a letter to Stoddard, see Grabo, "The Poet to the Pope," pp. 199–200.

103. Lowance, *Increase Mather,* p. 158.

104. *Ibid.*

105. Schafer, p. 332.

106. Lowance, *Increase Mather,* p. 159.

107. *Ibid.*

108. Quoted in Lowance and Emerson, p. 50.

109. Quoted in Schafer, p. 330. See P. Miller, *Harvard Theol. Rev.*, XXXIV (Oct. 1941), 316, 319. Also cf. Miller, *The New England Mind: From Colony to Province* (Cambridge, 1953), chaps. 15–16.

110. Walsh, p. 108. But cf. Larzer Ziff, *Puritanism in America* (New York, 1973), pp. 256, 262, for the view that the Conn. River valley, if not Northampton, was the frontier.

111. From the above-mentioned letter of Taylor to Stoddard (June 4, 1688), reproduced in entirety in Grabo, "The Poet to the Pope," p. 201.

112. Schafer, pp. 335 and 113 respectively.

113. *Ibid.*, p. 329. Schafer also notes, by way of stressing continuity between Stoddard's revivalism and that of the Awakening, that *The Safety of Appearing*, which he calls Stoddard's "finest work on conversion," was reprinted in 1729, the year of his death, and again in 1742 "at the height of the Great Awakening," pp. 332–33.

114. Alan Heimert and Perry Miller, eds., *The Great Awakening, Documents Illustrating the Crisis and Its Consequences* (Indianapolis, 1967), pp. 71n, 72.

115. Reproduced in entirety in Heimert and Miller. See p. 74 for this quotation.

116. *Ibid.*, p. 90.

117. Leo Lemay, *Ebenezer Kinnersley, Franklin's Friend* (Philadelphia, 1964), p. 43.

118. *Ibid.*, p. 43n.

119. Heimert and Miller, p. 576.

120. William Gerald McLoughlin, "The Great Awakening," *Encyclopedia Britannica*, XIX (Chicago, 1966), 248.

121. Ahlstrom, p. 350. See, too, Cushing Strout's excellent assessment of the Awakening in *The New Heavens and New Earth, Political Religion in America* (New York, 1974), chap. 3, esp. pp. 30, 42–49; and Martin E. Marty, *Faith of Our Fathers, Religion, Awakening & Revolution*, a Consortium book (1977), pp. 94, 96, 97, 99, 101, 103–104. Marty stresses the new value of the individual person, p. 94. None of these three or McLoughlin, however, mentions Whitefield's antislavery letter addressed "To the Inhabitants of Maryland, Virginia, and the Carolinas" and printed by Benjamin Franklin (Philadelphia, 1740).

122. George A. Cook, *John Wise, Early American Democrat* (New York, 1966), p. 64, believes this account was written to Increase Mather. See "The Narrative of Mr. John Wise, Minister of Gods Word at Chebacco," in *Mass. Hist. Soc. Proc.*, 2nd series, XV (1902), 282.

123. Cook, p. 71.

124. *Ibid.*, pp. 74–76. It was 1711 before some of Proctor's heirs had this property returned to them.

125. *Ibid.*, p. 84. Pp. 79–80 for the wrestling incident, which Cook thinks legendary.

126. See *ibid.*, p. 88, for activities of this organization.

127. The *Manifesto* professed adherence to the Presbyterian *Westminster Confession of Faith* of 1680 (although Wise himself resisted this profession) but it differed from doctrines of the orthodox association by advocating such points as the reading of the Bible without explanation in public worship, admission to church membership without public confession of a religious experience, and extension of the vote to all baptized adults in choice of a minister. *Ibid.*, pp. 93–94.

128. Cook, pp. 106–109.

129. *Ibid.*, pp. 109–10.

130. I am grateful to Cook, p. 119, for these examples. See pp. 109–27 for the detail of the argument and for remarks on the "humble" attitude, or tone, Wise used to ingratiate himself into his readers' good graces. For the dates of various editions of *The Churches Quarrel Espoused*, see Cook, p. 125.

131. Cook, pp. 151, 153. Both *The Churches Quarrel Espoused* and *A Vindication* were reprinted in 1772.

132. "Diary of Cotton Mather," *Mass. Hist. Soc. Coll.*, 7th series, VIII, 450.

133. Cook, p. 150, who also gives the adverse reaction of Nathaniel Stone.

134. See Evans 1941, AAS copy of *A Vindication* (Boston, 1717), pp. 34–35, 37–38, 39–40. Parenthetical citations that follow are to this text.

135. One other work of Wise's should be mentioned. This was *A Word of Comfort to a Melancholy Country* (1721), written under the pseudonym of Amicus Patriae and dealing with the diminishing purchasing power of paper currency.

Chapter Three

1. *The Friend*, IV (1831), No. 46, p. 363. Reproduced in Joanne Grant, *Black Protest: History, Documents, and Analyses 1619 to the Present* (Greenwich, Conn., 1967), p. 26. Thomas E. Drake, *Quakers and Slavery in America* (Gloucester, Mass., 1965), p. 1, says this law was "never enforced."

2. Reproduced in Samuel W. Pennypacker, "The Settlement of Germantown and the Causes which Led to it," *Pa. Mag. Hist. and Biog.*, IV (1880), 28–30. See Drake, p. 12, for evidence that Worrell was a Quaker; p. 14n for further information on the signers of this doc. Ahlstrom, p. 232, mentions that from 1686 to 1690 both Mennonites and Quakers occupied a common meeting house in Germantown. He adds that three of those who signed this doc. were "Friends," i.e., Quakers, and that the doc. was transmitted to the Quaker meeting at Burlington, "which quietly suppressed it." Ahlstrom, p. 232, describes Pastorius as a Lutheran Pietist.

3. See pp. 148–50.

4. Cf. *A Pastoral Letter to the English Captives in Africa* (Boston, 1698), p. 10, and *The Negro Christianized* (Boston, 1706), p. 3.

5. Kennerly M. Woody takes this position in "Bibliographical Notes to Cotton Mather's *Manuductio Ad Ministerium*," *EAL*, supp. to VI, no. 1 (Spring 1971), 3. For more information on Mather's views on, and personal experience with, slavery, Kenneth Silverman's *Selected Letters of Cotton Mather* (Baton Rouge, 1971) should be consulted. See especially pp. 161, 198–99, 214–15, 368–69.

6. Parenthetical page references which follow in the text are to the work or edition mentioned in the text, in this case to a three-page broadside edition, printed in Boston by Bartholomew Green and John Allen and dated June 24, 1700 (see Evans, 951). I have followed this method throughout.

7. Sewall gives as sources for these quotations Matthew 7:12 and 2 Thess. [chap.] 3, and [William] Ames, *Cas. Consc. Lib.*, Bk. V, chap. 23.

8. See George Henry Moore, *Notes on the History of Slavery in Massachusetts* (New York, 1866), pp. 251–56, reprinted by the Negro Universities Press, a branch of Greenwood Publishing Co. (New York, 1968).

9. See Drake, *Quakers and Slavery*, pp. 1–39, and William Sumner Jenkins, *Pro-Slavery Thought in the Old South* (Gloucester, Mass., 1960), pp. 8–9, for titles and further information on these five writers.

10. L. W. Labaree *et al.*, *The Papers of Benjamin Franklin*, I (New Haven, 1959), 189n.

11. *The Mystery of Iniquity in a brief Examination of the Practice of the Times* (1730), Evans 3349, Sabin XVIII, 435. Again Franklin's name did not appear on the title page, but he advertised this "Second Impression" for sale in his *Pa. Gaz.* (December 22, 1730). See *Papers of BF*, I, 189.

12. Edwin H. Cady, *John Woolman* (New York, 1965), p. 71. See Drake, pp. 43–48, 241, for more information on Lay.

13. Cady, p. 73.

14. The pages of the preface are unnumbered. The text begins on p. 6.

15. These quotations are from the title page. On p. 120 he also refers to slavery as a "Leprosy." But he also liked the figure of "Slave-keeping with all its Concomitants" as the whore of Babylon, "the Mother of Whores," p. 140.

16. Respectively, *John Woolman* (New York, 1969), pp. 49–54, in TUSAS and *John Woolman* (New York, 1965), pp. 66–69, 78–81, 108–13, in Great American Thinkers series, where circumstances of writing and publications as well as chief arguments of *Some Considerations* are presented. Rosenblatt, p. 53, says that Franklin published this essay and sold it at cost.

17. Janet Whitney, *John Woolman, American Quaker* (Boston, 1943), pp. 187–94, 280–82, 420, for discussion of this attribution, reasons for having part 2 of this work published by Franklin, and information on the end of Woolman's life.

18. P. 53.

19. P. 93.

20. Louis Ruchames, *Racial Thought in America, From the Puritans to Abraham Lincoln* (Amherst, 1969), p. 111.

21. Drake, *Quakers and Slavery*, p. 56

22. Cf. above, John Wise's "Immunities," two of which were Liberty or Freedom and the Equality of all men in a state of nature. Tom Paine was later to develop the economic as well as political aspects of this idea in his *Agrarian Justice* (1797).

23. Cady, p. 138, writes that "the aim of the voyage [to England] seems always to have been vague. . . ." Although Woolman lectured and wrote on other subjects than slavery during the brief period of his visit, the fact remains that one of his four antislavery works was written there.

24. Hornberger, Blair, *et al.*, *The Literature of the United States*, I, p. 347.

25. Christopher Sower of Germantown was the printer for both editions of *Observations* (1759 and 1760). *A Short Account* first appeared in Philadelphia (1762) in the form of a fifty-six-page pamphlet. No printer is listed on the title page. William Dunlap printed the second edition in the same year "with large additions and amendments"—80 pp. in all. The following year (1763) it was printed in German by the Society [of Friends] Press at Ephrata. The third ed., 80 pp., came out in London (1768) with W. Baker and J. W. Galabin listed as printers.

26. Henry Miller "in Second Street" was the first publisher. For the 1767 ed. Franklin's former partner, David Hall, and W. Sellers of the New Printing Office in Market Street repeated the 1766 version of Miller. London reprints of 1767 and 1784 do not specify the printer.

27. Philadelphia, 1771.

28. Printed by Crukshank, this predominantly pacifist tract extends to 48 pp. The *Library of Congress Cat. of Printed Cards* also attributes *Notes on the Slave Trade* [Philadelphia?, 178–] to Benezet.

29. The *LC Cat. of Printed Cards* attributes *Brief Considerations on Slavery and the Expediency of Its Abolition . . .* (Burlington, N.J. 1773), Evans 12701, to William Dillwyn. Two other anonymous works, both by David Cooper—*A Mite Cast into the Treasury; or, Observations on Slave-Keeping* (Philadelphia: Crukshank, 1772) and *A Serious Address to the Rulers of America, on the Inconsistency of their Conduct respecting Slavery* (Trenton: Isaac Collins, 1783), Evans 17839—have also at one time or another been attributed to Benezet. Both Dillwyn (sometimes spelled Dillyn) and Cooper were apparently Quakers.

30. Benezet adds that "under the Mosaic-Law Man-stealing was the only Theft punishable by Death," p. 10.

31. Page references are to the second edition "with large Additions and Amendments" (Philadelphia, 1762). Among the "several persons of Note" not specifically mentioned on the title page, appears William Bosman (p. 9), from whom Benezet had quoted in his *Observations* (see above).

32. Hutcheson (1694–1746) was the author of *An Inquiry into the Original of our Ideas of Beauty and Virtue* (1725) and of a posthumously published work entitled *System of Moral Philosophy* (1755). He developed some of the ideas of Shaftesbury, but with more emphasis on the theory of the moral sense.

George Wallis, according to Benezet (p. 30), wrote *A System of the Principles of the Law of Scotland*. Benezet (pp. 31–33) quotes extensively from him in support of the natural rights argument against slavery. For further information on Wallis, see David Brion Davis, "New Sidelights on Early Antislavery Radicalism," *WMQ* (Oct. 1971), 584–90, which treats of Benezet, including his borrowing from Wallis, and his influence on the French *Ephemerides du Citoyen* of 1769.

33. Philmore is not listed in either *DNB* or *DAB*. Davis, p. 593, states that Benezet altered the original dialogue of Philmore's *Dialogues on the Man Trade* (London, 1760). The speakers in these dialogues are J. Philmore (who typifies logic and knowledge) and Mr. Allcraft (a person involved in the slave trade). Davis adds that Benezet also omitted one of Philmore's most radical doctrines—that the slaves had the *right* to use force and violence against their oppressors, p. 594.

34. Ignorance of the white man's language is the principal reason here given.

35. Drake, p. 62, gives 1766 as the date for this work, but the copy accessible to me in the Houghton Library had 1767 on the title page. Page references are consequently to this latter edition (Philadelphia, 1767).

36. As one might expect, Whitefield's arguments are mainly based on scripture, but he also notes (from his own observations) that "your Slaves . . . work as hard, if not harder, than the Horses whereon you ride," p. 12. For differences between Whitefield and Benezet on the subject of slavery, see George S. Brookes, *Friend Anthony Benezet* (Philadelphia, 1937), pp. 96–97. Among other writers Benezet quotes are: Montesquieu, James Foster, George Wallis, Francis Hutcheson, William Bosman, Sir Hans Sloan (Franklin's friend), George Fox, Philmore, and William Warburton (the Bishop of Gloucester).

37. Reprinted in London in 1772 and 1788, in France in 1788, and again in London in 1815. The title is, of course, abbreviated.

38. Brookes, p. 107.

39. *Ibid.*, p. 83.

40. Apparently Benezet thought the colonists were not winning the war at this time and that their lack of success was due to a divine punishment for their sins—Negro slavery and bad treatment of the Indians. See p. 29.

41. P. 62.

42. See Drake, p. 91; also, Alice Felt Tyler, *Freedom's Ferment* (New York, 1962), p. 465.

43. David Freeman Hawke, *Benjamin Rush, Revolutionary Gadfly* (New York, 1971), p. 104.

44. *Ibid.*, p. 106. Evans gives *Nisbet* as the spelling of this author's

name. See Evans 24623 for an entry of a later work on slavery by Nisbet—*The Capacity of Negroes* (Baltimore, 1792). Evans fails to reproduce this work, noting only that it is an advertisement for a London edition.

45. Rush indicates relevant textual passages from Nesbit's *Defence* after each of the above quotations. I have omitted these in the interest of greater continuity of effect.

46. Hawke, p. 108.

47. IV, 81–82.

48. Hawke, pp. 360–61.

49. David Freeman Hawke, ed., Robert Beverley, *The History and Present State of Virginia* (Indianapolis, 1971), p. 141.

50. Evans 4816 is my text. See Dedication, p. iv, and p. 175. For further information about these three authors, see Clarence L. Ver Steeg, ed., *A True and Historical Narrative of the Colony of Georgia* (Athens, Ga., 1960), pp. xii–xxvii, xxix–xxx, xxxii–xxxiii.

51. Hawke, *B. Rush*, p. 14—although Hawke does not refer to any specific writing of Davies. See also pp. 19 and 405 for more information on Davies and the slavery question, which Hawke has taken from Winthrop D. Jordan, *White Over Black* (1968) p. 188.

52. Jenkins, p. 27.

53. Julian Boyd *et al.*, eds., *The Papers of Thomas Jefferson* (Princeton, 1950), I, 130.

54. Robert Douthat Meade, *Patrick Henry, Patriot in the Making* (Philadelphia, 1957), p. 299.

55. *Ibid.*, p. 300.

56. Philip S. Foner, ed., *The Complete Writings of Thomas Paine* (New York, 1945), II, 15. Page references are to this text. Cf. David Freeman Hawke, *Paine* (New York, 1974), pp. 36–37, for discussion of this essay written under the pseudonym of "Humanus."

57. Hawke, *Paine*, p. 36, states that this idea had become common since its appearance in Rush's *Address* (1773). We have already seen its generalized statement in Benezet. Paine's version was more specific—*viz.*, that God might punish the Americans (for tolerating slavery) by permitting the British to enslave them.

58. Foner reproduces this act of the Pa. Assembly, II, 21–22.

59. *Poor Richard's Politics* (New York, 1965), p. 80.

60. V. W. Crane, ed., *Benjamin Franklin's Letters to the Press, 1758–1775* (Chapel Hill, 1950), pp. 186–92), is the text I have used here. Page references are to this edition.

61. A. H. Smyth, ed., *The Writings of Benjamin Franklin* (New York, 1907), V, 431–32). The original manuscript is in the Library of Congress.

62. Smyth, *Writings of BF*, VI, 39–40. Original in APS coll. Richard Woodward was Dean of Clogher (1764–1781) and Chancellor of St. Patrick's (1772), according to Smyth, VI, 39n.

Franklin's antislavery activities in the post-Revolutionary period are better known. For discussion of these see my *Benjamin Franklin* (New York, 1962), pp. 82, 89, 92–93, 102–103, specifically for discussion of his satire entitled "On the Slave Trade." For discussion of another recently discovered satire and reasons for possibly attributing it to Franklin, see my article "A New Franklin Satire?" *EAL*, VII, no. 2 (Fall 1972), 103–10, and subsequent discussion with P. M. Zall in *EAL*, IX, no. 1 (Spring 1974), 96–98.

63. New York, 1969. The quotation which follows is from the second edition (N.Y. State Library). Later references are to this edition. The first edition was issued in Norwich, Conn., printed for Judah P. Spooner, 1776. See p. 8n for information that this work was published early in 1776, "before the declaration of our independence."

64. This work also appeared under the title of "A Letter written by a foreigner (1776) on the character of the English nation" in *The Miscellaneous Essays and Occasional Writings of Francis Hopkinson* (Philadelphia, 1792), pp. 98–111. Page references are to this edition.

65. My text is a modern edition—Everyman Library (London, 1945). Page references are to this edition.

66. *St. John de Crevecoeur* (New York, 1970), pp. 44–48. Philbrick concludes that the "melancholy scene" is probably imaginary—p. 48.

67. I have used the second American edition (Philadelphia, November 12, 1794), Evans 27162 (AAS copy).

68. Arthur P. Davis and Saunders Redding, *Cavalcade: Negro American Writing from 1760 to the Present* (Boston, 1971), pp. 17–18, give most of the little-known biographical information. The quotation is from p. 17. P. 18 mentions that abolition forces on both sides of the Atlantic used Vassa's *Narrative*.

69. *Ibid.*, p. 24.

70. Reprinted in *Negro Protest Pamphlets*, intro. by Dorothy Porter (New York, 1969), pp. 1–24. For biographical sketches of Rev. Richard Allen and Absalom Jones see Benjamin Brawley, *Early Negro American Writers*, (Freeport, N.Y., 1968), pp. 87–89.

71. He cites various instances of the success of such intermarriages—the Portuguese settlers in the Congo and Sierra Leone, for example, whose offspring had become assimilated in color.

72. See Lorenzo Dow Turner, *Anti-Slavery Sentiment in American Literature Prior to 1865* (Port Washington, N.Y., 1966), p. 32, for the statement that H. H. Brackenridge's *Modern Chivalry* was "the most significant" of the less numerous appeals for immediate emancipation.

Chapter Four

1. Quoted from the preface to *A Discourse Concerning Unlimited Submission and Non-Resistance to the Higher Powers* (Boston, 1750). The

remainder of the elongated title makes clear that it was directed against Charles I's "Saintship." Page references are to this edition.

2. Charles W. Akers, *Called unto Liberty, A Life of Jonathan Mayhew 1720–1766* (Cambridge, Mass., 1964), p. 82, says Edwards estimated with alarm that the Church of England had tripled its numbers during the previous seven years.

3. Bernard Bailyn and Jane N. Garrett, eds., *Pamphlets of the American Revolution 1750–1776* (Cambridge, Mass., 1965), I, 205–206.

4. *Ibid.*, p. 205.

5. *Ibid.* See, too, Akers, pp. 77–78, for details.

6. In the original text three of these quotations are footnoted with biblical references—one is attributed to Mr. Leslie, and one is unacknowledged.

7. *Pamphlets of the American Revolution*, p. 204.

8. See *ibid.*, pp. 209–11, for reaction to the sermon; also Akers, p. 93.

9. *The Puritans*, p. 792.

10. Akers, pp. 203–208, provides a description of this sermon and the complicated circumstances surrounding this incident.

11. P. 212. Mayhew died in 1766 and this was his last published sermon.

12. Dumas Malone, ed., *Dictionary of American Biog.*, hereafter *DAB* (New York: Charles Scribner's Sons, 1961), V, 219–20.

13. Bailyn, *Pamphlets*, pp. 356, 500, 713n, for background information and reprints of Hopkins's "Essay," which Merrill Jensen, *Tracts of the American Revolution 1763–1776* (Indianapolis, 1967), pp. 2–18, reproduces. See Bailyn, *Pamphlets*, pp. 361–77, for *Considerations Upon the Act of Parliament* (Boston, 1764), the "most comprehensive and readable" of all the protests against the Sugar Act, p. 358.

14. Bailyn, *Pamphlets*, p. 368.

15. *Ibid.*, p. 501.

16. See *ibid*, p. 729, for reference to Hopkins's "long career of conflict with the admiralty courts."

17. See Bailyn, *Pamphlets*, pp. 524–30, for an excellent sketch of this little-known Tory lawyer, who was hanged and burned in effigy in Newport and later forced to flee from his position as chief justice in North Carolina.

18. *Pamphlets*, p. 528.

19. *Ibid.*, pp. 529, 733. Bailyn says the "Vindication" totaled about 10,000 words.

20. *DAB*, VII, 205.

21. *Ibid.*, VII, 102.

22. *Ibid.*

23. Charles Francis Adams, ed., *The Works of John Adams* (Boston, 1854), X, 247. But cf. Robert J. Taylor *et al.*, eds., *The Papers of John Adams* (Cambridge, Mass., 1977), I, xxv, for a different view, that the case "actually made little impact at the time."

24. *DAB*, VII, 102.

25. *Ibid.*, VII, 104.
26. Bailyn, *Pamphlets*, p. 546.
27. *Ibid.*, pp. 409–10.
28. See Bailyn's comment, p. 410, that Otis's "untenable subtleties" were "the result of an unsure, incomplete application of seventeenth-century doctrines to eighteenth-century issues." How fair this comment is I leave to the reader to judge.
29. Otis nevertheless quotes from Grotius a passage written by Thucydides to the effect that the Greek colonies enjoyed the same rights as other cities, "but that they owed a *reverence* to the city whence they derived their origin, and were obliged to render her respect and certain expressions of honor, *so long as the colony was well treated*" (26). Bailyn quotes John Adams to the effect that Otis "was a passionate admirer of the Greek poets, especially Homer," adding that Otis "was well versed in Greek and Roman history, philosophy, oratory, poetry, and mythology," p. 410.
30. The first edition (Boston, 1765) did not have Otis's name on the title page, but that of London, 1769, did. Since the latter is in larger print, I found it easier to read. Page references are to this edition.
31. The passage Otis quotes is this: "In the midst of all this clutter and revolution, in comes Lord Peter with a file of dragoons at his heels, and gathering from all hands what was in the wind, he and his gang, after several millions of scurrilities and curses not very important here to repeat, by main force very fairly kicks them [Martyn and Jack] both out of doors, and would never let them come under his roof from that day to this."
32. See Bailyn, pp. 548–52, for brief descriptions of each of these three works and for the tragic end of Otis's career. Otis's *Considerations . . . in a Letter to a Noble Lord* answered Soame Jenyns's *The Objections to the Taxation of Our American Colonies . . . Considered* (London, 1765), which had been reprinted in America. Jenyns was an M.P. who attacked the colonists' objections to taxation without representation. He argued that Manchester and Birmingham and several of the richest towns in England had no representation in Parliament, but had nonetheless been regularly taxed. See Bailyn, pp. 600–601, 742.
33. Bailyn, pp. xvi, 598, gives Annapolis as the place for this publication. Neither the name of the author nor the place of printing appeared in the original edition. See John E. Alden, "The Boston Edition of Daniel Dulany's 'Considerations on the Propriety of Imposing Taxes,'" *NEQ*, XIII, no. 4 (1940), 705–11, for attribution of this anonymous work to Dulany. I have made use of the New York, 1765, ed., reprinted by John Holt, in the Houghton Library. The end of the preface of the New York ed. is unsigned, but dated "VIRGINIA, August 12, 1765." Jensen, *Tracts*, p. 94, states that Jonas Green, the publisher of the *Md. Gaz.*, printed the Dulany pamphlet on Oct. 14, 1765.
34. See Bailyn, pp. 599–603, for information on each of these, all of

whom were better writers than Dulany. The stylistic infelicities of the latter are well summarized on p. 599.

35. Edmund S. and Helen M. Morgan, *The Stamp Act Crisis, Prologue to Revolution* (Chapel Hill, 1953), p. 85. For more complete discussion the Morgans' chap. on Dulany, pp. 71–87, should be consulted.

36. P. 604.

37. P. 705. See pp. 705–11 for various editions and reprints—also Bailyn, p. 509.

38. Bailyn, p. 606. For the clash between Carroll and Dulany, see Elihu S. Riley, *Correspondence of "First Citizen"—Charles Carroll of Carrollton, and "Antilon"—Daniel Dulany, Jr., 1773, With a History of Governor Eden's Administration in Maryland, 1769–1776* (Baltimore, 1902). Dulany defended the proprietary right to collect revenue from all tobacco exported from the province of Maryland in his *Right to the Tonnage* (Annapolis, 1766). For Dulany's attempts at maintaining an independent position during the war, see Robert M. Calhoun, *The Loyalists in Revolutionary America, 1760–1781* (New York, 1973), pp. 135–46.

39. Bailyn, pp. 660, 662, 667.

40. *Ibid.*, p. 666.

41. For an index to the various authors quoted in Dickinson's long and numerous footnotes, see *ibid.*, p. 768.

42. Clinton Rossiter, *Seedtime of the Republic* (New York, 1953), p. 248.

43. Elsewhere, Rossiter refers to Bland as "an admirable representative of the Virginia aristocracy," See p. 251 as well as Rossiter's entire excellent sketch of the life and writings of Bland, pp. 247–80. At the end of his discussion he sees Bland as an "elder brother" to men like Mason, Madison, and Jefferson.

44. I shall cover only a few of the most important points, since James E. Pate, "Richard Bland's Inquiry into the Rights of the British Colonies," *WMQ*, 2nd series (1931), XI, 20–28, has already presented much of the argument in this document.

45. Jensen, *Tracts of the Am. Rev.*, pp. 127–28, is my source for the information in this paragraph. Cf. David Ramsay's statement that these letters were "universally read by the colonists." (See reproduction of Appendix No. 4 of his *History of the Am. Rev.*, 1789, in W. Thorp *et al.*, *American Issues*, 5th printing (New York, 1944), I, 113.

46. See sketch in *DAB*.

47. Morgan, *The Stamp Act Crisis*, pp. 94–98, for discussion of these resolutions. Cf. Meade's chap., "The Stamp Act Speech," pp. 158–82.

48. Evans 11239. *The Farmer's and Monitor's Letters, To the Inhabitants of the British Colonies* (Williamsburg, 1769). Page references are to this edition.

49. See Benjamin H. Newcomb, *Franklin and Galloway: A Political Partnership* (New Haven, 1972), 105–35; V. W. Crane, *BF's Letters to the*

Press-1758–1775, passim; and my own *Benjamin Franklin* (New York, 1962), the chap. on "Political Journalism," *passim*.

Chapter Five

1. Francis Bernard, *Letters to the Ministry from Governor Bernard, General Gage, and Commodore Hood and also Memorials to the Lords of the Treasury, From the Commissioners of the Customs. With Sundry Letters and Papers annexed to the said Memorials* (Salem, 1769). On the last page of this pamphlet, p. 24., a note explains that the second part of these *Letters* is still in press and will appear on Thursday and Friday of the following week. This particular edition which I have used contains only letters from Bernard. Here the quotations are from the letter of June 11, 1768.

2. *Ibid.*, p. 15. Letter of June 13, 1768. The Liberty Tree, according to Bernard, was "a large Old Elm in the High Street" from which effigies had been hung "in the Time of the Stamp Act," p. 17.

3. *Ibid.*, p. 23. Letter of June 24, 1768.

4. *Pamphlets*, p. 750, Houghton Library edition—Boston, 1770. J. Almon of London reprinted this edition. Bailyn, p. 750, gives 1769 as the date of the first edition and ascribes this work to Samuel Adams.

5. Quoted from the subtitle. William Cooper, the town clerk, wrote a statement which precedes the *Appeal* in which reference is made to the town meetings of Oct. 4 and Oct. 18, 1769, at which the *Appeal* was ordered published and transmitted to Isaac Barré, M.P.; Thomas Pownal, M.P. and ex-governor of Mass.; Benjamin Franklin; William Bollan, agent for the Mass. Council; Dennys De Berdt, agent for the Mass. House of Representatives; and Barlow Trecothick, M.P. and London alderman.

6. Another pamphlet, *True Sentiments of America*, which presents and answers other letters of Bernard, was published in Dublin by J. Millikin in 1769. Attributed to Samuel Adams, it calls on the Americans to boycott British goods: "Let us agree to consume no more of their expensive gewgaws. Let us live frugally, and let us industriously manufacture what we can for ourselves," p. 119. *The Extract of a Letter from the House of Representatives of the Massachusetts-Bay, to their Agent Dennys De Berdt, Esq.; with Some Remarks* (London, 1770) has also been attributed to Sam Adams. See, too, Jensen, *Tracts*, pp. 233–35, for the background of Adams's quarrel with Governor Hutchinson which eventuated in the celebrated "Hutchinson affair." Jensen reproduces, pp. 235–55, three of the four parts of *A State of the Rights of the Colonists* (1772), which he attributes to Adams.

7. Carl Van Doren, *Benjamin Franklin's Autobiographical Writings* (New York, 1945), p. 296.

8. The reader is referred to the chapter on "Political Journalism" in my

Benjamin Franklin, particularly to pp. 76–77, 82–89, 96. Franklin, like Cotton Mather, was fond of short political fables, several of which appeared anonymously in various British newspapers. See p. 96 for three of these which were printed in the *Public Advertiser* (Jan. 2, 1770). See, too, for further discussion of Franklin's work during the 1770s, V. W. Crane's *BF's Letters to the Press, 1758–1775*, Bruce Granger's *Political Satire in the American Revolution, 1763–1783* (Ithaca, 1960), Paul W. Conner's *Poor Richard's Politicks* (New York, 1965), and Francis X. Davy's excellent unpublished Ph.D. dissertation, "BF, Satirist: The Satire of Franklin and Its Rhetoric" (Columbia University, 1958). For Franklin's part in the affair of the Hutchinson Letters (1773), see James K. Hosmer, *The Life of Thomas Hutchinson* (New York, 1972), pp. 268–93.

9. Durand Echeverria, " 'The Sale of the Hessians.' Was Benjamin Franklin the Author?" *APS Library Bulletin* (1954), 428, states that the MS circulated in Paris before its first known printing in Neuwied on the Rhine. See p. 427.

10. Saul K. Padover, *Jefferson* [abridged by the author] (New York, 1964), p. 28.

11. *Ibid.*

12. Frederick C. Prescott, *Alexander Hamilton and Thomas Jefferson: Representative Selections* (New York, 1934), p. 186. Page references in the text are to this work.

13. The Boston Port Bill shut the port there completely until the tea destroyed in the Tea Party should be paid for; the Mass. Gov't. Act replaced Governor Thomas Hutchinson with a military governor, General Gage, who had power to appoint sheriffs and justices of peace and to limit Boston town meetings; the Quartering Act provided anew for the quartering of troops in all thirteen of the colonies; and the Administration of Justice Act provided that royal officers could be tried elsewhere at the discretion of the governor for capital offenses. These acts provoked the calling of the Continental Congress. See Marshall Smelser, *An Outline of Colonial and Revolutionary History* (New York, 1950), pp. 129–30.

14. Marvin Meyers, Alexander Kern, and John Cawelti, *Sources of the American Republic, A Documentary History of Politics, Society, and Thought* (Chicago, 1960), I, 137.

15. Edwin Gittleman, "Jefferson's 'Slave Narrative': The Declaration of Independence as a Literary Text," *EAL*, XIII (Winter 1974), 239–56.

16. *The Declaration of Independence* (New York, 1942), p. xiii, as quoted by Gittleman, p. 239. See pp. 194–223 for a critical discussion of Jefferson's limitations as a writer and for the 'Literary Qualities of the Declaration.'

17. Quoted in Richard Hofstadter, *The American Political Tradition and the Men Who Made It* (New York, 1974), p. 249.

18. Meyers *et al.*, *Sources*, I, 137. Becker, p. 203, sees the justification as embracing *moral* as well as *legal* grounds.

19. See *DAB* for sketch of Wilson's life and significance in the Constitutional Convention, etc.

20. My text is an abridgment from Samuel Eliot Morison's *Sources and Documents Illustrating the American Revolution, 1764–1788 and the Formation of the Federal Constitution* (New York, 1965), pp. 104–16, and references in text are to this book.

21. Bailyn, *Pamphlets*, p. 135.

22. I am indebted to Bailyn's *The Ideological Origins of the American Revolution* (Cambridge, Mass., 1967), p. 225, for this information. See Griffith J. McRee, *Life and Correspondence of James Iredell* (New York, 1949), pp. 205–20, for reproduction of Iredell's *Address*. Jensen, *Tracts*, p. lii, also mentions pamphlets by Jonathan Boucher and by William Henry Drayton of South Carolina in the period preceding the Continental Congress. See Bailyn, *Pamphlets*, pp. 750–51, for titles and dates of these.

23. Bailyn, *Pamphlets*, p. 747.

24. The long footnote beneath this relatively short passage accounts for the number of pages.

25. Printed in Philadelphia and then reprinted in Watertown, [Mass.], by Benjamin Edes, 1775. The copy I used in the Houghton Library was the reprint.

26. Morison, p. 143n, writes that this account of Lexington and Concord "is naturally biased."

27. Hancock was president of the Congress; Thomson, secretary.

28. George A. Peek, Jr., ed., *The Political Writings of John Adams, Representative Selections* (Indianapolis, 1954), pp. 26–78. Actually, Peek presents only four letters by each writer, a highly limited selection considering that Adams's letters alone appeared every week with but one exception—a total of twelve letters.

29. I have used as my text here *Novanglus and Massachusettensis* (Boston, 1819).

30. Cf. Peek, pp. 26–27.

31. Students interested in other political writings of John Adams should study carefully *A Dissertation on the Canon and the Feudal Law* (1765), in which he argues against tyranny (both ecclesiastical and civil) inherited from feudal times. He also argues in this work that the first American settlers were attempting to avoid both forms of these ancient tyrannies in the government which they set up. *Thoughts on Government* (Philadelphia, 1776) and *Twenty-Six Letters, Upon Interesting Subjects Respecting the Revolution in America. Written in Holland, in the Year 1780* should also be consulted.

32. Clarence L. Ver Steeg and Richard Hofstadter, *Great Issues in American History* (New York, 1969), p. 428.

33. Blair, Hornberger, and Stewart, *The Lit. of the U.S.* (Chicago, 1946), I, 309.

34. All quotations for this paragraph are from Prescott, p. xv. I have used the selection in Prescott for my text of *The Farmer Refuted*.

35. My italics. Hamilton's indictment also rests on another quotation from Blackstone, which states that the function of society (or government) is to secure *absolute* (or natural rights), See Prescott, p. 6. Samuel Seabury was an Anglican priest who later became presiding bishop of the Episcopal Church in America.

36. Prescott, p. 406. See pp. 33–36 for a reproduction of the first in this series, and pp. xx–xxi for Prescott's comment on their significance.

37. *Ibid.*, pp. xxi, xxiii.

38. Foner, *Writings of TP*, I, 3–4. Page references in the text are to Foner.

39. Hornberger, *Lit. of the U.S.* (1971), I, 384. Subsequent citations to this work refer to this edition—3rd, Heritage printing.

40. *Ibid.*

41. I, 412.

42. I, 49.

43. Hornberger, I, 412. I use Foner for my text.

44. I, 414n.

45. Here, for this one sentence, I follow the text as given in Hornberger, I, 418; Foner, I, 56, gives: "I thank God, that I fear not."

46. Foner, I, 48–239, reproduces the complete text of the 1776–1783 *Crisis* papers. For a convenient index to the general content of each paper the reader is referred to Harry H. Clark, *Thomas Paine: Representative Selections* (New York, 1944), pp. 414–20. Clark sees four main trends of thought in the series as a whole: 1. the insistence on "absolute independence"; 2. the attack on the English monarchy and system of government; 3. Paine's conclusion that the war could be won only with the support of the wealthy; 4. his sentiment in favor of union rather than for states' rights. See p. 420.

47. The error in Brackenridge's middle name on the title page (Montgomery instead of Henry) was probably occasioned by his authorship of a tragedy entitled *The Death of General Montgomery*, published in 1777.

48. See pp. 16, 38, 87, respectively, for these comparisons; p. 15 notes that "these discourses were held in the camp of the Revolutionary army." This may account for their pronounced religious and rhetorical cast.

49. Although Brackenridge figures more importantly in his postwar writings, at least two other works of his should be mentioned: *An Eulogium of the Brave Men Who Have Fallen in the Contest with Great Britain: Delivered on Monday, July 5, 1779* (Philadelphia, 1779), 23 pp., and *The United States Magazine: A Repository of History, Politics, and Literature*, vol. I (Philadelphia, 1779). The latter work contains numerous editorials by Brackenridge as well as propaganda poetry by his friend Freneau. See Jacob Axelrad, *Philip Freneau, Champion of Democracy* (Austin, Tex. 1967), pp. 100–102, for reasons why this magazine failed. For other works by

Brackenridge, see Charles Frederick Heartman, *A Bibliography of the Writings of H. H. Brackenridge* (New York, 1917).

50. Hornberger, I, 384n.
51. David Freeman Hawke, *Paine* (New York, 1974), p. 62.
52. I, 382.

Chapter Six

1. Richard Current, T. Harry Williams, and Frank Freidel, *American History, A Survey* (New York, 1965), p. 121.
2. *Ibid.*
3. Marvin Meyers, Alexander Kern, and John G. Cawelti, eds., *Sources of the American Republic: Documentary History of Politics, Society, and Thought* (Chicago, 1960), I, 154. For similar conservative views (both theological and legal) held by Noah Webster *et al.* on this rebellion see Thorp *et al.*, *American Issues* (Chicago, 1941), I, 164–73.
4. Meyers, I, 155.
5. P. 121.
6. Cf. Peek, pp. 105–107, for background. He quotes Adams as saying he received a copy of the Constitution only when his third volume was about to come off the press, p. 106.
7. Adams criticizes Locke's constitution for Carolina because in it Locke "gave the whole authority, executive and legislative, to the proprietors. . . ." He storms at Milton (quoting a long extract from the latter's *Ready and Easy Way to Establish a True Commonwealth*) for advocating elimination of the House of Lords. He objects to Hume's *Idea of a Perfect Commonwealth* as excessively aristocratic—more specifically for "1. Letting the nobility or senate into the management of the executive power; and 2. Taking the eyes of the people off from their representatives in the legislature." On this latter subject he adds, "The liberty of the people depends entirely on the constant and direct communication between them and the legislature, by means of their representatives" (I, 368–69, 371).
8. The quotations are from p. 3.
9. Most of these had to do with the ownership and disposition of farm land and the abolition of entail. See p. 48.
10. *DAB* (New York, 1932), VI, 327. This volume also contains sketches of the lives and other writings of the Livingston brothers.
11. Clinton Rossiter, ed. *The Federalist Papers* (New York, 1964), p. vii. I have used this work as my text.
12. *Ibid.*, p. xi.
13. *Ibid.*
14. *Ibid.*, pp. xi, xvii.
15. Jay simply means that the colonies were more closely connected, for example, than the various parts of the British empire, p. 38.
16. Here he cites their common ancestry, common language, similar

religious background, and similar principles of government, manners, and customs. *Ibid.*

17. Madison's method of controlling majority factions does not really answer the question about control of majorities as factions. He simply argues that the control of factions will be easier in a large republic than in a small one.

18. The sixteen points of this important document, probably slightly altered by the Virginia Convention, are reproduced in Richmond Croom Beatty *et al.*, eds., *The Literature of the South* (Chicago, 1952), pp. 24–25.

19. *Objections of the Hon. George Mason to the Proposed Federal Constitution. Addressed to the Citizens of Virginia* ([Richmond:] Printed by Thomas Nicholas, [1787]), Folio, Broadside. Listed by Evans as No. 45095, but *not reproduced*. I have used the six-page broadside copy given by Paul Leicester Ford in *Pamphlets on the Constitution of the United States* (Brooklyn, 1888), pp. 327–32.

20. Apparently because that state from which the vice-president came would have a greater power, because of his office in presiding over the Senate.

21. Curiously, he adds, ". . . There never was, nor can be a legislature, but must and will make such laws [*ex post facto* laws], when necessity and the public safety require them . . ." (pp. 331–32).

22. See Ford, *Pamphlets on the Constitution*, p. 327.

23. James D. Hart, *Oxford Companion to American Literature* (New York, 1946), p. 142.

24. See *The Letters of Fabius in 1788* (Wilmington, 1797), p. iii.

25. Ford at first identified Brutus as Thomas Treadwell but later as Robert Gates. See p. 116.

26. Attributed to Hanson by Ford, *Pamphlets on the Constitution*, pp. 221ff.

27. Respectively, Evans 21414, LOC copy, and Evans 22088, AAS copy.

28. Worcester, Mass., 1788. The title page indicates, "By a Native of Boston," but Harvard librarians have attributed this work to Minot. For other works by Tench Coxe, James Wilson, John Jay, *et al.*, see Ford, *Pamphlets on the Constitution*.

Chapter Seven

1. *Journal of William Maclay, United States Senator from Pennsylvania, 1789–91* (1800). All of the following material quoted in the text is from chapter one. See reproduction of this chapter in Thorp *et al.*, *American Issues*, I, 175–81.

2. *Papers of BF*, I, 52.

3. Samuel Eliot Morison and Henry Steele Commager, *The Growth of the American Republic* (New York, 1942), I, 346.

4. Peek, p. 175.

5. *Ibid.* In the quotations that follow I have used Peek as my text.

6. Paine's friend Johnson was the publisher; but he became frightened, and it was transferred to J. S. Jordan, a Fleet Street printer. Paine's friends Thomas Holcroft, William Godwin, and Thomas Hollis assisted in the publication. See Foner, I, 242, and H. H. Clark, p. 421. Clark's excellent notes on the *Rights*, pp. 420–26, should be consulted for further information on the circumstances attending publication of all three parts.

7. Foner, I, 249. Parenthetical pages in text refer to Foner.

8. Clark, p. 426.

9. See Foner, II, 517–620, for Paine's voluminous other writings in connection with the French Revolution.

10. Clark, p. 429, who gives 1797 as the publication date and 1795–96 as the time of composition (See Paine's preface.)

11. Clark, p. 337, gives this phrase as a convenient heading for the first part of the essay.

12. Cf. Clark, p. 338, and Foner, I, 605.

13. Quoted in Parrington, I, 384. For biographical information, see James Woodress, *A Yankee's Odyssey: The Life of Joel Barlow* (Philadelphia, 1958).

14. *Ibid.*, I, 383. As my text I have used the 1792 London edition.

15. Barlow regarded Burke as a traitor to the cause of liberty, as did Paine. See, for example, the long prose note to Barlow's poem "The Conspiracy of Kings," in which Barlow blames Burke "almost exclusively" for the "present war." *Political Writings of Joel Barlow* (New York, 1796), pp. 252–53.

16. The other four chapters in part one treat successively these topics: V. Revenue and Public Expenditure; VI. The Means of Subsistence; VII. Literature, Science and Arts; VIII. War and Peace (3–4).

17. See, for example, Barlow's *A Letter Addressed to the People of Piedmont, on the Advantages of the French Revolution, and the Necessity of Adopting its Principles in Italy*, translated from the French by the author (New York, 1795). In this important forty-five-page letter, written at Chambery in Savoy (Dec. 1792), Barlow urges his "fellow-creatures" in the Piedmont "to burst the bands of slavery" (5–6). For a brief analysis of some of the major ideas in Barlow's *A Letter to the National Convention of France* (New York, [1793?]), another work connected with the French Revolution, see Parrington, I, 386–87.

18. Prescott, pp. 304–305.

19. See Prescott, p. 304.

20. Prescott, pp. xviii–xix, 408 (footnote 23).

21. Prescott, p. 408.

22. *Ibid.*

23. Evans 23424, p. 3. Page references are to this ed.

24. See, for example, Prescott, p. 109.

25. *Ibid.*, p. 409.

234 AMERICAN POLITICAL WRITERS: 1588-1800

26. Evans 26245 [Richmond, 1793] is the text I used.

27. Philadelphia, 1794. Evans 26861 from original in John Carter Brown Library, p. 5.

28. Taylor also lists other bad effects of the paper system—for example, it is "adverse" to the rights of labor and to the mass of the people. It increases taxes and debts. It pretends to secure private property but is really a system of plunder for itself. It "imposes all taxes, receives most taxes, and pays no taxes." It can renew the bank charter for its own purposes. It can make laws to acquire wealth for itself. And it will destroy the union "if the union should obstruct its designs," pp. 14–15.

29. See Evans 27782 for the original. The quotation is from Merle Curti, *The Growth of American Thought* (New York, 1943), p. 175.

30. Curti, p. 175. This quotation is also Curti's.

31. John Chester Miller, *The Federalist Era, 1789–1801* (New York, 1960), p. 168. See Miller, pp. 155–82, for more information.

32. *Ibid*. See also Prescott, pp. 151–53, 411, for reproduction of one of these papers.

33. Krout, p. 66. See pp. 61–69 for a good, succinct review of the historical background of this rather complicated decade.

34. My text here is *The Letters of Fabius in 1788 . . . and in 1797* [title abbreviated] (Wilmington, Del., 1797). See especially letters three and four in the 1797 series.

35. Prescott, p. 142–44, reprints one of this series of seven letters in which Hamilton defended Washington's neutrality policy against American supporters of the French.

36. Hart, p. 267.

37. See Axelrad, *Philip Freneau*, pp. 326, 328–29, for a list of those editors and writers whom the Federalists actually "got." At one point the lists apparently became confused, because John Adams considered deporting one of his own writers, William Cobbett (see *infra*). See *DAB*.

38. Only Vol. II, part of which was published in 1801, after Jefferson's election, was available at the Houghton Library in 1967 when I read there.

39. Thorp *et al.*, p. 188. Manning also includes a short account of Shays' Rebellion in his *Key*.

40. Larzer Ziff, "Revolutionary Rhetoric and Puritanism," *EAL*, 13 (Spring 1978), 45–49.

41. *Ibid.*, pp. 47–49, 46.

Selected Bibliography

Detailed bibliographical information for numerous primary sources has already been supplied in the text. Consequently, because of the large scope and restricted space of this book, only a few of the most important primary and secondary sources can be mentioned here.

PRIMARY SOURCES

BAILYN, BERNARD, ed. *Pamphlets of the American Revolution*, I (1750–1765). Cambridge: Harvard University Press, 1965.

BOYD, JULIAN, *et al.*, eds. *The Papers of Thomas Jefferson*. Princeton: Princeton University Press, 1950–.

CRANE, VERNER W., ed. *Benjamin Franklin's Letters to the Press, 1758–1775*. Chapel Hill: University of North Carolina Press, 1950.

FONER, PHILIP S., *The Complete Writings of Thomas Paine*, 2 vols. New York: Citadel Press, 1945.

FORD, PAUL LEICESTER, ed. *Pamphlets on the Constitution*. Brooklyn: n.p., 1888.

GUMMERE, AMELIA MOTT, ed. *The Journal and Essays of John Woolman*. New York: Macmillan Co., 1922.

HALL, DAVID D., ed. *The Antinomian Controversy, 1636–38, A Documentary History*. Middletown: Wesleyan University Press, 1968.

HEIMERT, ALAN, and MILLER, PERRY, eds. *The Great Awakening: Documents Illustrating the Crisis and Its Consequences*. New York: Bobbs-Merrill, 1967.

JENSEN, MERRILL, ed. *Tracts of the American Revolution, 1763–1776*. Indianapolis: Bobbs-Merrill Co., 1967.

LABAREE, LEONARD W., *et al.*, eds. *The Papers of Benjamin Franklin*. New Haven: Yale University Press, 1959–.

MARSH, PHILIP M., ed., *The Prose Works of Philip Freneau*. New Brunswick: Scarecrow Press, 1955.

MCREE, GRIFFITH R., ed. *Life and Correspondence of James Iredell*. 2 vols. New York: Peter Smith, 1949.

MEYERS, MARVIN, *et al.*, eds. *Sources of the American Republic: Documentary History of Politics, Society, and Thought*. Vol. I. Chicago: Scott, Foresman and Co., 1960.

MILLER, PERRY, and JOHNSON, THOMAS, eds. *The Puritans*. Boston: American Book Co., 1938.

MORISON, SAMUEL ELIOT, ed. *Sources and Documents Illustrating the American Revolution, 1764–1788, and the Formation of the Federal Constitution*. New York: Oxford University Press, 1965.

MURDOCK, KENNETH B., ed. *Selections from Cotton Mather*. New York: Hafner Publishing Co. reprint, 1960. Originally New York: Harcourt Brace, 1926.

PEEK, GEORGE A., JR., ed. *The Political Writings of John Adams, Representative Selections*. Indianapolis: Bobbs-Merrill, 1959.

PRESCOTT, FREDERICK C., ed. *Alexander Hamilton and Thomas Jefferson: Representative Selections*. New York: American Book Co., 1934.

ROSSITER, CLINTON, ed. *The Federalist Papers*. New York: New American Library of World Literature, 1964.

RUCHAMES, LOUIS, ed. *Racial Thought in America: From the Puritans to Abraham Lincoln, A Documentary History*. Vol. I. Amherst, Mass.: University of Massachusetts Press, 1969.

SYRETT, HAROLD C., et al., eds. *The Papers of Alexander Hamilton*. New York: Columbia University Press, 1961.

THORP, WILLARD, et al., eds. *American Issues*. Vol. I. New York: J. B. Lippincott, 1944.

WISH, HARVEY, ed. *The Diary of Samuel Sewall*. New York: G. P. Putnam's Sons, 1967.

WOOLMAN, JOHN. *The Works of John Woolman*. Philadelphia: Joseph Crukshank, 1774.

SECONDARY SOURCES

AHLSTROM, SIDNEY E. *A Religious History of the American People*. New Haven: Yale University Press, 1975.

AKERS, CHARLES W. *Called unto Liberty, A Life of Jonathan Mayhew, 1720–1766*. Cambridge: Harvard University Press, 1964.

BAILYN, BERNARD. *The Ideological Origins of the American Revolution*. Cambridge: Harvard University Press, 1967. The first chapter, "The Literature of Revolution," pp. 1–21, is an excellent introduction to pamphlet and other literature of the period.

BATTIS, EMERY. *Saints and Sinners: Anne Hutchinson and the Antinomian Controversy in the Massachusetts Bay Colony*. Chapel Hill: University of North Carolina Press, 1962.

BERCOVITCH, SACVAN. *The American Jeremiad*. Madison: University of Wisconsin, 1978.

BROOKES, GEORGE S. *Friend Anthony Benezet*. Philadelphia: University of Pennsylvania Press, 1937.

CADY, EDWIN H. *John Woolman*. New York: Washington Square Press, 1965.

COOK, GEORGE A. *John Wise, Early American Democrat*. New York: Octagon Books, 1966.

DUNN, MARY MAPLES. *William Penn: Politics and Conscience*. Princeton: Princeton University Press, 1967.

EMERSON, EVERETT H. *John Cotton*. New York: Twayne, 1965.

GRABO, NORMAN. *Edward Taylor*. New York: Twayne, 1962.

HAWKE, DAVID FREEMAN. *Benjamin Rush, Revolutionary Gadfly*. New York: Bobbs-Merrill Co., 1971.

————. *Paine*. New York: Harper and Row, 1974.

HOSMER, JAMES K. *The Life of Thomas Hutchinson*. New York: DaCapo Press, 1972. This valuable reprint contains many original letters.

JENKINS, WILLIAM SUMNER. *Pro-Slavery Thought in the Old South*. Gloucester, Mass.: Peter Smith, 1960.

LOWANCE, MASON. *Increase Mather*. New York: Twayne, 1974.

MARTY, MARTIN E. *Religion, Awakening, and Revolution*. Wilmington, N.C.: McGrath Publishing Co., 1977.

MEADE, ROBERT DOUTHAT. *Patrick Henry, Patriot in the Making*. Philadelphia: J. B. Lippincott Co., 1957.

MILLER, JOHN CHESTER. *The Federalist Era, 1789–1801*. New York: Harper and Brothers, 1960. Definitive for this period.

MILLER, PERRY. *Orthodoxy in Massachusetts, 1630–1650*. Boston: Beacon Press, 1959.

————. *Roger Williams, His Contribution to the American Mind*. New York: Atheneum, 1965. This valuable little book contains much primary material, in addition to being an excellent abridgment of Williams's life and thought.

MOORE, G. H. *Notes on the History of Slavery in Massachusetts*. New York: Greenwood Publishing Co., 1968. This is a reprint of the original volume first published by Appleton in 1866.

MORGAN, EDMUND S. *The Birth of the Republic*. Chicago: University of Chicago Press, 1956.

————. *The Puritan Dilemma, The Story of John Winthrop*. Boston: Little, Brown and Co., 1958.

————. *Puritan Political Ideas: 1558–1794*. Indianapolis: Bobbs-Merrill, 1965.

————, and MORGAN, HELEN M. *The Stamp Act Crisis, Prologue to the Revolution*. Chapel Hill: University of North Carolina Press, 1953.

MURDOCK, KENNETH B. *Increase Mather, The Foremost American Puritan*. New York: Russell and Russell, 1966. Originally published in 1926, this is still the most nearly complete book available on Increase Mather. Should be supplemented by Lowance's more recent work.

NASH, GARY B. *Quakers and Politics; Pennsylvania, 1681–1726*. Princeton: Princeton University Press, 1968.

NEWCOMB, BENJAMIN H. *Franklin and Galloway: A Political Partnership*. New Haven: Yale University Press, 1972.

POPE, ROBERT G. *The Half-Way Covenant*. Princeton, N.J.: Princeton University Press, 1969.

ROSENBLATT, PAUL. *John Woolman*. New York: Twayne, 1969.

ROSSITER, CLINTON. *Seedtime of the Republic: The Origin of the American Tradition of Political Liberty*. New York: Harcourt, Brace and Co., 1953. Reliable and eminently readable.

STEWART, DONALD H. *The Opposition Press of the Federalist Period*. Albany: State University of New York Press, 1969.

WATERS, JOHN J., JR. *The Otis Family in Provincial and Revolutionary Massachusetts*. Chapel Hill: University of North Carolina Press, 1968.

WERTENBAKER, THOMAS JEFFERSON. *The Puritan Oligarchy*. New York: Charles Scribner's Sons, 1947.

WILSON, JEROME D. and RICKETSON, WILLIAM F. *Thomas Paine*. Boston: G. K. Hall. 1978.

BACKGROUND INFORMATION

BERCOVITCH, SACVAN, ed. *The American Puritan Imagination: Essays in Revaluation*. New York: Cambridge University Press, 1974. Contains an excellent bibliography as well as good chapters on the jeremiad and on other aspects of Puritanism.

CURRENT, RICHARD N., *et al. American History, A Survey*. New York: Alfred A. Knopf Co., 1965.

MORISON, SAMUEL ELIOT and COMMAGER, HENRY STEELE. *The Growth of the American Republic*. Vol. I. New York: Oxford University Press, 1942.

PARRINGTON, VERNON LOUIS. *The Colonial Mind, 1620–1800*. New York: Harcourt, Brace and Co., 1927.

Index

This index includes: (1) principal writers and their works (abbreviated); (2) important general subjects; and (3) authors of secondary sources who have been quoted from and named in the text.

No attempt has been made to index the extensive bibliographical information in the *Notes and References*. However, important nonbibliographical information and statements have been indexed.

The individual chapters contain brief recapitulations: see pp. 34, 39–40, 62–63, 65, 71–72, 115–16, and 203–206.

Anne Ward Amacher assisted with the index.